LABOUR AND LEISURE IN THE SOVIET UNION

The Soviet Union is experiencing a severe labour shortage which is adversely affecting the rate of economic growth. With the highest rate of labour-force participation in the world, the possibilities for increasing the labour supply are limited. In spite of the fact that there appears to be full employment, there are several alternative ways that Soviet planners are trying to increase the labour force. Their attempts often conflict with the goals of Soviet citizens, who want more leisure. Planners use temporary and seasonal employment, part-time employment, old-age pensioners and summer employment of students to meet short-term labour-force deficiencies.

This book argues that there is a conflict between economic planners and individual households. The analytical framework shows how private households make decisions on how to trade off leisure against work, given the availability of leisure facilities and alternative labour-market options. It is shown that the work–leisure trade-off is different in urban areas than in rural areas, primarily because of the private plot, low farm incomes and considerably fewer recreational opportunities in the countryside. It is also shown that Soviet women have to make different work–leisure decisions because of their dual responsibilities as workers and housewives. The Soviet service sector does little to help them.

William Moskoff has been Ernest A. Johnson Professor of Economics and Chairperson of the Department of Economics and Business at Lake Forest College, Illinois, since 1983. Prior to that he was Professor of Economics at Sangamon State University, Illinois, for eleven years. Moskoff has published about twenty articles on the Soviet Union and Eastern Europe, mostly in the labour field. He spent 1976 in Romania under the auspices of a Fulbright Senior Research Grant. He is the author of *Comparative National Economic Policies*. His publications range from articles on Soviet divorce and urban labour problems to Soviet economic trade relations with the Third World and an evaluation of CIA publications on the Soviet economy. His articles have appeared in *Soviet Studies* and *Slavic Review*. He has also been a Visiting Professor of Economics at the University of Illinois-Urbana-Champaign.

LABOUR AND LEISURE IN THE SOVIET UNION

The Conflict between Public and Private Decision-Making in a Planned Economy

William Moskoff

St. Martin's Press   New York

© William Moskoff 1984

All rights reserved. For information write:
St. Martin's Press, Inc., 175 Fifth Avenue, New York, NY 10010
Printed in Hong Kong
Published in the United Kingdom by The Macmillan Press Ltd
First published in the United States of America in 1984

ISBN 0-312-46241-7

Library of Congress Cataloging in Publication Data

Moskoff, William.
  Labour and leisure in the Soviet Union.

  Includes bibliographical references and index.
  1. Labour supply—Soviet Union. 2. Leisure—Soviet Union. 3. Labour policy—Soviet Union. 4. Women—Employment—Soviet Union. 5. Households—Soviet Union—Decision making. I. Title.
HD5796.M67   1984   331.13′6′0947   83-24701
ISBN 0-312-46241-7

This book is dedicated to the three teachers who most touched my life

EDGAR L. FEIGE
DAVID GRANICK
DOROTHY L. THOMSON

Contents

Acknowledgements	viii
Introduction	ix
1 Household Time Budgets	1
2 Non-traditional Sources of Labour: Women, Pensioners and Students	25
3 Seasonal and Temporary Work	51
4 Overtime Work	66
5 Leisure	81
6 Holidays	113
7 Women and the Service Sector	134
8 The Rural Sector	157
Conclusion	196
Endnotes	199
Index	221

Acknowledgements

I am no different from anyone else who has brought a book to a conclusion; I would probably still be crouching in the starting-blocks had it not been for all the help I have received from so many able and generous people. I apologise to those whose names I inadvertently omit; they deserve a better fate than to be victimised by my lapse of memory.

Four people were of the greatest importance. First, Veronica Shapovalov served as my research assistant. But she was even more than that. She was my *referent*, my reader. She was an assiduous comber of libraries and books, a detective of ideas and words. Second, I want to thank Sue Dezendolet, formerly the Vice President for Academic Affairs at Sangamon State University, who not only provided financial support for my work, but also gave continuing moral encouragement. Two colleagues submitted to reading and criticising the entire manuscript. I am very grateful to Roy Wehrle for his surgical skills as an editor. Finally, I want to thank Carol Gayle, who not only edited the manuscript with meticulous care, but was also a patient sounding-board for my ideas. Her voluminous knowledge of Russian and Soviet history served me well.

I would like to thank Alice Gorlin, Ken Gray, Roger Skurski, Robert Sipe and Robert Stuart for their assistance. I am also indebted to John Collins, Director of the Center for Policy Studies and Program Evaluation at Sangamon State University, for his perpetual support.

The University of Illinois at Urbana–Champaign is a goldmine for a Sovietologist and the librarians in the Slavic Language Reading Room are as valuable as the book collection. In particular I would like to thank Harold Leich, Larry Miller and Mary Stuart for their assistance. I would also like to thank Nancy Stump, who handled all 'as soon as possible' inter-library loan requests with grace.

Finally, I would like to thank Donna Tucker and Patty Montgomery for typing draft after draft after draft. Their competence made my work that much easier.

WILLIAM MOSKOFF

Introduction

One of the major economic problems confronting the Soviet Union today is a serious shortage of labour. The absence of new labour resources is one of the reasons why an economic growth rate which is already low is likely to remain low for a number of years. The chronic nature of the labour-supply problem constitutes a threat not only to the health of the Soviet economy but is also a threat to Soviet national security, given the dependency of military power in any country on the overall strength of the national economy.

This book examines the problem of the labour shortage within a specific context. It is the contention of the analysis that there is a fundamental conflict between Soviet planners who want to increase the labour input into the economy, and Soviet households who supply labour. Individual households try to maximise income subject to two major constraints. The first constraint is the household's desire for leisure, which implies the desire to control the distribution of time between work and leisure. The second principal constraint is the obligation to run a household and to take care of children.

While the labour force grew at an average annual rate of 1.8 per cent from 1961 to 1970, and about 1.6 per cent from 1971 to 1980, it is expected that during the period 1985–2000 there will be no net additions to the labour force. This is largely a demographic problem. Low birth rates in the recent past and the continuation of this pattern have predetermined the falling number that will enter employment.

In addition there are several problems of labour misallocation that adversely affect the size of the labour force:

1. Labour turnover is extremely high. Fully 20 per cent of the industrial labour force and 30 per cent of all construction workers annually either quit their job or are fired for disciplinary reasons. In other words, on average the industrial labour force turns over every five years. In the US labour turnover averaged only 4.3 per cent during the period 1959–80.

2. Absenteeism also is very high, Soviet workers are absent about 18 days a year or about twice as much as American workers.
3. There is an incentive for enterprise management to maintain a labour force which is larger than that demanded by an efficiency criterion. The standard of enterprise success under Soviet central planning has been overwhelmingly tied to some measure of gross output calculated in physical terms, rather than using a pecuniary measure, such as profits or the rate of return on capital. A particular feature of Soviet planning has been a chronic problem with the uneven delivery of material inputs over the course of a month, which is the basic production planning period. In general, this unevenness has led to intense production activity at the end of the month, known as 'storming'. When the concentration of production is tied to the inevitable emphasis on short-run results, there is an incentive for the enterprise director to maintain a labour force that will be able to cope with end-of-the-month production pressures, even though during the rest of the month many workers will be idle. A second aspect of this is the demands placed on urban industrial enterprises to supply workers for the autumn harvest in the countryside. It is not always in the best interests of enterprises to do this, but they must meet their assigned quotas. A redundant labour force eases the pain of temporarily releasing workers for agricultural work. Finally, enterprise managers maintain more workers than necessary as a protection against anticipated high leaving rates. In 1975 Gosplan estimated that enterprise employment targets built in a redundancy equivalent to 2.5 million workers.
4. The Soviet system has bred a very high ratio of auxiliary workers to production workers. These are workers who do warehouse, transportation and repair work. In the Soviet economy there are 85 auxiliary workers for every 100 production workers, in the US only 38 auxiliary workers per 100 production workers.

In sum, there is a shortage of labour, partially determined by demographics and partially rooted in systemic causes. For the purposes of this book it is not important whether the shortage is something of a fiction because a more efficient allocation of labour would reduce the problem. The shortage must be accepted as a given of the Soviet scene.

The demographic issues can be resolved only in the long run and therefore bear little relationship to the short-term labour shortage. If Soviet planners decide to pursue aggressive pronatalist policies this would probably reduce the number of women in the labour force. To that extent, the demographic issue would be very relevant to the short-run labour shortage. More women at home bearing and rearing children means a reduction in the labour force. But there are no serious moves in the direction of pursuing a dramatically different set of population policies.

The problems of labour misallocation mainly have to do with systemic economic problems that can be solved only by significant structural reforms in the economy. Even if such reform does take place it will not fully compensate for the labour shortage. Soviet economic planners will still have to cope with this problem.

There are several ways in which Soviet policy is trying to increase the labour supply. The norm that prevails in the Soviet Union is the full-time, year-round worker. This does not exhaust the potential work schedules that can be adopted. Overtime employment, seasonal and temporary employment and part-time employment are alternative labour supply models from the perspective of Soviet planners. These models will be analysed within the context of the conflict that is created between the Soviet labour planners' attempts to increase the labour supply, the relative success of these policies, and the degree to which Soviet policy violates the expectations of Soviet households.

The conflict that exists between planners and households is that for individuals there is a trade-off between work and leisure. In general, individuals offer their labour in return for income. The fact that people work reflects their higher valuation of work in relation to leisure. If leisure were more highly valued, then less labour time would be offered. As the wage rises the cost of leisure rises and economic theory predicts that workers will be most likely to substitute work for leisure. Common sense suggests that beyond a certain point the desirability of working additional hours declines. Moreover, when household income reaches a certain point, the benefits of additional income also decline.

In the Soviet Union workers have experienced substantially rising incomes over time. This is reflected in the 3.5 per cent average annual rate of growth per capita consumption during the period 1951–80, although in the decade of the 1970s it has slowed down rather considerably. Most importantly the present-day Soviet family has a good deal of discretionary income. This is partially reflected in the constantly rising level of savings. Moreover the standard work week has declined. In 1955 the typical industrial worker worked 47.8 hours a week; in 1980, 40.6 hours.

Thus the Soviet Union has reached a stage of development where consideration of the issue of the trade off between work and leisure is not only reasonable, but of great significance. This is true not only of the ordinary Soviet citizen but for the society as a whole.

There are several subthemes that are developed in this book. The first is that economic planners define the range of choice of individuals so that the decision whether to work or engage in more leisure is restricted by the priorities of those who allocate state resources to leisure activities.

Secondly, the work–leisure trade off is a mixture of voluntary choice and involuntary obligation. For example, in Chapter 2 we will see that little part-time work is made available because of Soviet fears that it will lead to a decline in the labour force. Therefore, for a certain part of the labour force, full-time employment is the only realistic choice. Old-age pensioners, on the other hand, are offered the possibility of employment on an absolutely voluntary basis. Similarly, in Chapter 3, seasonal employment is shown to include industrial workers who must assist in the autumn harvest as well as workers who take their construction skills to the rural areas and sell them at very high free market wages.

A second major theme is that women best exemplify the conflict between public and private decision-making in the labour market. Soviet women have the highest labour force participation rate of any industrialised nation in the world. About 85 per cent of all able-bodied Soviet women work. Because of their traditional roles as wives and mothers, there are additional pressures placed upon women. Public policy towards the service sector affects women's choices in an immediate way. Any improvement in the service sector (e.g. public child care facilities, laundries, etc.) benefits working women in particular because it reduces their domestic responsibilities. It also creates an incentive for non-working women to enter the labour force. Investment in the service sector also reflects a commitment of resources by planners who have historically given this sector low priority. As a result, it will be shown that even though life has been eased for everyone, women still lag behind men.

Thirdly, we will show that there are major differences between the urban and rural sectors of the economy. The rural analysis deals mainly with Soviet collective farms. The major structural difference between the two sectors is the existence of the private plot. The private plot constitutes another lever for public policy makers to pull in attempting to affect the labour supply. The plot also adds another choice to the decision-making process of Soviet farmers because it is an alternative to both leisure and work in the socialist sector of agriculture. It will be shown that in general farmers work harder than urbanites. In particular the lives of rural women are considerably more difficult than those of urban women. This results from an even greater deficiency of public services and household appliances in the countryside than exist in the cities. Beyond this the recreational and cultural facilities are much less available to farmers, particularly for private consumption; the community is a relatively more important provider of leisure-time activities in the cities.

Fourthly, we will show a consistent pattern of the importance of income, education and occupation as determinants of how much freedom Soviet citizens have in making the choice between work and leisure. Within the broad category of leisure these personal resources also widen the possibilities of what can be consumed. There is less leisure and more housework for those with the lowest incomes and levels of educational attainment. There are class differences in the Soviet Union; money and education buy time.

Finally, the Soviet perspective on work and leisure bears no resemblance to the lofty but rather vague ideals Karl Marx set forth in his writings. Labour is probably the most important category in Marxist analysis. It is the basis for the labour theory of value and his theory of exploitation. Within the framework of his critique, most of his views of labour under capitalism are negative, e.g. the idea of workers being inherently alienated. Under capitalism the worker is alienated from the object of his production, i.e. workers give form to what is produced but it is appropriated by the capitalists. Moreover, work is but a means to an end under capitalism, while under socialism it is an end unto itself. Finally, under capitalism only a few skills are developed and thus the individual is a dwarf, a mere shadow of what could be. Under socialism, to use Marx's metaphor, the worker will hunt in the morning, fish in the afternoon, raise cattle in the evening and criticise after dinner.

Leisure emerges logically as a residual in the Marxist analysis. Marx called leisure free time and it is defined as non-work time. Free time can only occur under communism when automation will create the capacity for time away from work. It must be remembered that the work day in Europe was 12–14 hours long when Marx wrote about free time. Workers did little else but eat, sleep and work. At the highest stage of communist society said Marx, the measure of wealth would be the amount of free time.

Free time has increased in capitalist society. The 40-hour work week, or less, has replaced the 70–80-hour work week. Yet from the neo-Marxist point of view labour remains underdeveloped. Herbert Marcuse has argued that leisure time is really manipulated by the capitalist society. Leisure accords with the worst values of capitalism, e.g. it is competitive and hierarchical. Leisure under capitalism does not allow individuals to be fully human, to be constantly creative.

The data that unfold in the course of this book do not testify to the abundant success of the Soviet system in meeting Marxist ideals. On the contrary, typical Soviet citizens are subject to substantial restrictions on their options during their free time. These restrictions reflect two elements within the society. First, the low priority given to the production of recreational and cultural goods. This is true of those leisure goods available on a day-to-day basis as well as facilities for holidays. Moreover, they reflect the relative inadequacies of the service sector.

But they also represent a philosophical perspective of the directors of the Soviet system. Work is still considered the most important category in the life of an individual. It is certainly viewed as more important than leisure. As one Soviet writer put it: 'material production and labour of a person comprises the basis of his development'.[1] In the strictest sense the end of life is work and time off or leisure is for the purpose of getting ready for work again. One source uses the term *prostoe vosproizvodstvo* (simple reproduction) about non-working time during which other kind of work is being done, e.g. housework. There is much the same implication in the term *rasshirennoe vosproizvodstvo* (large-scale reproduction) which stands for free time or leisure time.[2] Free time is thus regarded as the time in which one regenerates for the real purpose of life, which is work.

There are also philosophical strictures on leisure itself. There is a very judgemental strain in the criticisms of what people do with their free time. Some activities are seen as better than others. In assessing the Soviet critique it is important to keep in mind that to a substantial degree planners can control what people do with their time. If D. H. Lawrence violates socialist morality, then planners have sufficient control not to publish any of his books. If certain kinds of television are 'harmful', then they are left off the air. Thus, people are criticised for engaging in athletic activity in front of their television sets while watching sporting events.[3] There are those who admit that defining a 'first-rate' and 'second-rate' activity is realistically impossible.[4] Yet it is a common complaint that people spend too much time 'passively', that is, as spectators at sporting events, television watchers and cinemagoers.[5]

The judgemental posture of the Soviet perspective is tied to an equally puritanical outlook, which is explored in Chapter 1. Thus, leisure can be used 'as a means toward spiritual wealth and growth' pursuing 'lofty civic goals' or can be materialistic in a direction where 'wittingly or unwittingly, [people] erect artificial barriers for themselves, barriers that hinder them from turning their free time into true wealth'.[6] Or it can take the view that night clubs should not exist because if people stay up late at night they will not be able to get up in the morning.[7]

The final major concept that underlies the Soviet view of leisure is the emphasis on the collective rather than the private nature of the consumption of leisure. There are two meanings to this concept. One is that people should engage in more collective activities, i.e. consuming leisure not as an individual, but participating jointly in organised, group activity.[8] The other aspect is the idea that there are social obligations and what one does during non-working time should be consistent with those responsibilities. At the 24th Communist Party Congress in 1971, First Secretary Leonid Brezhnev said, 'Free time is not time free from responsibility for the society'.[9] The rather amorphous idea that the individual should make choices that accord with social values has been spelled out more recently: 'Individual development of a worker is connected above all with the effectiveness of socially useful activity. That is why the society requires of its members conscious submission of personal interests to social interests. This affirms not only the value of free time in all its richness, but also the value of human life . . . What definite set of values finds its realisation in the activity of youth in free time? It is interested in definite orientation to basic social values of the society. And that defines the limits of possible activity of a young worker's leisure activity.'[10]

Explicitly, the public can regulate free time through collectivising leisure; implicitly, society rules leisure through adherence to its values. It is true that Soviet planners regulate leisure consumption through control over production. However, this control is highly imperfect. In fact attempts at control are resented. Ultimately, within the constraints of the Soviet leisure economy, individuals make free choices. The largest problem is that in controlling the supply of leisure, insufficient resources have been devoted to recreation; the general choices are limited.

A final introductory word about the methodological approach taken in the book. The questions being raised are not only complex, they demand that one uses the research findings and data of more than one discipline. The analysis is therefore multidisciplinary; materials have been drawn from both economics and sociology in an attempt to weave together the natural interaction that occurs in dealing with an issue like the conjuncture of private and public decision-making. To exclude the viewpoint of either discipline would be to produce reductionist conclusions about the conflict between planners and households.

1 Household Time Budgets

This chapter establishes the quantitative base for studying the trade-off between work and leisure by analysing the household budget of time in detail. It is an analysis of how much time people spend working, travelling to work, eating and sleeping, and how much time they have for leisure after work and on their days off. In particular, a substantial part of the analysis deals with sex differences. It will be seen that time pressures weigh very heavily on Soviet citizens. This is especially true for women whose options on a daily basis are extremely limited because of their dual roles as worker and homemaker. This information is collected using a standard methodology that has been used for a long time in the Soviet Union: simply asking people how much time they devote to each of these activities and viewing the results as the household's or individual's time budget. These time budget studies represent the West's primary source of knowledge on how Soviet citizens spend their lives.

Our treatment of the subject focuses on urban households. A later chapter analyses the work–leisure trade-off in the Soviet rural sector. There is no shortage of budget studies in the Soviet Union. They are not always as recent as one would like (there do not appear to be any studies from the 1970s), and the nature of the sample is not always perfectly defined, but there are a lot of numbers. As a result, there is an enormous amount of material on housework in the USSR and how that is broken down by activity, sex, etc. The large number of budget studies also allows us to present material on the profile of the household's time budget by such variables as sex, type of job, marital status, level of education, etc. We also analyse the changes that have taken place over time. Soviet researchers have been collecting these data since the early 1920s. In some cases we benefit from longitudinal studies from the same geographical area or among the same group of workers.

It would make little sense to present all the data that are available on time budgets. It is virtually impossible to do so and it would be boring and confusing. Moreover, the definition of categories often differ from one study to another which eliminates meaningful comparisons. What I try to do is to either present results which are representative of a certain type of study or present the average of several similar studies. In those cases where a budget study focuses on a single variable, the study is presented by itself.

Throughout it must be remembered that from the perspective of the individual a time budget is always the result of both constraints imposed from the outside and voluntary choices made by the household. A fixed obligation to work an eight hour day and a five or six day work week represents the imposition of a social dictate in the work–leisure trade-off. This is true whether we are talking about the Soviet Union or a western democracy. The choice of whether to go to the cinema or to the local library or to visit friends is a choice made either by an individual or a household that negotiates decisions between its members' competing desires. Even here choice is limited by the number of leisure activities from which to choose; a society with few cars reduces the possibility of a weekend drive into the countryside as a prominent leisure activity.

The great defect in Soviet time budget studies is that we cannot tell if they have controlled for the other relevant variables when we look at the effect of any individual variable. That is, if the relationship between the level of education and the amount of free time is being studied, have they held such variables as age and sex constant? It appears that Soviet social science does not apply this kind of rigour to its survey research. While this limits the definitive quality of any conclusions, the results are nevertheless illuminating. Moreover, these data are all we have to work with at this point.

Time budget studies in the Soviet Union can be divided into three historical stages.[1] The first stage is the early 1920s. This work was directed by the famous Soviet social scientist, S. G. Strumilin. His research was aimed at measuring the influence of the 1917 revolution on both urban workers and peasants. The second stage is the period of the late 1920s and the 1930s. In 1927 the Soviets began the transition to a 7 hour work day which was actually carried out between 1930–2. The change in the length of the work day is the distinguishing feature of the budget studies of this period. Otherwise the main ideas of the classification system remained unchanged. In 1933–4 the time budgets of collective farmers were studied for the first time. The third stage coincides with the post-Stalin period and the first study in this era was carried out in 1957.

The studies carried out during the Stalinist period are puritanical and by language and conceptualisation rigidly work-orientated. The research of the post-Stalin period conforms more closely with Western methodology particularly in the sense that the categories are not so stringently defined.

It is worth going through the Strumilin schema to see the biases of Soviet social science in the early 1920s:

A Necessary Time
  I Productive labour:
    in the social economy
    in the private economy
  II Housework (in the family):
    cooking
    care of children
    other
  III Wastes of time:
    transportation to work and back
    shopping
  IV Unavoidable requirements:
    eating (at work and home)
    sleep (night and day)
B Free Time
  I Physical development:
    athletics and sports
    walks, tourism
  II Cultural amateur activity:
    social work
    education, lectures, museums
    reading
    amateur artistic activity
  III Cultural leisure activities:
    cinema, theatre and other performances
    home games: chess, draughts and others
  IV Other entertainment:
    inviting guests and visiting
    other wastes of time
  V Doing nothing

In the first part, 'Necessary Time', the Russian term for 'unavoidable requirements', is *neustranimye potrebnosti* which is a very strong term implying these activities are an obstacle to alternative uses of time, e.g. more 'productive labour'. This is very much a Stalinist conception. There is a similar implied criticism of non-work activities. The term 'wastes of time' (*poteri vremeni*) literally means that these activities are useless expenditures of time as opposed to being in the labour force or doing housework. Within the other major category, Free Time, there is the implication that these also are irrelevant activities. There is the term 'other wastes of time' (*prochie poteri vremeni*) implying that all the other activities falling within the concept of free time are a waste of time. That kind of judgemental rigidity has declined in the last quarter of a century, although it has not entirely disappeared. Thus in the 1959 study of time budgets in the Krasnoiarsk *krai* which was also supervised by Strumilin, the most blatant of the value-loaded terms did not appear.[2]

Finally, it should be noted that time budget studies no longer appear in the social scientific literature of the 1970s. While it would obviously be very useful for comparative purposes if more recent work were available, most Soviet research in this area is clustered within the period of the first half of the 1960s.

TIME BUDGETS OF SOVIET URBANITES

We begin by looking at the time budgets of Russian Republic (RSFSR) urban workers in 1930 and 1963. The 1930 data are for Moscow and the 1963 data are for the Ivanov, Gorky, Rostov and Sverdlovsk *oblasts* (see Table 1.1). Non-working time connected to production usually refers to commutation time. On occasion it may also include the time it takes to

TABLE 1.1 *Time budgets of urban workers in the RSFSR, 1930 and 1963, hours per week*

	1930		1963	
	Men	Women	Men	Women
Work time	44.0	44.0	41.1	40.3
Non-working time, connected with work; housework and work on the private plot	20.2	45.4	24.7	42.8
Time for satisfying physiological needs	63.8	61.5	67.0	63.3
Free time	40.0	17.1	33.3	20.1
Other expenditures of time	—	—	1.9	1.5
TOTAL	168.0	168.0	168.0	168.0

SOURCE V. G. Baikova *et al.*, *Svobodnoe Vremia i Vsestoronnee Razvitie Lichnosti* (Moscow, 1965) p. 5!.

get to one's shift and leave the work place. While we generally associate the private plot with the rural peasantry many urbanites kept private plots, particularly in 1930 when so many Soviet urban workers had only recently left the farms. Even today, many urbanites keep some kind of a garden. In Chapter 5 we discuss the collective garden associations so common among urbanites. Physiological needs generally refers to eating and sleeping, but may at times include personal hygiene. Free time should be regarded as a residual after all other expenditures of time have been accounted for. It should also be noted that 'work time' means work for pay. Work on the private plot is not considered work for pay. It is placed in the same category with housework, though an imputed income is earned from the agricultural output produced by urban plots and women's lives are dramatically affected by the amount of unpaid housework they must do.

Over the period of 33 years, there was a decline in the amount of work time; about 3 hours for men and close to 4 hours for women. There was an increase in the amount of time men spent in the broad category of time spent travelling to work, doing housework and work on the private plot, which was slightly greater than the decline in the hours expended by women within this category. As is shown in Table 1.2, this is due much more to the fall in the time devoted to private plot agriculture than it is to increased male assistance with housework. Both sexes experienced increases in the time available for eating and sleeping. The

TABLE 1.2 *Monthly utilization of nonworking time, in hours, by sex, 1923–4 and 1960–1*

	Women		Men	
	1923–4	1960–1	1923–4	1960–1
Non-working time	527.3	550.0	521.8	550.0
Round trip to work	20.4	30.0	20.9	36.3
Housework	141.4	114.0	46.9	38.0
Work on private plots and trade	23.0	2.0	15.1	5.0
Free time	72.5	119.0	133.9	177.0
Physiological needs	270.0	285.0	305.0	293.7
Sleep	212.7	220.0	238.3	229.0
Eating	40.0	42.0	47.7	45.0
Personal hygiene	17.3	23.0	19.0	19.7

SOURCE V. G. Kriazhev, *Vnerabochee Vremia i Sfera Obsluzhivaniia* (Moscow, 1966) p. 79.

amount of free time for men declined by almost 7 hours, while women's free time rose by about 3 hours.

A more detailed study compares time budgets of men and women in the time periods 1923–4 and 1960–1. The data in Table 1.2 are stated in terms of monthly expenditures of time. On a net basis, both men and women experienced an increase in the amount of non-working time, with men gaining slightly more than women during this period of nearly 40 years. In the early 1920s both sexes had to do less travelling to work than they did in the early 1960s. This is particularly true of men whose round trip to work almost doubled during this time period. Housework fell for both sexes, by 27 hours a month for men and 9 hours for women. But women were still doing three times as much housework as men. The decline in the amount of housework for women is due to technological changes, e.g. household appliances, and institutional changes, e.g. the growth of day care centres. Predictably the assimilation into urban life was accompanied by a decline in the role of private plot agriculture. In the 1960s the Soviet household devoted only about 7 hours a month to a plot compared with 48 hours a generation before. The amount of free time rose by 47 hours a month for women and 43 hours a month for men. But men still had 58 hours more free time than women in 1960–1. The entire difference was easily absorbed by the 76 hours more of housework women had to do. In the 1920s men had about 35 hours a month more time to sleep, eat and take care of basic personal needs. This changed over the period and women were getting more time to do all three while men experienced a decline in the time available to them for personal hygiene. Men were still getting a bit more sleep every morning and a little more time to eat a meal.

In general, however, there is evidence not only of a decline in the general work burden of Soviet men and women, but a fall in the difference of work time between the sexes. This is seen in Table 1.3 where production work is added to housework to arrive at a figure for the daily work load of men and women. In 1923–4 women had a total work load of 78 hours – 19 hours more than men. In the mid-1930s this difference rose to a high of 21 hours and then the difference fell steadily so that by the period 1967–70 the difference was 14 hours a week. But it took 30 years for this 7 hour decline in the difference in the total male–female work load to take place. More remarkably it took about 45 years for the weekly work load of women to fall 13 hours from 78 hours to 65 hours a week. At 65 hours a week, the work load of women in 1967–70 was 6 hours longer than men worked in 1923–4.

A 1959 study in Moscow and Novosibirsk confirms these findings.[3]

TABLE 1.3 *Work load in blue collar families in large cities of the European parts of the USSR, hours per week*

Year	Kind of work	Male workers	Female workers	Difference of work time	Non-working housewives
1923–4	Production work	46	44		—
	Housework	13	34		70
	Weekly work load	59	78	19	70
1936	Production work	41	40		—
	Housework	12	34		41
	Weekly work load	53	74	21	41
1963	Production work	40	40		—
	Housework	12	30		—
	Weekly work load	52	70	18	—
1965–8	Production work	40	39		—
	Housework	12	27		—
	Weekly work load	52	66	14	—
1967–70	Production work	41	38		—
	Housework	10	27		52
	Weekly work load	51	65	14	52

SOURCE L. A. Gordon et al., *Cherty Sotsialisticheskogo Obraza Zhizni: Byt Gorodskikh Rabochikh Vchera, Segodnia, Zavtra* (Moscow, 1977) p. 152.

The time spent at work plus travelling to work was 38.7 per cent of a man's average work day but only 31.9 per cent of a woman's typical work day. The two categories where there were major differences were in housework and personal hygiene where men spent 2 hours a day, or 8.3 per cent of their time. Women spent 5 hours and 3 minutes, or 23.5 per cent of their time at these activities. Both sexes spent virtually the same amount of time sleeping and eating. Men had more than 4 hours a day free time (17.2 per cent of the day) and women had just under 2.5 hours (9.9 per cent) for leisure.

A 1963 study of four *oblasts* in the RSFSR compared the time budgets of men and women on a typical work day with the distribution of their time on a day off, when Sunday was the only day off (see Table 1.4). Aside from the obvious fact that people do not work on their day off, there are three interesting differences between a work day and a day off. The first is that housework increased, particularly for women. While men devoted an additional hour to the house on their day off, women seem to need the day off to catch up with household chores, spending 6.5 hours a

TABLE 1.4 Time budgets of industrial workers, 1963, by sex, four RSFSR oblasts, in hours and minutes and per cent of total day

	Men				Women			
	Work day		Day off		Work day		Day off	
	Hours and minutes	Per cent of total time	Hours and minutes	Per cent of total time	Hours and minutes	Per cent of total time	Hours and minutes	Per cent of total time
Work time	6:54	28.7	0:03	0.02	6:48	28.3	0:03	0.02
Non-working time connected with work	1:38	6.8	0:04	0.03	1:23	5.8	0:04	0.03
Housework	2:02	8.5	3:02	12.6	4:37	19.2	6:25	26.7
Satisfying physiological needs	9:11	38.3	11:23	47.5	8:43	36.3	10:47	44.9
Free time	4:02	16.8	8:37	35.9	2:17	9.6	6:20	26.5
Other expenditures of time	0:13	0.9	0:51	3.5	0:12	0.8	0:21	1.4
TOTAL	24:00	100.0	24:00	100.0	24:00	100.0	24:00	100.0

SOURCE V. A. Artemov et al., *Statistika Biudzhetov Vremeni Trudiashchikhsia* (Moscow, 1967) p. 56.

day when they do not work instead of the more usual 4.5 hours. Both sexes spent more time sleeping and eating, about 2 hours more for each sex, with men having about half an hour longer than women on both work days and the day off to sleep and eat. Finally, leisure time rose for both sexes, although men benefited more than women. Men gained about 4.5 hours free time and women about 4 hours from having a day off.

TIME BUDGETS AND MARITAL STATUS

Several studies from the 1960s focus on the question of the relationship between marital status and the time expended for various activities (see Table 1.5). The data for Pskov are from 1965, while those of other cities seem to be from the early 1960s. Each study indicates that being married changes the shape of the individual's time budget in the USSR. Moreover, the impact of marriage is different upon women than it is upon men.

There is no consistent relationship between the amount of time worked and marital status, though there is such a relationship between marital status and housework. In all cases, married people devote more time to housework than do those who are single. The impact on housework is greatest when there are children; the presence of children adds almost 1 hour to the work load of men but in the case of women it means 3 hours more housework than for single women and close to 2.5 hours more than married women who have no children. There is also a positive correlation between being unmarried and the amount of time people sleep and eat. The Yerevan data suggest that the presence of children reduces this time for women more than men. When children enter the life of a married man he loses about 20 minutes a day for sleeping and eating. But the mother loses 1 hour and 20 minutes. Finally, marriage reduces the amount of time for leisure, and children decrease it even more. In the three cities, single men had an average of 5 hours and 27 minutes for leisure, while single women had 4 hours and 21 minutes. Marriage costs married men about 1 hour a day in free time, but women lose about 2 hours when they are married.

TIME BUDGETS AND OCCUPATION

The time budget of Soviet citizens is also partially determined by the type of work done by the individual (Table 1.6). Those who do

TABLE 1.5 *Time budgets of workers by marital status and sex, various RSFSR cities, in hours and minutes*

	Free time	Work time	Housework and care of oneself	Sleeping and eating
Pskov				
Men:				
Married	4:36	6:12	1:42	9:24
Single	6:00	5:48	0:54	9:00
Women:				
Married	2:06	5:42	4:36	9:06
Single	3:48	5:54	3:00	9:12
Yerevan				
Men:				
Married, no children	4:41	7:07	1:50	8:37
Married, with children	3:54	7:04	2:40	8:18
Single	4:54	7:02	1:30	9:11
Women:				
Married, no children	3:15	7:08	2:58	8:36
Married, with children	1:55	7:04	5:17	7:18
Single	4:24	6:34	2:20	8:37
Kostroma				
Women:				
Married	1:48	7:47	4:20	8:17
Single	4:51	7:39	1:31	8:34

SOURCES Pskov – B. T. Kolpakova and V. D. Patrusheva (eds), *Biudzhet Vremeni Gorodskogo Naseleniia* (Moscow, 1971) p. 212; Yerevan and Kostroma – G. S. Petrosian, *Vnerabochee Vremia Trudiashchikhsia v SSSR* (Moscow, 1965) p. 103.

intellectual work are at their place of work longer and spend more time commuting. Male intellectual workers in particular spend close to 1 hour a day more than male manual workers in these two activities. With respect to housework, there is a substantial difference between manual and intellectual workers. Whereas the difference between male and female manual workers is 1 hour and 49 minutes a day of housework, the difference in the time spent on housework by male and female intellectual workers is 1 hour and 11 minutes. This is overwhelmingly due to the fact that women intellectual workers do less housework

TABLE 1.6 *Time budgets by type of work and sex, Leningrad 1968, in hours per day*

	Manual workers		Intellectual workers	
	Men	Women	Men	Women
Work time	7.98	8.02	8.24	8.14
Non-work time connected with production work	1.16	1.18	1.34	1.46
Housework	1.32	3.13	1.34	2.52
Satisfying physiological needs	8.4	8.3	8.75	8.58
Free time	4.62	2.77	3.52	2.68
Other expenditures of time	0.53	0.78	0.8	0.62

SOURCE I. P. Trufanov, *Problemy Byta Gorodskogo Naseleniia SSSR*, pp. 111 and 113. Those who do physical work are: (1) unskilled workers who do physical labour, (2) skilled workers who primarily do physical labour employed on machines, (3) skilled workers who primarily do manual labour. Those who do intellectual work are: (1) workers whose work requires mostly intellectual skills, (2) highly skilled workers who do scientific–technical work, (3) administrators of production collectives.

than their female manual worker counterparts. Intellectual workers spend more time sleeping and eating than manual workers. In both cases men have a bit more time than women for these activities. Male intellectual workers also have less leisure time than manual workers; manual workers enjoy more than an hour a day free time. There is little difference in the free time of the two groups of women.

THE EFFECT OF EDUCATION, INCOME AND TYPE OF APARTMENT

A study done in the second half of the 1960s analysed the difference in time expended on various activities by level of education, income and the living conditions of workers (see Table 1.7). The number of categories of activities are not as complete as other studies, but the study does shed additional light because it includes the weekend, when leisure activities increase relative to work. Finally this study makes a distinction between 'leisure' and such activities as 'physical culture, sports' and 'meeting friends, guests, dance'. I have lumped all these activities together under the heading of 'free time'.

TABLE 1.7 *Time budgets by level of education, income and type of apartment 1965–8, in hours per week*

	Least educated workers	Most educated workers	Poorly paid workers	Well-paid workers	Workers living in the worst conditions	Workers living in the best conditions
Housework and work in the private plot	45.0	34.6	41.5	37.1	46.0	32.4
Free time	28.7	45.2	37.0	40.2	31.4	42.8

SOURCE   L. A. Gordon et al., *Cherty Sotsialisticheskogo Obraza Zhizni: Byt Gorodskikh Rabochikh Vchera, Segodnia, Zavtra* (Moscow, 1977) p. 150. Least educated workers – 4 classes or less; most educated workers – middle special, unfinished higher and higher education; poorly paid – less than 50 roubles per month per household member; well-paid – more than 75 roubles per month per family member; worst living conditions – homes without communal conveniences; best living conditions – homes with the communal conveniences.

Poorly educated workers spend more time doing housework and have less time for leisure activities than do well-educated Soviet citizens. The poorly educated spend about 1.5 hours more every day doing housework. This accounts for most of the 2.3 hours less free time available to them. The differences in the amount of time spent on these two broad activities is less when household incomes are compared. As might be expected, the poor spend more time on housework and this almost exactly corresponds to the lesser amount of free time they have available. The difference between the two groups is about half an hour a day. The type of apartment people live in makes a big difference in their lives. Those who live in apartments equipped with conveniences spend about an hour a day less doing housework than those who live in less comfortable housing. The free time difference is greater; those living in the well-outfitted apartments have more than an additional 1.5 hours for leisure.

HOUSEWORK

We have firmly established that women have much greater responsibility than men for housework. The two tables which follow detail how household responsibilities are shared within the family and how much time families devote to the major household responsibilities. The data in Table 1.8 averages the results of three studies, one done in 1966 among

TABLE 1.8 *Division of household responsibilities in the family, late 1960s, in percentages*

Kind of work	Per cent of families in which work is done by:			
	Wife only	Husband only	Together	Others
Keeping house				
Shopping	65	3	18	13
Preparing breakfast	64	8	16	12
Preparing dinner	71	2	12	14
Washing dishes	31	10	30	27
General cleaning	39	11	36	16
Everyday cleaning	67	4	14	11
Minor repairs	32	54	3	9
Laundry	74	1	14	10
Paying bills	47	30	13	11
Child care				
Bringing child home	57	17	22	4
Washing, dressing, feeding	71	4	20	7
Taking child to nursery	63	10	22	5
Going to parent–teacher conferences	68	11	21	1
Helping with homework	61	18	18	3

SOURCES G. A. Slesarev and Z. A. Iankova, 'Zhenshchina na Promyshlennom Predpriiatii i v Sem'e' in G. V. Osipov and Ia. Shchepan'skii (eds), *Sotsial'nye Problemy Truda i Proizvodstva* (Moscow, 1969) p. 430; A. G. Kharchev and S. I. Golod, *Professionalnaia Rabota Zhenshchin i Semia* (Leningrad, 1971) p. 74; Ia. Andriushkiavichene, 'Zhenskii Trud i Problema Svobodnogo Vremeni', *Problemy Byta, Braka i Semi'i* (Vilnius, 1970) p. 82.

married working women in Moscow, Leningrad and Penza, the second in Leningrad and Kostroma in 1968, and the third in Vilnius at the end of the 1960s.

All the studies examine the basic household tasks; only the 1966 study and the Vilnius research looked at the issue of child care. Notwithstanding anecdotal tales of how Soviet husbands also carry a bag with them when they go to work, shopping is overwhelmingly a woman's job. Shopping takes a great deal of time. In a Kiev study in 1965–6 only 22 per cent of households spent half an hour a day shopping; 40 per cent spent 1–1.5 hours and the rest 2–2.5 hours a day.[4] Meal preparation is also the wife's responsibility. Because husbands are even less help with dinner than they are with breakfast, more women cook dinner by themselves than breakfast. In addition to these jobs, women also have disproportionate responsibility for everyday cleaning of the house and laundry, which means washing and ironing. In a world without permanent press clothes and fully automatic washers and dryers, laundry is the most tedious task in a Soviet household.

Washing dishes and general cleaning, e.g. cleaning windows and floors, are the household chores most shared, although they are still mostly women's work. They are also areas where others in the home such as children and grandparents lend assistance. Husbands do most of the repair work around the house by themselves, although a sizeable minority of wives also do this work. Finally, wives are mostly responsible for family finances, although a substantial minority of households have husbands doing this.

It is apparent from the data on child care that where there are young children who need the attention of family members, women have the primary responsibility in most households. This is most true in the basic washing, dressing and feeding of a child as well as for going to parent–teacher conferences. There is not even one job involving child care where the parents share the role in more than about 20 per cent of Soviet households.

A number of studies were done in the early 1960s on the amount of time devoted to each of the household tasks. The results were all remarkably close to one another, and so I cite only one of those studies because it also provides 1922 data as a comparison (Table 1.9). This study shows that for both men and women, shopping and cooking dominate their household responsibilities. Remarkably, in the period of 40 years there was only a 2 hour decline in the amount of time women spent shopping and cooking over an entire week. Men experienced a similar decrease in the time they allocated to this work. Women experienced more of a gain in cleaning clothes, shoes, etc. This probably reflects the increase in the availability of appliances to assist in doing housework and state production of certain goods and services. However, only a negligible decline was enjoyed in the time spent on house cleaning. Finally, there was a small decline in the time a woman devoted a child care, with husbands picking up virtually no responsibility over the 40 year period. In sum, there was but a small decrease in the amount of time devoted to house and child care. More importantly, male and female roles remained virtually unchanged over the 40 year period.

Earlier data showed that women, who do more housework than men,

TABLE 1.9 *Expenditures of time on different household tasks, by sex, 1922 and 1963, hours per week*

	Men		Women	
	1922	1963	1922	1963
Shopping and cooking	6.6	4.7	18.0	15.9
Cleaning house	2.5	1.7	4.6	3.9
Cleaning clothes, shoes, furniture	0.5	0.5	7.6	4.8
Caring for children	0.7	0.9	4.5	3.3
TOTAL	10.3	7.8	34.7	27.9

SOURCE V. G. Baikova *et al.*, *Svobodnoe Vremia i Vsestoronnee Razvitie Lichnosti* (Moscow, 1965) p. 61.

also have less free time. A detailed study in Moscow in the early 1960s showed that as the time spent on housework increases, the amount of free time goes down. Time pressures are so great that any additional time spent on housework can only come out of time which would otherwise have been used for leisure. For example, people who do less than 1 hour of housework a day have 4 hours and 53 minutes of free time; those who do between 2 and 2.5 hours of housework have 2 hours and 32 minutes of free time and those who do 3 to 3.5 hours have only 1 hour and 28 minutes of leisure.[5] The estimates are that half the increase in free time achieved during the period 1960–7 was a result of reducing housework and the other half was a result of the decline in the length of the work day.[6]

We also showed that married women with children do more housework than married women without children and single women. More detailed data show that the number and age of the children also affect the amount of time spent on housework. The first child, not surprisingly, leads to the largest increase in housework. Thereafter, each additional child increases housework by diminishing increments. For example, in one study, the first child increases housework by 56 per cent, but the second child adds 'only' 10 percentage points and the third another 7 points.[7]

The age of children also affects the time spent doing housework. In a Moscow study the presence of an infant under the age of 1 year is associated with a woman doing 5 hours and 40 minutes of housework, with a child 1 to 3 years old, 2 hours and 30 minutes, with a child 3 to 7 years old, 4 hours and 15 minutes and with a child 7 to 16 years old, 3 hours and 5 minutes. The average time for housework of the families with preschoolers is 4 hours and 8 minutes, about 1 hour longer than those families with school age children.[8] A Novosibirsk study found that families with school age children had 3 hours and 5 minutes housework, exactly the same as the Moscow study, but households with preschool children had housework of 4 hours and 54 minutes, a little less than 2 hours longer.[9] Finally, a 1965 study of married women in Pskov compared the time expended on housework in houses where all the children were over the age of 4 years with those households where there was one child under the age of 4 (see Table 1.10). Four years is a significant age for a Soviet child because it is at this age that children can begin to go to a day care centre (*detski sad*) and in principle relieve the mother of some responsibilities. I have not seen any study estimating whether the day care centre reduces housework. The Novosibirsk study to which we just referred claims that the number of children does not affect the free time of parents if they are in a school or preschool institution.[10] In the Pskov research, it is clear that having a child under the age of 4 increases the housework burden of women. The differential is greatest if there are two or three children in the household; mothers in this situation spend about 1.5 hours more on housework when there is a child under 4 than in one in which all children are over that age.

TABLE 1.10 *Expenditures of time on housework of married women, Pskov, 1965, hours per day*

Women with all children over the age of 4 years			Women with one child under the age of 4 years		
Number of children in household			Number of children in household		
1	2–3	3+	1	2–3	3+
4.2	4.8	5.9	4.6	6.4	6.3

SOURCE B. T. Kolpakova and V. D. Patrusheva (eds), *Biudzhet Vremeni Gorodskogo Naseleniia* (Moscow, 1971) p. 73.

Household income is also a determinant of the time spent on housework. Data from a study of the early 1960s (see Table 1.11) showed that the higher the per capita household income, the less the time spent on housework. The differences are quite substantial. In a later commentary on this study it was argued that the differences in housework can be attributed to the lesser capacity of the low income

TABLE 1.11 *Influence of per capita household income on time spent on housework, early 1960s*

Per capita household income, roubles per month	Housework, hours and minutes per day
Less than 35	5:00
35–50	3:45
50–75	2:40
More than 75	2:15

SOURCE V. G. Kriazhev, *Vnerabochee Vremia i Sfera Obsluzhivaniia* (Moscow, 1966) p. 109.

households to buy labour-saving household appliances as well as their relative inability to consume certain social services.[11]

The data in Table 1.12 show that there is an inverse relationship between the level of education and time spent on housework. Two things should be noted. The best educated women (women with university degrees have been excluded from this study) do about 60 per cent more housework than the least educated men. Moreover, while the amount of housework keeps decreasing for women as their level of education increases, the relative payoff is uneven. The percentage decrease is greatest for women who finish elementary school.

Soviet budget studies concentrate on people in the work-force. This makes sense in view of the fact that the labour-force participation rate is about 90 per cent for men and about 85 per cent for women. When people are unemployed the additional time they have shows up partially in the form of more time doing housework. Thus in 1965 in Pskov, working men did 1.4 hours of housework a day while unemployed men

TABLE 1.12 *Hours of housework by sex and level of education, Krasnoiarsk Krai, 1959 (hours during six working days)*

	Level of education			
	Up to 4 classes	5 to 9 classes	Middle and unfinished higher education	Higher education
Men	14.8	13.2	11.1	10.9
Women	32.4	26.7	23.6	—

SOURCE V. D. Patrushev, *Vremia Kak Ekonomicheskaia Kategoriia* (Moscow, 1966) p. 112.

did 2.9 hours. The comparable figures for women were 4.1 hours and 5.9 hours.[12]

Finally, we examine the question of whether the type of living facility affects the amount of housework. Unfortunately, there is no overall measure of how different living arrangements in the Soviet Union alter housework responsibility. The only data available relate to cleaning the house. Interestingly, the data show very little difference in the time spent on cleaning, whether people have their own apartment, live in a communal situation or own their own home (see Table 1.13). There is almost no difference between large cities and the small city of Pavlov-Posad. The only difference of any consequence is the one hour more that women living in the small city in a private home spend on housework.

TABLE 1.13 *Time devoted to cleaning the house by type of living space, hours per week*

	In large cities			In Pavlov-Posad		
	Separate apartment	Room in communal apartment	Private house	Separate apartment	Room in communal apartment	Private house
Women	4.1	4.1	3.5	4.1	4.4	4.4
Men	1.0	1.3	1.2	1.4	1.3	1.0

SOURCE L. A. Gordon and E. V. Klopov, *Chelovek Posle Raboty* (Moscow, 1972) p. 122.

The housework burden has been shown to be substantial, occupying a large portion of the non-working time of Soviet households, particularly women. Earlier data showed that even over a period of 45 years housework had only declined by seven hours for women. Given the socialist goal of substituting public facilities for private responsibility, the Soviet record in this area is hardly illustrious. Nevertheless, the goal remains. Writing from the vantage point of 1968, at some unspecified future date it was forecast that housework will drop from 27.4 hours (1963 figure) to 19.2 hours, which is about 8 hours less, essentially the decline that it required 45 years to accomplish. Of the 19.2 hours, 4.5 hours, or 23 per cent are to be absorbed by the socialist sector, the remainder coming from the mechanisation of housework.[13]

THE EFFECT OF THE FIVE DAY WORK WEEK ON TIME BUDGETS

There have been several notable changes in the length of the work week in the USSR. As Table 1.14 shows the average work week before the Revolution was 58.5 hours. By 1955 it had fallen to 47.8 hours, which meant essentially a worker worked 6 days a week, for 8 hours every day. In 1956 the work day was reduced by 2 hours for days immediately preceding days off and official holidays. From 1956–60 all workers were transferred to 7 and 6 hour work days. As a result the work week fell from 47.8 hours to 41.6 hours. In March 1967 a major change took place in the life of the ordinary Soviet citizen; the work week declined from 6 days to 5 days, with the work day lengthened to 8 hours. For the typical industrial worker this meant that the work week fell by one hour to 40.7 hours a week and if one adds in the somewhat shorter work day of teachers, doctors and other professionals, then the overall work week in the Soviet Union was lowered to 39.4 hours, where it stands today.[14]

The introduction of the 5 day work week had a rather remarkable impact on workers. Table 1.15 shows the results of a massive time budget study carried out in December 1967 and January 1968 covering 2480 workers in the large Leningrad electronic equipment complex, Svetlana, which was transferred to the 5 day work week. These data are compared with the time budgets of workers from Dnepropetrovsk, Zaporozhe, Odessa, and Kostroma from a study done in 1965–6 when these workers were under a 6 day work week regime. The results are shown for the 5 work days, Saturday, which was formerly a work day, Sunday, which was always the day off and the total for the week.

TABLE 1.14 *Average length of the work week in the Soviet Union*

	Industrial workers	All blue-collar and white-collar employees
1913	58.5	—
1955	47.8	—
1960	41.6	—
1963	41.6	—
1969	40.7	39.4
1970	40.7	39.4
1975	40.7	39.4
1977	40.6	39.4
1980	40.6	39.4

SOURCE   *Narodnoe Khoziaistvo SSSR*, various years.

TABLE 1.15 *Time budgets of workers after the transfer to a five day week and workers under a six day week (in hours and minutes)*

	Work day			Saturday			Sunday			Total for the week		
	Five day	Six day	Difference	Five day	Six day	Difference	Five day	Six day	Difference	Five day	Six day	Difference
Women												
Work time	7:30	6:55	+0:35	0:45	5:00	−4:15	0:09	0:10	−0:1	38:24	39:45	−1:21
Time connected with work	2:14	2:20	−0:06	0:39	1:45	−1:06	0:15	—	+0:15	12:04	13:25	−1:21
Housework	2:59	4:21	−1:22	5:07	5:05	+0:02	4:49	6:05	−1:16	24:51	32:55	−8:04
Physiological needs	9:00	8:31	+0:29	11:35	9:40	+1:55	11:50	11:05	+0:45	68:25	63:20	+5:05
Free time	2:17	1:53	+0:24	5:54	2:30	+3:24	6:57	6:40	+0:17	24:16	18:35	+5:41
Men												
Work time	7:32	6:54	+0:38	0:35	4:55	−4:20	0:08	0:40	−0:32	38:23	40:05	−1:42
Time connected with work	2:17	2:38	−0:21	0:20	1:55	−1:35	0:09	0:10	−0:01	11:54	15:15	−3:11
Housework	1:09	2:03	−0:54	2:41	2:20	+0:21	2:41	3:30	−0:49	11:07	16:05	−4:58
Physiological needs	9:26	8:44	+0:42	12:32	10:10	+2:22	12:02	10:45	+1:17	71:44	64:35	+7:09
Free time	3:36	3:41	−0:05	7:52	4:40	+3:12	9:00	8:55	+0:05	34:52	32:00	+2:52

SOURCE A. V. Netsenko, *Sotsial'no-Ekonomicheskie Problemy Svobodnogo Vremeni Pri Sotsializme* (Leningrad, 1975) p. 44.

The length of the work day increased for both men and women under a 5-day schedule, although it declined for the week as a whole. The time connected with work, which mainly involves travelling to and from work also declined. This is due to one less day of travel to work. The weekly savings in travel time was one hour and 21 minutes for women and for men, who typically travel further to work, a saving of over 3 hours under the new system.

The time devoted to housework changed sharply. On a work day, women reduced the time spent on housework by a little more than 1 hour, which one Soviet author characterised as a decline in women's productivity.[15] The fact that a woman's work day lasted longer meant that she had to cut down on her housework. Men also reduced their time on housework by almost 1 hour. The free time of women rose by almost half an hour and men's free time remained about the same. The great changes on a Saturday went beyond the absence of work. There were also large increases in the time spent sleeping and eating; almost 2 hours for women and 2.5 hours for men. In addition there were large increases in leisure time; over 3 hours for both sexes. What should be noted is that there was essentially no change in the time spent on housework. Apparently Soviet families traded off market work for leisure, not home work, when the 5 day week went into effect. Moreover, on Sundays women also spent more than 1 hour less on housework and men almost 1 hour less. On Sundays, both spent more time sleeping and eating.

For the week as a whole, the major changes show up very clearly. Women spend 8 hours less and men 5 hours less on housework. Soviet citizens do not use the extra block of time a 5 day work week has given them to 'catch-up' with housework; they use it to enjoy themselves. If you add free time to the time spent eating and sleeping, women spend almost 11 more hours a week on these activities and men now spend 10 hours a week more on the same things.

Two other studies confirm the results of this detailed research. In one study men's free time rose by 5.5 hours a week and women's free time by 4.1 hours.[16] In the other, women's average weekly leisure time rose from 21 to 27.5 hours with the shift to a 5 day week.[17] Only one source has suggested that women have not benefited as much as these other data suggest. According to a 1977 article, men gained 5 hours of free time during the week and women only 1 hour, which they have used for housework, while men have 'tended to while away the hours playing dominoes, lounging and drinking'.[18]

Soviet citizens overwhelmingly support the 5 day work week. In a 1972–3 Sverdlovsk study, 70 per cent of the men and 67 per cent of the women said they did not want a 6 day week with 1 day off. Sixteen per cent of the men and 17 per cent of the women said they wanted a 6 day week. The rest professed indifference.[19] There is at least one major reason why 16–17 per cent wanted to go back to the old system. Primarily, I suspect it has to do with the fact that some of the shift schedules either do not allow both spouses to work the same shift on the same day or do not allow them to have the same days off.[20] Much less importantly, the lunch break has been shortened so that effectively workers have about 20 minutes to eat. This is blamed on the poor organisation of enterprise public catering facilities.[21]

WAITING AND COMMUTING

There are two other issues that should be examined before we leave the subject of time budgets: the enormous amount of time Soviet citizens spend simply waiting in queues for most everything they do and the substantial time many Soviet workers spend travelling to and from work. Both of these facets of Soviet life are well known and jokes about Soviet citizens standing in queues abound ('What's fifty metres long and eats cabbage?' 'The queue outside a Soviet butcher shop'). The time that it takes to travel to work is really another part of working. Lengthy commuting increases the work day. Both waiting and commuting reduce the time available for leisure activities and place more pressure on a household to accomplish all the other things that are involved in family life.

In a 1963 study in the city of Krasnoiarsk workers were asked how much of their time was spent on round-trip transportation, waiting in queues, and actually using a particular service enterprise. With respect to dining out, men spend 39 per cent of the time and women 26 per cent of their time waiting in queues. For a public bath, both sexes spend about 30 per cent of the time waiting in queues and at the hairdresser's both sexes spend about 40 per cent of the time waiting for their turn.[22] Another source says that about 30 per cent of the time at service enterprises involves waiting.[23] In Novosibirsk it was reported that in restaurants people stand in queues for 2 hours.[24] It should be added that all these figures exclude the time waiting for the transportation to travel to these facilities. About one-third of the time is used to travel to and from a service enterprise.[25]

The official view on commuting is that the round trip to work should be no more than 8 per cent of all non-working time, i.e. approximately

1.5 hours a day.[26] Yet it seems unrealistic to hold out one number as the appropriate benchmark. Commuting time is a function of how far workers live from their place of employment and this is often determined by the size of the city. Indeed, it appears in the Soviet Union that the larger the city the longer it takes to get to work. This is not only true because many people commute from suburban to central areas in cities like Moscow and Leningrad, but it also applies to people who live and work within the largest cities. For example, the data in Table 1.16 show that those requiring the longest period of time to get to work are those in Moscow and the large cities of over 500 000 population. For those who commute to large cities from the suburbs, round trip transportation takes three to four hours.[27]

TABLE 1.16 *Expenditures of time for commuting to work, round trip, as percentage of total surveyed*

	Up to 1 hour	1–2 hours	More than 2 hours
Moscow	32.4	34.3	12.3
500 000 or more population	55.6	16.4	5.6
100 000–500 000 population	61.8	11.3	2.1
10 000–100 000 population	75.3	7.2	1.1
0–10 000 population	63.5	8.2	4.7

SOURCE B. Grushin, *Svobodnoe Vremia: Aktual'nye Problemy* (Moscow, 1967) p. 49.

In the medium-size city of Pskov commuting took only 4.9 hours a week for men and 4.2 hours a week for women, figures which were essentially the same as in 1922. But workers live close to their jobs in this city. Seventy-five per cent live less than two kilometres from their job and only 9 per cent live more than five kilometres from work. By international standards, this is very close to one's place of work.[28] By contrast 35 per cent of Muscovites lived more than 12 kilometres from their job.[29] A 1963 study carried out in four **RSFSR** *oblasts* estimated the average round trip to work to be 96 minutes, about twice what it was in 1922. Interestingly, only a little more than a third of the time was actually spent riding to and from work. Workers spent 40 minutes walking to the bus stop and another 19 minutes waiting for a bus. In addition, at the large enterprises, it takes about 35–45 minutes to go from the factory entrance to the work place.[30]

SUMMARY

We have seen the broadest outlines of how Soviet workers spend their day. There have been declines in the work week and concomitant increases in the time for leisure. There are major differences for men and women. In examining the basic time budget as well as housework, we saw that income, education and type of job are among the important determinants of how time is spent. The five day work week has had an important impact on the labour market decision of Soviet households. The data suggest that families chose leisure rather than market work or homework with the change in their work schedule. Even so the time pressures are far from gone. Urban residents still spend a great deal of time waiting in lines and commuting. There is no doubt that this limits their options every day of the year.

2 Non-traditional Sources of Labour: Women, Pensioners and Students

This chapter is the first of three which are devoted to the exploration of two major questions. The first question deals with how decisions are made by individuals when choosing forms of employment either alternative to or in addition to their normal full-time, year-round job. From this perspective the analysis is about the decision-making process between work and leisure that is made from below by the Soviet household. We are looking at the individual through a microscope. The second question in a real sense represents the flip side of the first. It is an explanation of policy-making at the apex of the Soviet system. Here we look through a telescope to find the kinds of policies that are being pursued to deal with the seemingly insoluble labour shortage facing the nation.

There are three groups which not only represent sources for increasing the Soviet labour supply but also involve individuals who must make clear-cut decisions about the trade-off between work and alternative activities. They are women, old-age pensioners and students, as potential part-time or full-time workers.

Each group, in its singular way, is a non-traditional source of labour. Soviet women already have the highest labour force participation rate in the world. Thus, the question in this case is not one of how to increase the percentage who want to work full-time, but how to attract to part-time work those who are still in the home to work part-time. This is our interest in women as workers in this chapter. The second group is old-age pensioners who must choose between the fruits of retirement and the benefits of a higher income. We examine the changing nature of state policy as Soviet planners seek to induce more old-age pensioners to remain in the labour force. Finally, we examine Soviet policy toward students. Students are a potential source of labour during the school year as part-time workers and during the summer as full-time or part-time employees. During the school year income is an alternative to leisure and study time while during the summer it competes with the universally coveted summer break. Before the three groups are discussed separately, we begin with a general discussion of part-time work, since each group is in one way or another a potential source of part-time employment.

PART-TIME WORK

Soviet efforts at enlarging the labour pool through additional part-time workers are a development of the last 10 to 15 years. Part-time (*nepolnyi rabochii den'*) is defined as an individual working less than the legal norm, where remuneration is proportional to the amount of time worked or is dependent on output produced. The length of work time, whether it be a part-time work day or a part-time work week is determined by agreement between the enterprise management and the worker.[1]

Part-time work is to be distinguished from a reduced work day (*sokrashchennyi rabochii den'*). The latter is defined as a reduction in the number of hours worked, but with full-time pay along with all other perquisites associated with a full-time work status. Moreover, a reduced work day is established by law, e.g. youths aged 16–18 years may not work more than 36 hours a week.[2] If the medical commission says a worker must work a reduced work day then the management is obliged to find part-time work for him or her with maintenance of full pay.[3]

Part-time workers are entitled to the state social insurance allowances, a pension on retirement and an annual paid holiday.[4] The length of the latter is unaffected by the part-time work status of the employee, although holiday pay is reduced to accord with the proportion of time worked by the individual.[5] The calculation of the length of lifetime employment for a retirement pension is unaffected by whether the work took place under full-time or part-time work conditions.[6] While part-time workers obviously receive less absolute pay, their wage rate may not be reduced from what it would be if they were full-time workers.[7] However, they do not have to be paid overtime compensation; only those who work a 'normal' week are entitled to overtime pay.[8] Typically, part-time employees work every day but a few workers work a part-time week, e.g. work full-time for three days, and have the other two days off. Blind workers and senior scientific researchers fall into this category.[9] The management also grants certain groups of students one or two days off, without reducing their wages.[10]

While part-time work has existed for a long time, it was not until 1971 that the basic labour code legislated the right of individuals to do such work.[11] Prior to 1971, part-time work was established by special acts.[12] For example, a 1964 regulation gave management the right to employ part-time workers in the service sector of the economy.[13] Part-time work already existed in the industrial sector prior to this. A number of enterprises in the Estonian clothing industry have had part-time workers for 20 years.[14] However, the only group which has ever had a definitive right to part-time work is invalids.[15] The law does not oblige management to offer part-time work to pregnant women, women with children less than 1 year old, mothers with large families or persons taking care of disabled family members,[16] in spite of the fact that this is the clear intention of the law.[17] As is shown below, the demand by women for part-time work far exceeds its availability.

For the nation as a whole, the proportion of all workers doing part-time work in the Soviet Union was miniscule: 0.32 per cent in 1974, 0.41 per cent in 1976, and 0.32 per cent in 1979. It was much higher in some of the service sectors of the economy: 1.02 per cent in education and 1.9 per cent in communications.[18] This is in vivid contrast to the United States where the proportion of part-time workers (less than 35 hours work per week) has risen in the last two decades from 8 per cent to 14 per cent.[19] In 1961 part-time workers were about 9 per cent of the total East German labour force.[20] In the RSFSR, in 1970, approximately 0.1 per cent of all workers were employed in part-time work, a figure which rose by 1974 to 2.0–2.5 per cent.[21] In the mid-1970s about 1 per cent of all those employed by the Estonian Ministry of Light Industry were part-time workers.[22] Three conclusions stand out:

1. part-time work is of minimal importance in the labor force
2. the service sector, in which women predominate, is the principal employer of part-time workers[23]
3. the geographical distribution of part-time workers is uneven.

A number of factors have contributed to keeping down the use of part-time workers. A distinction has to be made between those already in the labour force as full-time workers who would like to become part-time workers and those not currently in the labour force. From the point of view of economic planners, the latter group represents a welcome addition to active labour resources. However, the possibility that full-time workers might want to change their work status to part-time is a clear threat to the already low rate of economic growth. Soviet data show that if the government allowed 50 per cent of the female labour force to have one additional free day every month that would be the equivalent of an annual reduction of 950 000 workers for the USSR. A one-hour reduction of the working day for women would be the equivalent of an annual loss of 2.5 million workers.[24]

There are a number of reasons given by enterprise management for not increasing the availability of part-time work, but they largely involve a concern for meeting the various plan targets. Most notably, labour productivity is often measured by dividing gross output by the average number of production personnel and part-time personnel are counted in the same way as full-time employees.[25] This kind of accounting system creates a disincentive for management to hire part-timers since their presence can lower reported productivity. Of lesser importance is that some administrators do not know that they have the right to hire part-time help and that they do not need the authorisation of superiors to hire part-timers.[26]

Similar to the experience of Western countries, several Soviet studies show that the labour productivity of part-time workers is higher than that of full-time workers. For example, a study done by the Central Labour Resources Research Laboratory (TsNILTR) showed that the average hourly output of part-time workers was 10–15 per cent higher than those employed for a full shift.[27] One Estonian study showed that two workers on a half shift produced 20 per cent more than a single full-time worker.[28] This is mainly attributed to the fatigue that sets in during the last part of the working day,[29] although one Soviet study claimed that worker fatigue sets in 2.5–3 hours after the start of the shift.[30] In the service sector the higher productivity of part-timers is attributed to their greater sales experience and the fact that they usually work during peak hours.[31]

Many enterprises have not set up part-time jobs or schedules which would accommodate part-time employment.[32] A recent article suggests that anti-part-time attitudes emanate mainly from enterprises where part-time work has never existed. Typically, these managers argue that part-time work is associated with the under-utilisation of capital equipment, the stunting of the development of workers' skills, and the necessity to increase enterprise infrastructure investment in such areas as housing and preschool establishments as well as the need to employ additional administrative personnel.[33] More than 12 per cent of those who want part-time work cannot get it because of management's opposition.[34]

The notion that part-time work plays havoc with enterprise work schedules is contradicted by an isolated Estonian experience closely resembling the popular West European flexitime system in which a number of variants of part-time shifts are fitted into the regular pattern of enterprise experience. For example, women with children can work 4–5 hours a day or occasionally 6–8 hours a day, or several full days in a row followed by several days off. When work schedules are developed, attention is paid to those times when other family members who are supervising children in the absence of the mother are free. If a woman urgently needs to leave work for a day or two, the request is always granted.[35]

In the household sector there are at least two deterrents to the greater use of part-time work. The major one, of course, is the resulting decline in family income. The Soviet wage structure and its absolute level is designed to oblige both a husband and wife to work full-time. Less important in its impact is the apparent lack of knowledge of part-time jobs and of the associated regulations.[36]

WOMEN AS PART-TIME WORKERS

Having looked at the barriers which exist at the enterprise level and in the planning system, we turn now to examine why women want part-time work, how many of them want such work and the socio-economic groups from which they come. Two studies carried out about 1970 looked at the motivations of women to work.[37] The results, shown in Table 2.1, are very similar. It is clear that the family's need for income is

TABLE 2.1 *Women's motives for working, as percentages, circa 1970*

	Iankova	Kharchev and Golod
Need for additional family income	53	53.5
Desire to be in a collective	24	21.5
Use of special skill for society's good	9	—
Desire to be independent	8.3	—
Desire to be independent of husband	—	11.4
Desire to participate in social labour	—	13.6

SOURCES   Z. A. Iankova, *Gorodskaia Sem'ia* (1979) pp. 50–1; A. G. Kharchev and S. I. Golod, *Professional'naia Rabota Zhenshchin i Sem'ia*, (Leningrad, 1971) p. 42.

the overriding motive for working. Those who cited their need for independence (8.3 per cent and 11.3 per cent, respectively), are probably also associated, at least partially, with a desire for income.

A study was also conducted among part-time workers who had previously worked full-time. Somewhat more than half (53.5 per cent) worked because of the family's need for income; 32.1 per cent either because they wanted to work daily, function in a collective or use their skills, and 12.1 per cent were seeking seniority in order to qualify for a pension.[38]

Working women face different pressures than men and this makes part-time jobs more attractive to them. First, we have already seen that women do most of the housework. A second major pressure is the care of children. Two Soviet studies showed that the obligation to care for children was a dominant factor in causing women to switch to part-time work. In one study, almost half of the women said they transferred to a part-time schedule because of the need to care for children or sick family members[39] and in the other, 62 per cent said they preferred part-time work because they had young children. In the latter study another 10 per cent moved to part-time employment to care for a large family.[40] A complaint voiced in the press is that when a child becomes ill, a full-time working mother has to take unpaid leave, even though the availability of part-time work could have better met the joint need for work and income as well as time to be with the child.[41]

The importance of family obligations in reducing female participation in the labour force is verified by the fact that 61 per cent of the non-working women are under the age of 35.[42] It is contended that 8–9 per cent of all able-bodied urban women are 'lost' to the labour force because they have young children.[43] But the Estonian experience suggests that the availability of part-time work attracts this group into the labour force. Within that Republic's Ministry of Light Industry, 74 per cent of the part-time workers are women aged 21–40, and three-quarters of this group had shifted to a reduced work load because they had young children.[44] Other less important reasons which show up consistently in Soviet studies are the illness of family members, trying to combine work with study, and working on the private plot.[45]

We now consider the number of women who want to work part-time. Currently only 0.5 per cent of all working women work part-time.[46] Ninety per cent of those who want part-time work in the Soviet Union are women.[47] Various Soviet studies indicate the interest in part-time work. According to one author, up to 22 per cent of the women who are not working or who are in school and 10 per cent of currently employed women want part-time employment.[48] A survey of women workers in a Moscow watch factory and in a number of Moldavian enterprises revealed that about 6–12 per cent of the women, mostly with either preschool or young school-age children, wanted to transfer to part-time work.[49] In another study, about 20 per cent of the workers in the service sector expressed a desire to do part-time work, but only half of them would take a reduced workload because of the need for a full salary.[50] Among new brides, 50 per cent said they wanted to work part-time after the birth of their children.[51] In another group of non-working women, 40 per cent said they would be willing to take part-time work if it was offered to them and another 16 per cent said they would be willing to work at home.[52] In half of these cases the women said their willingness to work was contingent upon being able to place their children in a preschool establishment; another 9 per cent said they needed a school with an extended day and 27 per cent said they needed a job nearer home.[53] Thus, a prerequisite for drawing women into employment is meeting their needs as mothers.

A major Soviet study has analysed how long non-working women have been out of the labour force.[54] Over 38 per cent had been out of work for less than a year, 27 per cent for 1–3 years, 15.8 per cent for 3–5 years, and the other 18.9 per cent for over 5 years. Half of all of these women were raising children under the age of 5, and 19 per cent were the mothers of children aged 7–9 years. While 44 per cent of the group had no intention of working in the 'near future', 62 per cent of the mothers of young school children wanted part-time work. Thus the absence of preschool age children in the home has a significant effect on the desire to work and is therefore of some benefit to the state.

A second part of this same study looked at women who were now doing part-time work in terms of what they had planned to do if part-time work had not come along. Nearly half the women (45.6 per cent) had decided not to work, 29.3 per cent planned to take home work, 17.4 per cent were going to resume full-time work eventually and 7.7 per cent were hoping to find a 'more comfortable work schedule'. These data imply that the existence of part-time work attracts women into the labour force. We have already seen that the desire to work part-time partly depends on the age of a woman's children. One study suggests that it is also determined by a woman's income.[55] Table 2.2 shows that the lower a woman's income, the more likely she is to want part-time work. This may be attributed to the lower opportunity cost of giving up full-time employment experienced by women who earn low incomes.

The data also indicate that about 70 per cent of the women who

TABLE 2.2 *Income of women who want part-time work, Vilnius (Lithuania) 1967*

Income group	Percentage of total
30–50 roubles	13.4%
50–70 roubles	58.9%
70–90 roubles	21.8%
90+ roubles	5.9%
	100.0%

SOURCE   N. V. Panova, 'Voprosy Truda i Byta Zhenshchin', *Problemy Byta, Braka i Sem'i* (Vilnius, 1970) p. 91.

formerly did full-time work and were currently doing part-time work would return to their previous work schedule. On average, those women who leave full-time employment to care for an infant will do part-time work for 4 years and then return to full-time work.[56]

Yet planners are apparently reluctant to encourage the availability of part-time work for fear it would drive full-time women workers into part-time status, given the earlier projections of the implications of widespread part-time work.

In recent years, there has been an increased drive to employ women on a part-time basis as home workers, that is, working for an enterprise in their own home during hours which are convenient for them because of their domestic responsibilities. This has been broached in the press as a way of dealing with the labour shortage[57] and at the same time allowing mothers to care for young children or elderly or sick relatives.[58] While the concept of home work for women with children dates legislatively from 1928, the recent rash of regulatory action suggests a renewed interest in it. For example, regulations promulgated in 1972 in Latvia specifically declare that various categories of mothers (e.g. those with several children and single mothers) can be employed for home work. Earlier, in 1959, an all-union decree gave management the right to employ various groups as home workers, including invalids, old-age pensioners and housewives.[59] Women have long been known to work at home for the folk-art industries,[60] and for the sewing industry, apparently being paid on a piece-rate basis.[61] The suggestions for home work appear to be mainly confined to various branches of the clothing industry.[62]

It is interesting to note how reminiscent this is of the British Industrial

Revolution and the putting-out system under which textile merchants took raw materials to workers in their homes, often provided them with the spinning wheels and looms, paid piece-rate wages and then sold the final product. The system is generally regarded as highly exploitive and, in Marxist terms, would be categorised as primitive capitalist accumulation.

Not only do the Soviets propose this as a solution to getting more unemployed women into the labour force, but in a study of non-working women, 16 per cent said they would be willing to work at home.[63] The actual number of home workers for the country as a whole is not known. However, in the mid-1970s, it was estimated that there were no more than 10 000 home workers in the RSFSR, 70 per cent of whom were women[64] and there is almost no home work available for women in Moscow.[65] In the much smaller Latvian Republic there were an estimated 5000 home workers in 1978.[66] In 1979, there were 10 000 home workers in Belorussia, 1000 of whom were said to be raising children.[67] This latter figure suggests that offering home work is not solely for the purpose of attracting women with small children into the labour force; a large number of home workers are simply unskilled individuals. However, this varies from place to place. Thus, 1.8 per cent of the workers employed by the Leningrad sewing combine 'Tribuna' were home workers, 68 per cent of whom were mothers taking care of young children.[68]

'Tribuna' started a program which was geared to women who work at home. They have a special shop where they train women to do home work. The factory places the appropriate equipment in their homes, the material is brought to them and somebody picks up the finished product.[69] Almost nothing is known about the reward system except that they work on a piece-rate system. One article says they earn more than other women who work for the same factory and suggests this is also true of another factory.[70] They can also earn bonuses of up to 60 roubles a month for knitting and up to 100 roubles for those working with amber.[71]

There is a conflict of opinion on the efficiency of home work. There are those who argue that home work is profitable because it does not require any capital investment.[72] An Estonian study claimed that home workers' productivity was 20 per cent higher than the women who worked in the factories. Moreover, home workers had a lower leaving rate.[73] However, data from a pillow factory show a profitability rate almost twice as high in the factory than among home workers. In part this is because the capital endowment of home workers is so low.[74]

OLD-AGE PENSIONERS

The second major non-traditional group of workers is old-age pensioners. Soviet policy toward pensioners has vacillated over the past quarter of a century, reflecting the changing priorities of the regime in recruiting workers from this group. In this section, we look at the number of pensioners who have remained in the labour force, why they choose to continue to work or elect retirement, the nature of the reward system, what kind of work schedules are available, and the way the pension systems have operated as inducements or deterrents to work.

The pension is a monthly payment to retirees, the size of which is determined by previous income. For non-working pensioners the pension is the only source of income and for working pensioners it is extra income. Men ordinarily have the right to a pension at age 60, women at age 55. Those whose work is connected with harmful or dangerous working conditions have the right to a pension at the age of 50 or 55 for men, 45 or 50 for women, depending on the occupation.[75] The potential labour to be obtained by successfully recruiting pensioners increases as the percentage of individuals of retirement age increases concomitantly. In 1950, 1960 and 1970 the proportion of the total population which had reached retirement age was 10.4 per cent, 12.4 per cent and 15.1 per cent, respectively. Estimates for 1980, 1990 and 2000 are 15.5 per cent, 17.6 per cent and 19.2 per cent.[76]

The proportion of working pensioners as a percentage of all pensioners has tended to move in response to the presence or absence of incentives in the pension system. As Table 2.3 shows, after 1956 there was a dramatic decline in pensioners' participation in the labour force,

TABLE 2.3 *Working pensioners as a percentage of all pensioners, USSR, 1956–75*

1956	59.0	1968	15.9
1957	28.6	1969	18.9
1958	19.2	1970	19.0
1959	15.1	1971	20.5
1960	11.7	1972	21.3
1964	10.1	1973	22.3
1965	12.5	1974	23.4
1966	14.0	1975	24.3
1967	15.2		

SOURCE M. S. Lantsev, *Sotsial'noe Obespechenie v SSSR* (Moscow, 1976) pp. 127, 131 and 137.

which continued until 1965, when the participation rate began to rise steadily, so that by 1975 one quarter of all pensioners were in the labour force.

The rise in participation rates is reflected in the increased relative importance of pensioners in the labour force. Table 2.4 shows that from 1960 to 1975, the percentage of the total Soviet labour force which was pensioners rose from 0.8 per cent to 4.3 per cent, constituting more than a five-fold increase. It should be pointed out that about 60 per cent of those who have recently reached retirement age choose to remain in employment.[77]

Table 2.5 shows where pensioners work in the economy by sector. The

TABLE 2.4 *Old age pensioners as a percentage of the total Soviet labour force, 1960–75*

1960	0.8	1972	3.4
1965	1.3	1973	3.7
1970	2.8	1974	4.0
1971	3.2	1975	4.3

SOURCES Lantsev, pp. 127, 137, and *Narodnoe Khoziaistvo SSSR v 1975g*, p. 531.

TABLE 2.5 *Percentage of a sector which is pensioners (1 June 1973)*

	55–59 years old	60 years and over
Total economy	3.9	3.1
Industry	2.9	2.0
Agriculture	4.4	3.1
Transportation	4.2	2.5
Communications	3.3	2.6
Construction	2.6	1.7
Trade, public catering, material, technical supply and sales	4.3	3.7
Public utilities and daily services	6.9	8.3
Health, physical culture and social security	4.6	4.0
Education and culture	4.1	3.2
Art	4.6	5.0
Science and scientific services	3.3	3.2
Credit and state insurance	5.0	3.9
Administration	4.6	3.2

SOURCE A. A. Ustenko, *Trudovye Resursy Neproizvodstvennoi Sfery* (Lvov, 1976) p. 101.

first column, which deals only with those aged 55–59 years, is essentially comprised of women since men do not ordinarily retire until the age of 60. The group that is over 60 years includes both men and women. The importance of working pensioners as a share of the Soviet labour force drops significantly after age 60, which makes sense given the progressive decline in ability as people age as well as the statistical implication of having those over 60 years clustered in one group. In general, pensioners are relatively more important in sectors which are service-orientated or are dominated by white-collar employment. As might be expected, pensioners are less important where work is likely to be more physically rigorous, such as industry and construction. Studies of working pensioners done in 24 light industry enterprises all over the country confirmed the notion that they stayed on where the work was easiest. About 85 per cent of the working pensioners were employed as auxiliary workers, engineering–technical workers, white-collar workers and junior service personnel.[78]

The unexpectedly high figure for agriculture should be noted. In spite of the fact that farm work requires so much physical labour, the importance of pensioners is greater in this sector than it is in the overall economy. While this might partially reflect a tradition of older people working in agriculture, it is more likely it results from the structural imbalance in age groups in agriculture; there are simply relatively more older people in rural areas than in urban areas.

Data from Moscow for the period 1967–73 (see Table 2.6) reveals that elderly men are more likely to be in the labour force than women. Overall, 27 per cent of all men who are of pensionable age are in the labour force as opposed to 21 per cent of the women. Of course, women have something of a 'head start' since they are eligible for pensions 5

TABLE 2.6 *Working pensioners as a percentage of all pensioners, Moscow, 1967–73, by sex and age group*

Age group	Total	Men	Women
All pensioners	24	27	21
55–59 years	26	—	33
60–64 years	36	44	18
65–69 years	16	22	12
70 years and over	6	6	6

SOURCE V. Kogan, 'Pozhilye Liudi na Rabote' in *Zdorov'e Pozhilykh Liudei* (Moscow, 1978) p. 84.

years earlier than men. Thereafter, beginning at age 60, men dominate until the age of 70 years when 6 per cent of both groups work. Why is there a higher percentage of pension-age males who stay in the labour force? Since women have a higher life expectancy than men, and therefore are presumably healthier, the issue of physical capabilities cannot be germane. And because the service sector is the principal demander of pensioners and women dominate employment in this sector before retirement, one might expect retired women's participation to be relatively greater than men's. Yet it is not. There are two explanations for this. One is that women acquire the role of grandmother and with it the responsibility for taking care of small children and a house again. This double burden is a difficult feat at the age of 30; it is even more taxing at the age of 60. Secondly, since women are more likely to be the surviving spouse they receive survivor's insurance, which may reduce their need for a job after retirement.

In general, capital cities and large cities have a higher percentage of working pensioners because the service sector is a greater component of large urban economies than it is in small cities or rural areas. In small cities, the structure of the local economy works against pensioners being in the labour force in two ways: the lower level of development of the service sector and the greater availability of private plots which pensioners prefer to the state sector.[79] Soviet pension law has played an important role in determining the participation of pensioners in the labour force. For purposes of analysis, the critical years are 1956, 1964 and 1970.

Before the introduction of the 1956 pension law, working pensioners received their full pension, independent of the level of their earnings.[80] The new law substantially reduced pension payments. Moreover, after 1956 while taxes were not taken out of pensions, they were taken out of wages and thus the incentive to work was further eroded.

After a steady decline in pensioners' participation rates, a reform was introduced in August 1964. Pensioners who decided to work were paid half of the pension to which they were entitled in addition to their wages. In the Urals, Siberia and the Far East, 75 per cent of the pension was paid. Underground workers were allowed their full pension plus wages. However, the sum of wages plus the pension could not exceed 200 roubles monthly. Pensioners in agriculture were allowed to continue receiving any state pension they were being paid regardless of what they earned from agricultural work.[81] It is clear that this reform reversed the flow of pensioners out of the labour force and there was a slow but steady rise in the proportion of pensioners who continued to work. In

1966–7 the right to receive 100 per cent of the pension was extended to a small number of groups in the health field and the food and meat preparation industries during their most intensive processing period.

The efficacy of reducing the pension penalty of working is shown by the fact that the growth of the number of working pensioners during the period 1964–9 was 77 per cent in those regions where 75 per cent of the allowable pension was paid, while in the regions where 50 per cent of the pension was paid, the increase in working pensioners was 46 per cent. The Soviet authorities claimed that experience during this period showed that:

1. the key determinants of whether pensioners remained in jobs were working conditions and pay, not the size of the pension
2. the pension plus wages arrangement was an incentive for those workers who were in low-paying jobs
3. the pension plus wages system did little to increase the participation rate of engineering–technical workers, since so many of these workers already remained in the labour force
4. once workers left the labour force it was virtually impossible to persuade them to return.

In order to keep more pensioners at work the Soviet authorities introduced another pension reform in 1970. There were two basic elements in the 1970 system: (a) the right of almost all pensioners to 100 per cent of their pensions and (b) an increase in the upper limit of wages plus pension from 200 to 300 roubles a month. As a result, the percentage of working pensioners receiving 100 per cent of their pension rose from 34.4 per cent in 1968 to 91.4 per cent in 1973. Concomitantly, the proportion receiving 50 per cent of their pension declined from 30.8 per cent to 5.7 per cent. The remainder were either people receiving less than 15 roubles a month or those who did not receive a pension.

A Soviet study argues that 39.2 per cent of the increase in the number of working pensioners between 1963 and 1973 can be accounted for by an increase in the pension paid, the rest of the increase being attributable to the growth in the total number of pensioners (50.8 per cent) and a rather vague, catch-all variable which includes an increase in the period of able-bodiedness, an improvement in working conditions and an increase in the difference between the level of the pension and wages (10.0 per cent). The claims for the virtues of the 1970 reform appear dubious. In reality the rate of increase in the relative participation of pensioners seems unaffected by the new system.

It may well be that the Soviet Union is simply reaching the upper limit of the proportion of pensioners who may reasonably be expected to continue work after retirement. This is consistent with Lantsev's suggestion that any change in the pension payments system should be directed towards those who are already working. One study, however, does offer the possibility that the USSR has not fully tapped the pool of non-working pensioners. In a poll of such pensioners 24 per cent indicated a desire to work part-time, 1.3 per cent to work at home, and 9.9 per cent to work full-time.[82] This suggests that more than one-third of non-working pensioners are in principle interested in working. A more recent Belorussian study indicated that more than half of the employees who want to leave employment after receiving their pension could continue to work if the work were part-time.[83] In a Tashkent study 20 per cent of the non-working pensioners wanted part-time employment, 60 per cent with a preference for jobs in the retail trade.[84] On the surface, these expressions of interest in work after retirement appear to be insignificant in view of the small increases in actual labour force participation that have taken place.

What motivations do workers have for continuing in employment or dropping out of the labour force permanently? About 90 per cent who reach retirement age are eligible to continue working as well as receiving a pension. The other 10 per cent are administrators and white-collar workers who are not entitled to a pension because their salary is too high.[85] Thus the Soviet pension system creates a disincentive against work for some of its most highly skilled people. Soviet studies all demonstrate that income is the overriding reason for pensioners continuing to work, particularly for men. In one study 53.4 per cent of the men in the service sector and 55.6 per cent in industry cited income as the principal reason for working. The comparable figures for women were 39.2 per cent and 23.6 per cent, respectively.[86] Another study said that 54 per cent of pensioners work because of the higher income which can be earned. Moreover, this same study suggested that the higher the family's per capita income, the more likely it was that reasons such as the 'companionship of fellow workers and the need for self-expression' would be decisive in the work-versus-retirement decision.[87]

Another important determinant of whether pensioners work, especially on a part-time basis, is the proximity of the job to home. Between 76.5–79.8 per cent of pensioners doing part-time work travel less than 30 minutes between their residence and their job; 16.3–19.5 per cent must travel 30 minutes to 1 hour and only 0.8–3.6 per cent travel more than 1 hour.[88]

There are several special categories of workers who have the privilege of early retirement and higher pension levels. This is designed as an inducement to enter less desirable employment, work in less pleasant places and as a reward for having endured employment in these selected areas. For example, the age of eligibility for a pension is 5–10 years lower and the required length of service is 5 years less for workers who work underground or in harmful conditions. Those in categories with the early retirement privilege are more likely to continue working than ordinary workers. In 1972, 56.3 per cent of all pensioners continued working. While 54.1 per cent of those who received a pension on a general basis continued working, 72.4 per cent of the workers in one of the special retirement categories remained in the labour force.[89]

The final determinant of a pensioner's presence in the labour force is whether or not they decide to retire when they become eligible. The data show that 84 per cent of working pensioners never retired; only 16 per cent returned to work after first retiring.[90]

The decision not to work is governed by a number of variables. In a survey of workers who were about to receive their pension and had made a decision not to work, 70 per cent indicated that it was to avoid heavy physical labour, 16.2 per cent cited the absence of part-time work, and 8.8 per cent blamed the absence of home work.[91]

Women retire for different reasons than do men. They are four times more likely to retire because of family considerations.[92] Most notably, women often become eligible to retire at the moment they become grandmothers and they acquire a new familial role. However, the absence of grandchildren is no guarantee that they can continue in the labour force free of home pressures. For there is an implied obligation for elderly women to give more time at home in order to allow the younger family members time to study or engage in recreation.[93]

For both men and women, health is another factor dictating retirement. Soviet studies have shown that many people in ill health try to stay at work after they receive their pension but are often obliged to resign after a year or two. In part this is largely because they are compelled to choose between full-time employment or no job at all, rather than having part-time employment routinely available as a work option.[94] Health was cited as the most important reason for retiring by 57 per cent of pensioners, which was more than twice the 27 per cent who cited family problems.[95]

The average length of the work life after retirement is presently about 5 years, which is longer than it was a few years ago. This suggests that the improved financial incentives are also producing long-run benefits for the state as well as short-run incentives to keep pensioners from retiring.[96] As regards the health issue, there is an additional benefit for those pensioners who continue working. According to the Soviet Academy of Medicine, working pensioners are half as likely to experience emotional problems (e.g. apathy, dissatisfaction with life) than non-working people in the same age group.[97]

The absence of part-time work as an option is crucial to understanding why more pensioners do not continue to work; 58 per cent of them said that if they were to be drawn back into the labour force during the first 5 years of retirement, the main contributing factor would be a shorter working day.[98] No other reason even approached the importance of part-time work. Similarly, we cited earlier the Belorussian study which showed that more than half of the workers who planned to retire would have remained at work if they had had the possibility of a part-time job.[99] A majority of pensioners want to work 3–4 hours a day and 70–80 per cent of them want to work during the first part of the day.[100] A Belorussian study of 13 enterprises showed that not a single one had a work schedule for pensioners which conformed to these needs.[101]

Working pensioners generally work at the same kind of job they did before retirement. About 91 per cent are said to use their special skills at work.[102] This is less likely to occur if the job was physically demanding manual work.[103] The higher the skill level of the workers, the more likely they are to work at the same enterprise after retirement. This is due to the strong demand for skilled pensioners.[104] However, an enterprise has no obligation to rehire a pensioner who formerly worked at that enterprise.[105] Pensioners are also being employed as home workers. Three-quarters of the workers at the Special Goods and Accessories Production Association in the Lvov Province are home workers, as are 80 per cent of the workers at a Minsk clothing factory.[106] How significant home work is as a share of the total employment of pensioners and what potential there is for expanding this avenue of employment is unknown.

There is apparently some discrimination against pensioners, mostly due to the belief that their low standard of health impairs their productivity. One attempt at measuring this found that the productivity of pensioners was 96 per cent of the enterprise average.[107]

WORKING PENSIONERS IN AGRICULTURE

In the economic and social history of the Soviet period, collective farmers have always been treated worse than non-agricultural employees. While their situation is improving, it is still not as good as in the state sector. For example, collective farmers did not become eligible for old-age pensions until 1964.[108] The law developed a set of guidelines for collective farm workers. Pensions were supposed to reflect productivity. As a result pensions are based on the actual average monthly income of the collective farmer for any 5 year period during the 15 years preceding retirement. Only those who are members of a collective farm at the time they become eligible for a pension have a right to a collective farm pension. Those who left the *kolkhoz* have no right to a pension in that sector, with the exception of those who joined during the early years of collectivisation (the exact dates are not mentioned), but because of old age or disability no longer live on a collective farm. In addition, those former members of *kolkhozy* whose farm was changed into a state farm or an industrial site can assert their right to a pension from a collective farm.[109]

In general the terms of pensions on collective farms are less generous than in the state sector. For example, the age of eligibility for retirement is 5 years higher on collective farms, although with the same number of years of work life required: 65 years old for men with at least 25 years of work and 60 years of age for women with at least 20 years of work.[110] There are additional eligibility conditions for collective farm personnel beyond the general age and length of service requirements. *Kolkhoz* chairmen must have been working for the 10 years prior to retirement on a collective farm and for at least 5 of those years as a farm chairman. *Kolkhoz* specialists must be working in that position at the time they apply for a pension and *kolkhoz* mechanics must have been working at least half their work life as a mechanic to qualify for a pension.[111]

Originally agricultural old-age pensions were equal to 50 per cent of earnings up to 50 roubles a month plus 25 per cent of the remaining monthly income. The minimum pension was set at 12 roubles a month and the maximum at 102 roubles a month. Even when collective farmer pensions were raised in July 1971 they were still well below the levels paid to non-agricultural workers. For example, the new minimum of 20 roubles was less than half of the 45 rouble minimum paid to non-working pensioners outside collective agriculture. In addition, the higher level only applied to new farmer–pensioners; those already receiving pensions remained at the previous level. As a result collective farms themselves began to supplement the state pension paid to collective farmers.[112] This supplement is not a fixed amount but is determined by each farm. They give some kind of pension to those who are not entitled to a state pension and provide an additional cash amount to those who receive minimum pensions. The supplements come from the farm's social consumption funds, i.e. from collective farm income.[113]

Nominally urban workers and collective farmers having the same earnings were to be paid the same pension. But the new pension schedule imposed a penalty on retired collective farmers who had a private plot over 0.15 of a hectare and reduced their pensions by 15 per cent.[114] This action has apparently reduced their participation in agricultural work. Twice in 1977 *Izvestia* argued that the restriction on pensioner activity was doing more harm than good and should be dropped.[115] The current law may have some negative impact on output given the fact that 36 per cent of those who work in agriculture said they wanted to work after retirement.[116] Yet pensioners do work. They work in vegetable gardens and do other kinds of field work. It is simply that they have reduced their inputs into private agriculture and the number of livestock have declined because of the penalty.

The Soviet position at first glance seems very confusing. Pensions paid to collective farmers are really quite low, and this has been admitted in the press. Even the stipend they get from the collective farm is extremely small and therefore not much help in providing a decent retirement income. For example, at the end of 1969, people were receiving 3–5 roubles a month as a pension supplement from collective farm funds.[117] One study done in Kalininskaia Oblast (between Moscow and Leningrad) showed that two-thirds of the more than 3800 old age pensioners were only receiving what was then the minimum pension of 12 roubles.[118] Thus, on the one hand, pensions are really extremely low and provide every incentive for pensioners to keep working, but on the other hand, the restriction on the size of private plots that can be worked without penalty reduces incentives to supply labour in a highly productive area of agriculture. What one would expect has in fact happened; pensioners have been 'forced' into field work in the socialist sector.

Several proposals have been made for increasing pensioners' participation on both a full-time and a part-time basis. The one which received the most attention at the end of the 1970s in both the scholarly and popular literature was a system of deferred pension payments to be funded out of retained profits of enterprises. For each year that a pensioner works there would be a percentage addition to the original pension entitlement.[119] For example, if an individual qualifies for a monthly pension of 100 roubles and decides to continue working, he or she might receive a 10 per cent addition to a deferred pension for each year of work, but receive no pension while working. Thus, if the individual were to work for 4 years and then retire, the pension would be 140 roubles a month. Another suggestion is that, given the obvious reluctance of management to create daily half-shift work for pensioners who want to work part-time, enterprises could perhaps offer a schedule of full-shift work on alternate days.[120]

What went into effect in 1980 was something of a compromise plan, but one clearly designed to sweeten the pot. A supplement to pensions has been introduced at the fixed rate of 10 roubles a month for each year that an individual works after retirement. The total supplement may not exceed 40 roubles a month. There is a ceiling of 150 roubles a month for the total of the pension and supplement. The supplement to the pension begins after the pensioner has stopped working. Pensioners who work will have the choice of receiving their regular pension while they work or foregoing their pension while they work in order to earn the right to a pension which has been increased by the supplement.

WHITE-COLLAR WORKER PENSIONS

The Soviets also increased the number of occupations in which workers can receive pensions while working. For the first time office employees are eligible for a pension as long as their pension and salary is no greater than 150 roubles. Finally, in an effort to make part-time work more inviting, pensioners who do such work will have the same fringe benefits as full-time workers.

STUDENT WORKERS

The final major group from which the Soviet economy can draw part-time workers is students. Their potential period of employment can be divided into work during the academic year and work during the summer. The Russian term for the organised recruitment of students working during the summer is *tretii semestr* or third term. Table 2.7 shows the extent of summer employment of higher education students in the so-called student construction detachments. The student construction detachments were first formed in 1959 at which time there were only 339 students working on 16 construction projects. The programme grew rapidly in the 1960s and by 1974 almost 620 000 students worked in the summer programme. It was estimated in 1973 that the construction

TABLE 2.7 Number of higher education students working in the summertime, 1959–74, 1977

Year	Total number of workers	Percentage of workers in construction detachments	Total number of higher education students	Percentage of students doing summer work	Number of construction projects worked on
1959	339	100.0	2,179,000	0.0	16
1960	520	100.0	2,267,000	0.0	23
1961	1,260	100.0	2,396,000	0.0	90
1962	9,560	100.0	2,640,000	0.4	919
1963	19,000	100.0	2,944,000	0.6	2,480
1964	30,000	100.0	3,261,000	0.9	3,860
1965	40,000	100.0	3,608,000	1.1	4,200
1966	60,000	100.0	3,861,000	1.6	5,000
1967	100,000	100.0	4,123,000	2.4	5,400
1968	270,000	100.0	4,311,000	6.2	7,145
1969	265,600	100.0	4,470,000	5.9	8,346
1970	351,800	87.8	4,550,000	7.7	10,350
1971	428,000	85.5	4,581,000	9.3	13,300
1972	526,016	80.5	4,597,000	11.4	14,404
1973	584,549	77.3	4,630,000	12.6	16,273
1974	619,674	72.3	4,671,000	13.2	17,751

SOURCES A. Ia. Semenchenko et al., *Tretii Semestr* (Moscow, 1975) pp. 172–3; *Narodnoe Khoziaistvo SSSR* (various years).

detachments added the equivalent of about 100 000 workers to the labour force. This amounts to roughly one-tenth of 1 per cent of the Soviet labour force.[121] With the exception of one year, the percentage of higher education students participating has increased, to the point where 13.2 per cent of this group worked in 1974. For 11 years all the students organised for summer employment worked in the student construction detachments. Then in 1970, students began doing non-construction work as well.[122] Students have been put to work in canning, harvesting vegetables, processing fish, working as passenger train conductors and doing maintenance work.[123] The proportion of all students involved in construction work declined rather rapidly so that by 1974, it was down to 72.3 per cent. However, over 90 per cent of the value of output produced by these students is still in construction.

The student construction detachment is a voluntary organisation of students. It is organised by the local Komsomol (Young Communist League) groups in schools and is under the authority of the central committee of the Komsomol.[124] Full-time day students constitute the bulk of the summer workers recruited from higher educational institutions. In 1977, over 61 per cent of the full-time day students worked in the All-Union Student Work Group during the summer.[125] The lure of a summer income is the single most important reason for the high rate of voluntary participation in the programme. There is, however, at least one restraint on student enthusiasm for summer work. While the program is designed to alleviate labour shortages in the less hospitable areas of the Far North, Siberia, Kazakhstan and the Far East, students want to work closer to home. As a result only 10 per cent of the students move from one republic to another and even within the RSFSR only about 20 per cent of the students work outside their home province. Students are discouraged from moving by local employers, who are reluctant to part with students who live in their area. As a by-product of student unwillingness to work in distant areas during the summer, brigades of freelancing moonlighters have gained more importance as a source of labour.[126]

Until about 1973, the student construction detachments comprised solely of higher education students. Now students from the *tekhnikums*, vocational–technical schools, and high schools work on the detachments.[127] In 1977, 32 per cent of the students in the specialised secondary schools worked during the summer in both construction and non-construction work.[128] The high school students work for only 1 month during the summer,[129] and there is some attempt made to have students work at jobs connected with their education. In 1974, about

80 000 students, or 13 per cent of the total, worked in their future specialisation.[130]

The actual work develops out of a contractual relationship between an educational institution and an enterprise. The contract can be either of a short-term nature (one summer) or a long-term relationship. For example, in 1970, a 5 year contract was signed between the Kazan Engineering Construction Institute and the Kama Hydroelectric Station. In 1971 the Primorsky Medical Institute signed a 5 year contract with *Glavdal'vodstroi* (the main organisation dealing with water construction projects in the Far East).[131] While a contract will be signed with a particular institution simply because it can supply a certain number of people to do physical labour, there are also instances when a contract develops because the institution has expertise in planning and design work. For example, the Perm Polytechnic Institute has students developing plans for agricultural facilities.[132]

Summer employment is not the only systematic means by which the state uses students in the labour force. Both high school and university students are recruited to work at harvest time. Students can spend anything from several days up to a month every year doing agricultural work during the school year. There has been concern for some time that the costs in lost classroom time outweigh the value of the agricultural output involved. In effect, over the course of an academic career, students could conceivably lose up to one term's worth of work because they are working in the fields.[133] In an apparent effort to deal with balancing conflicting needs, the Ministry of Higher and Specialised Secondary Education issued an order in 1979 prohibiting the use of first-year students. In spite of this regulation, farms have continued to use these students under the guise of emergency conditions.[134]

Not all summer employment is organised by the state. Brigades of 10–20 students do freelance contract construction work in high wage areas such as the North and the Far East. Generally, these are older students with experience in construction work. Unfortunately the total number involved in this type of summer work is unknown.

WORK DURING THE SCHOOL YEAR

There is not a great deal of employment of day-time students in the Soviet Union, which reflects the relative underdevelopment of part-time employment in the country. University and high school students represent the largest pool of individuals available for part-time employment. There are about 3 million full-time day students in higher education institutions (VUZy) and 2.9 million in the *tekhnikums*.[135] It is generally agreed that there is an inadequate effort made by the state to recruit them for part-time work.[136] There is a committee at Moscow State University which helps students find jobs. But managers want students who can work a full day, which is unacceptable to the university.[137] In spite of this reluctance, students still comprise about half of all part-time workers, with about 7 per cent of them ranging in age from 20 to 24 years. For 74 per cent of the students the main reason they work is to earn money; about one half of all students do not have the benefit of a stipend, and 12.7 per cent have a family. About two-thirds earned more than 60 roubles a month. Three-quarters of the students work in the service sector, which is where part-time jobs are most available. There is conflicting evidence about the desire for work in the service sector, as there is a strong student prejudice against such work. Construction work is considered respectable, and even has a certain mystique associated with it, but many students consider service work to be beneath their dignity.[138] They are encouraged in this elitism by their teachers who say they have not spent ten years educating children 'to serve vodka and salads'.[139] On the other hand, the fact that little else is available for students seems to account for the 40 per cent of university, *tekhnikum*, and secondary school students in Tashkent Province who said they would like to work in the service sector.[140]

STUDENT PAY

The wages paid to students during the summer have changed over the years. Since about 1973 they have been paid according to the wage rates prevailing for regular workers.[141] Previously they had been paid according to the lower wages applied to temporary workers.[142] In addition, students who were receiving stipends during the school year continue to receive them during the summer.[143] Students can also earn bonuses; before 1975 they could receive bonuses of up to 20 per cent of their pay.[144] Since 1975, the bonus system has operated on the basis of awarding 40 per cent of the student pay if the work is 'excellent', up to 30 per cent with a grade of 'good' and 10 per cent with a grade of 'satisfactory'. These bonuses are paid within the constraint that no more than 10 per cent of the general wage fund be distributed as bonuses. The current notion is that bonuses for student workers should not exceed

25–30 per cent of their salary.[145] Since 1973 students have been exempt from paying taxes on their summer earnings.[146]

The only estimates found on overall summer pay indicate that it averaged between 300 and 400 roubles in 1969, with a minimum of 100–200 roubles and income as high as 1000 roubles for those working in the North and Far East.[147] If these average earnings figures are correct, then summer construction work is lucrative for students. They work for two months, which means their average monthly income would have been 150–200 roubles, considerably higher than the 136.6 roubles year-round construction workers earned in 1969.[148] The explanation for the differential may lie in the inclusion of bonus payments in the student data. In any case, the high summer earnings of students appears to explain their high voluntary participation in the programme.

SOME COSTS AND BENEFITS OF USING STUDENT WORKERS

Both individual students and the state clearly benefit from the use of student workers. Students also gain experience as well as high wages from work in the construction detachment. In a survey carried out about 1970, 41 per cent said they learned a construction skill, 27 per cent said they acquired organisational skills and 22 per cent said they learned to do physical work.[149] The state also benefits from having students working in rural construction, where there is a serious labour shortfall. In addition, the costs associated with transporting and housing students are considerably less than those associated with employing regular workers. In part this reflects the fact that students do not need housing to accommodate a family. As a result, the cost of a million roubles worth of construction done by students in the Far East and the Far North is 35–40 per cent less than when non-students do the work.[150]

The summer programme is not without its problems. Many students who are sent to construction sites have never used construction equipment or power tools, or handled farm machinery.[151] This has led to two outcomes: low productivity and a large number of work-related injuries.[152] Moreover, there are some traditional Soviet inefficiencies such as the occasional failure to organise independent projects for students so that they were obliged to do relatively unproductive auxiliary jobs. Sometimes student brigades have nothing to do because machinery and materials are not available at the job site.[153]

In sum, there is a much greater commitment to recruiting students for full-time summer work than to developing a systematic effort at finding part-time employment during the school year. In spite of certain problems, the summer programmes appear to benefit both the state and the individual. Student part-time work runs into essentially the same set of barriers associated with the absence of part-time opportunities to women and pensioners. It is tempting to conjecture that Soviet planners do not want students working because they want them studying. In 1970, students spent an average of less than 1 per cent of their time working (12 minutes a day) but spent one third of their time (7.8 hours) as students.[154] The only systematic deviation from this pattern is the use of students at harvest time when they are taken out of school altogether for up to a month. The fact that so many are out of school during this period may foster an unwillingness to allow more work and an even greater inattention to school.

In general it may be concluded that policy makers have not done a great deal about exploiting the possibilities of more part-time employment or student employment. They have been much more successful at persuading pensioners to remain in the labour force, largely because they have been willing to pay the additional money necessary to attract them into the labour force. The unwillingness to be as generous with part-time work suggests that many of the women who remain unemployed are unskilled or that Soviet planners fear a wholesale shift of women from full-time to part-time status.

In Chapter 3 the attempts by policy planners to meet certain very short term labour deficiencies is treated in an analysis of seasonal and temporary employment.

3 Seasonal and Temporary Work

The labour shortage in the Soviet Union has not only led the state to experiment with increasing the number of workers by tapping non-traditional sources of labour, but it has also led to an increasing use of seasonal and temporary employment to meet immediate needs. On the demand side, seasonal and temporary employment allows state economic planners to fill gaps in the labour force in jobs that do not require year-round employment. In the case of seasonal employment the need for labour is more or less predictable, such as during the peak times in agriculture. At times, the seasonal nature of work merges with the temporary status of a job and the distinction is strictly legal rather than functional. On the supply side such employment taps several wide ranging sources of labour, including collective farmers who are idle in the off-seasons, urbanites on holiday, workers who take unpaid leaves of absence and housewives who want a few months' work. Seasonal employment can be voluntary, in which case work is chosen over leisure (e.g. holiday-makers and housewives) or workers substitute one form of employment for another (e.g. moonlighting urbanites). It can also be involuntary, as in the case where industrial workers are assigned to the autumn harvest.

Temporary and seasonal employment have existed throughout the Soviet period. Indeed, it might be pointed out that there is a long tradition of shifting labour back and forth between countryside and urban settings, both under serfdom as well as during the industrialisation drive at the end of the nineteenth century. Their presence today is justified simply by the nature of the required work done within these categories. But along with the benefits from seasonal and temporary work there are also several important costs to the state. These costs and benefits are the focus of this chapter. In addition, we examine several other aspects of seasonal and temporary employment: the number of workers involved, the kind of work performed, the sources from which such workers are drawn, and the legal framework within which seasonal and temporary workers function. Seasonal employment receives most of the attention because it is of much greater importance than temporary employment.

WHAT IS SEASONAL AND TEMPORARY WORK?

Seasonal workers are employed in jobs which, because of natural and climatic conditions, do not exist during the entire year but only within a specific time period, a 'season', which by law may not exceed 6 months.[1] If the period of work exceeds 6 months the person automatically becomes a permanent worker and then comes under the jurisdiction of a different set of labour laws.[2] The major area where seasonal workers are found is in agriculture, not only for planting and harvesting, but also for construction on collective farms.[3] To a lesser degree they are also found in timber-cutting, timber-rafting, peatbogs, railroad track maintenance, ice-breaker work and snow clearance.[4]

Throughout the Soviet period, temporary workers have been those workers hired for a period not to exceed 2 months. If workers are hired to substitute for other workers who are absent because they are temporarily (and legally) absent from the job, then the temporary replacement can be hired for up to four months. If the actual period of work goes beyond these limits then the individual becomes a permanent worker.

The individual is not a temporary worker if the same enterprise hires her to work two different time periods separated by less than a week and the total work time exceeds 2 months. In this case the worker is considered permanent and acquires the more generous benefits accruing to regular status.[5] Labour contracts for both seasonal and temporary work are usually for a fixed period, but they can be concluded for an indefinite length of time.

Temporary workers are hired to do two basic categories of work: (a) auxiliary work such as loading and unloading, hauling, harvesting, and repair work, and (b) work involving natural disasters.[6] There is supposed to be either a sense of urgency about the need for the worker or the hiring must be of an occasional (*sluchainyi*) nature.[7]

The data on employment of temporary and seasonal workers is neither systematic nor at a sufficiently aggregated level to provide definitive insights into the number involved in the Soviet economy. Nevertheless, the data suggest certain conclusions. First, the number of workers sent from non-agricultural enterprises to help with the harvest on both state and collective farms has increased dramatically since 1960. In 1978 the number of these seasonal workers was about 3.4 times higher than in 1960, increasing at an average annual rate of 13 per cent for 18 consecutive years. In 1979, 15.6 million people were sent to harvest crops, half of whom were employed in material production.[8] Second, most of this increase may be taking place on collective farms since there is some evidence suggesting that while the number of seasonal and temporary workers on state farms is still large, it is a declining share of the state farm labour force. The large numbers of workers doing temporary work during the harvesting period mainly reflects the shortage of labour in rural areas caused by migration to Soviet cities and the correlative failure of capital to compensate for the loss in productivity provided by these workers. In 1940, the proportion of the total state farm work force accounted for by these two groups was 29.6 per cent, a figure which declined to 29.1 per cent in 1953 and in 1961 to 17.4 per cent.[9] These figures appear to refer to field work. State farms and collective farms also hire workers to do construction work. In 1969, about one million seasonal and temporary workers were hired by state farms.[10] This amounts to about 12 per cent of the *sovkhoz* labour force in that year.[11]

Third, there are violations of the law regarding the amounts of time that an individual can be employed and still be classified as a seasonal or temporary worker. This can be seen in Table 3.1. Seasonal workers are supposed to work no more than 6 months. However, at least 56 (15.7 per cent) of the 351 seasonal workers on one farm and 30 (23.3 per cent) of the 129 seasonal workers on the other farm worked beyond 6 months. Temporary workers should work no more than 2 months. This law was also violated although to a lesser degree. At least 10 (3.5 per cent) of the 288 temporary workers on one farm and 16 (4.4 per cent) of 364 temporary workers on the other were employed beyond the legal limits.[12] A number of the so-called seasonal workers are in essence year-round workers. It should also be noted that seasonal workers are numerically more important than temporary workers. The total number of seasonal worker days on Sovkhoz Besdetski was 42 471 compared to 6048 temporary worker days, a ratio of roughly 7:1. In Sovkhoz Moevski, the total number of worker days was 20 085 and 9537, respectively, a ratio of 2:1. A collective farm in Moldavia used 4000 labour days worth of seasonal workers in 1961.[13]

Finally, seasonal workers account for only a small proportion of the non-agricultural labour force. In 1974, there were only 28 500 in the

TABLE 3.1 Seasonal and temporary workers by number of days worked per person on two state farms of the Vinitski Oblast, 1961

Group of workers by number of days worked in a year	Sovkhoz Besdetski				Sovkhoz Moevskii			
	Seasonal workers		Temporary workers		Seasonal workers		Temporary workers	
	Number of workers in a group	Average number of days worked per worker	Number of workers in a group	Average number of days worked per worker	Number of workers in a group	Average number of days worked per worker	Number of workers in a group	Average number of days worked per worker
Up to 50	60	20.8	259	13.1	11	14.8	315	14.7
51–100	79	89.8	19	70.3	11	79.3	33	71.1
101–150	116	114.3	9	121.8	41	129.3	9	128.4
151–200	40	168.3	1	169.0	38	167.9	5	179.0
201–250	26	227.3	—	—	14	242.2	1	206.0
251–300	26	266.4	—	—	11	275.3	1	289.0
Over 300	4	320.2			3	318.3	—	—
TOTAL	351	121.0	288	21.0	129	155.7	364	26.2

SOURCE V. Litvinova, 'Ob Uluchshenii Ispol'zovaniia Rabochei Sily v Sovkhozakh', *Ekonomicheskie Nauki*, no. 2 (1964) p. 35.

RSFSR; 15 000 worked in logging enterprises, 10 000 in the fishing industry and the rest were scattered among peat work, dock work, etc.[14]

There are two broad groups of people who become seasonal workers: those who are recruited through formal state channels and those who develop contractual relationships on their own, 'spontaneously' as the Soviets put it. Organised recruitment is carried out by the State Committees of the Council of Ministers of the Union Republics for the Utilisation of Labour Resources and their local organs at the *oblast*, *krai*, and autonomous republic levels and at the city level in the case of Moscow and Leningrad. They recruit workers at the request of various ministries which do seasonal work, such as the fish industry, the meat and milk industry, and the sugar and canning branches within the Food Ministry.[15]

The organised recruitment of workers is supposed to be strictly voluntary; workers are not compelled to work in any enterprise.[16] But it is hard to imagine that a trip to a collective farm to do tedious field work is voluntarily engaged in by all those sent to the countryside to do seasonal work. On the other hand, collective farmers cannot do seasonal work outside the *kolkhoz* without permission of the management board and the farmers must have a certificate (*spravka*) before being hired for seasonal work.[17] Thus the voluntary nature of movement by collective farmers is associated with the restrictive counterweight of administrative prerogative.

Otherwise workers sign on to do seasonal work on a one-to-one basis and the contractual relationship is strictly between employer and employee. The same is true of temporary workers. There is no organised recruitment of this latter group.[18] Unfortunately, there are no data on the relative importance of organised state recruitment and private initiative in the employment of seasonal workers.

The seasonal work force is comprised of two main groups: collective farmers and urbanites. As indicated above it is in agriculture that most seasonal workers are to be found. Overwhelmingly they do construction work either on other collective farms or in areas of the country which have serious labour shortages, such as the Far East.[19]

The second group is composed of urbanites who are either sent to the countryside by their enterprises or go on their own seeking high incomes for short-term work. These are two distinct groups. In the autumn industrial enterprises have an obligation to send workers to villages to harvest the crops. This is a mix of blue-collar workers, engineers and drivers who go '*na kartoshku*', literally, to the potatoes.[20] As we showed earlier this process now involves millions of workers who are sent to the countryside during rush weeks.

There are neither formal regulations nor a contract governing the relationship between a factory which supplies workers to a collective farm and the farm which uses them. As a result, there are several crucial questions still unanswered at the end of the 1970s. For example, who gets credit for the value of output produced, the collective farm or the factory? What is the salary system used? Who is responsible for the living conditions of the workers? None of these questions has been answered on a routine, systematic basis.[21]

The movement to the countryside of state-recruited industrial workers for seasonal field work is viewed as both virtuous and necessary by the Party. There are ambivalent views, however about those who go on their own to do seasonal work. These workers are often called '*shabashniki*', the Russian word for moonlighters and, depending upon the context, can have either a positive or pejorative connotation. Some of these urbanites use their summer vacation to work on construction projects in rural areas. Often they will work without official documents, although there will be an oral agreement between themselves and the farm management.[22]

How do urbanites and villagers know where to go for seasonal work? There seems to be at least three different mechanisms for conveying information on job availability. The first is word of mouth. A group that successfully finds work for a short period comes home with enough money to build a house and creates an envied example for others in the same locality to follow.[23] The second method is the use of a representative of a group of seasonal workers who spends the winter and spring finding employment for clients. This individual, often regarded as a shady figure engaging in arcane machinations, generally puts together several brigades of workers (perhaps five to eight in number) in the spring and in the autumn he pays them for their work, keeping a certain percentage for himself.[24] Finally, some cities have organisations which unofficially serve as brokers between seasonal workers and potential employers.[25] From the worker's perspective, the need for informal mechanisms is necessitated by the long distances they often travel to do seasonal work, as much as 1000 kilometres.[26]

THE INCOME OF SEASONAL WORKERS

There are two systems of compensation of seasonal workers, each corresponding to the way in which workers are hired. There is a state wage scale associated with the organised recruitment of workers, while the wages of freelancing moonlighters are determined by market supply and demand.

When workers from the cities go to collective farms under the aegis of the state they receive 75 per cent of their average monthly income plus the wage paid to temporary workers. This first part is comprised of their salary plus their bonuses. It is calculated from the average of the 3 months prior to being sent to the countryside. They can also receive bonuses on the collective farm but no more than 20 per cent of the wages based on temporary workers' pay.[27] Since the base pay of temporary workers is low,[28] it is possible that some of these workers will not earn the income they received in their regular non-agricultural job.

In the area of rural construction where private enterprise is dominant in the use of seasonal workers, wages are strictly determined by the interaction of supply and demand. Since the demand for such workers is intense, earnings are quite high. The intensity of demand is due to three interrelated factors: the general shortage of labour, the failure of rural vocational schools to produce enough graduates, and the shortage of construction specialists in rural areas.[29] These shortages are themselves a direct result of the chronic out-migration of young people from villages to cities.[30]

There is a good deal of evidence that seasonal workers who do construction work in villages, the Virgin Lands in Soviet Central Asia and such remote areas as the Far East make a great deal of money. Moonlighters in general apparently earn two or three times what regular construction workers earn.[31] This is substantiated by some specific data. One team of 13 freelancing construction workers (*vol'nonaemniki*) averaged 12 000 roubles each during a season, although it is not clear how many months they worked. This group also earned 20 000 roubles from buying construction materials illegally and selling them to the *kolkhoz*. During a period of several years another construction team made 1500 roubles a month per person. Over the years they received 558 854 roubles, which was 256 584 more than would have been paid using official state pay scales.[32] There is a good deal of additional anecdotal evidence of large sums of money being earned by individual workers. For example, one *sovkhoz* was reported as paying seasonal construction workers 1940 roubles for a month's work and another source said the staggering sum of 17 000 roubles might be earned in a single season in the Virgin Lands.[33] High incomes are earned in spite of the fact that seasonal construction workers are not eligible for either the 30 per cent increment for difficult construction work or for bonuses. In contrast to regular construction workers who are paid on the basis of a 7 hour work day, moonlighters are paid on a contract basis and they work whatever hours they choose. Since it is in their interest to finish a job with as much speed as possible in order to move on to another lucrative construction job, they typically work a great deal of overtime. Collective farm managers often do not record the output of the seasonal worker brigades. Since they produce so much more in a day than the regular construction crews the inclusion of their high level of production activity would endanger future production plans for the enterprise because of the possibility that planners would raise future output targets.[34]

As a result of the premium wages stemming from the labour shortage, in 1969 the wages of seasonal construction workers on state and collective farms constituted 60 per cent of the total cost of the buildings they constructed while regular workers' wages were 21.9 per cent of planned construction costs.[35] In 1965 RSFSR collective farms signed contracts with seasonal construction workers worth more than 80 million roubles.[36]

These high wages are in direct contradiction to the attempt to regulate the wages of a portion of these workers. On 9 June 1973, a resolution was issued, 'On Regulating the Movement of *Kolkhozniki* to do Seasonal Work', which in essence stated that the wages of collective farmers who do seasonal work on other collective or state farms should accord with the wage rates paid to workers doing analogous jobs in these enterprises. The administration of the *kolkhozy* and *sovkhozy* were charged with implementing the resolution.[37] Faced with the reality of labour shortages, farm managers routinely ignore the resolution's intent.

In addition to wages there are other forms of monetary and in-kind compensation of seasonal workers. First, seasonal workers in several industries are eligible for bonuses.[38] Second, there are one-time bonuses awarded to workers who sign up to do peat work, timber cutting and logging and work in the fish industry. These bonuses range between 10 roubles and a month's wage depending on the length of commitment of the worker and the distance they must travel to get to their seasonal job. Thus, if an individual signs a contract to do peat work for the season in the area where he lives, he receives only ten roubles. If this person signs a contract to work for the next season he receives a bonus equal to three weeks' wages, and a month's wages if he agrees to work the next two seasons.[39] Finally, there are several forms of in-kind payments. If collective farmers working in the peat industry stay until the end of their contract they have the right to buy bread for themselves and feed for their livestock at state purchase prices in the same quantity as is available to collective farmers who have remained on the *kolkhoz*.[40]

Individuals who work as seasonal vegetable growers (*sezonnye ovoshchevody*) are allowed to keep a certain portion of the output from the fields they tend. The farm provides seed, fertiliser, machinery and water. These growers, in turn, hire workers at about 5–6 roubles a day and still make large profits.[41] Sugar refineries dispense fuel and bagasse to seasonal workers who complete the season.[42]

FRINGE BENEFITS

There are also fringe benefits for doing seasonal work, although they are not always as generous as those available to permanent workers. For example, seasonal workers have old-age pension rights. For the typical worker who is employed year-round at the same job, each year of work counts towards the requisite number of years needed to qualify for a pension. However, seasonal workers can work no more than 6 months at a given job. Prior to 1967, although seasonal workers were eligible for pensions, only the actual time worked counted towards the old-age pension. That is, if you worked three and a half months, that was the amount of time that was credited to your service record. Beginning in that year, however, the pension system was liberalised.[43] If a worker stayed throughout the season, the time worked counted as a full year of service in the calculation of a pension.[44] Thus, in principle, a person could work only 6 months a year for 30 years and would be credited with 30 years towards a pension. In a 1974 decree that marked something of a retreat, this was modified so that, in general, workers not only had to work the entire season but also had to sign a contract for the following season and fulfil the contract to qualify for continuity towards a pension. The exceptions are workers in the timber industry and forestry; for them, one season's work equals one year towards the right to a pension without any obligations for future seasons.[45]

A worker's average monthly earnings constitutes the basis for calculating the pension to be received upon retirement. In the case of seasonal work this calculation uses both the 6 month period which is defined as 'the season' and the 12 months of the calendar year. For example, if an individual worked a full season (6 months) and earned 1080 roubles, this sum would be divided by 12 to find the average monthly earnings of 90 roubles. If a worker works for only part of a season, in order to find the average monthly earnings for the current year, earnings from the preceding year are used. For example, suppose a woman worked 4 months in 1981 and earned 600 roubles. In 1980, let us say she worked a full season (6 months) and earned 1080 roubles. We add the 600 roubles from the 4 months of 1981 to 2 months-worth of 1980 or 180 roubles, for a total of 780 roubles. This is divided by 12 to yield average monthly earnings of 65 roubles. Upon retirement, the pension is calculated from the average monthly earnings of any 5 successive years during the last 10 years, that is, on the basis of a 60 month period.[46]

Disability insurance is also available for seasonal workers. They have the right to an allowance if they worked for not less than 3 months during the year prior to the onset of the disability or not less than 10 months during the last 2 years. Temporary workers are not subject to any social insurance eligibility requirement regarding their length of work because of the short duration of their employment. In general, the allowances seasonal and temporary workers receive come under the general state social insurance system applied to permanent workers. The only way a seasonal worker can maintain disability benefits in the off-season is by contracting to return the following season. Otherwise, the time period in between seasons leaves them without disability insurance if they are unemployed. If a seasonal worker is injured or becomes ill during the period between seasons, their disability insurance starts the first day the contract goes into effect the next season.[47]

The amount of maternity benefit is the same for permanent and seasonal workers although eligibility requirements for seasonal workers were tightened in the 1970s. Formerly, if a pregnant woman's right to a leave of absence arose before the start of the season and she had contracted to work, then she received maternity benefit starting the first day she was supposed to begin employment.[48] This benefit has been made somewhat more restrictive by the requirement that one of the parents must have worked at least 3 consecutive months prior to the birth of the baby. There is no maternity allowance granted if the baby is born between seasons.[49] The new maternity leave regulation for seasonal workers is essentially the same as the one which has been applied to temporary workers for quite some time.[50]

Seasonal workers do not have the right to a paid holiday. Under Soviet labour law, a worker is granted leave only after 11 months of uninterrupted work at the same enterprise and seasonal work can last no longer than 6 months.[51] Temporary workers, whose period of work is even shorter, are also ineligible for paid holidays.[52]

Seasonal workers receive severance pay equal to 1 week's average earnings and temporary workers receive 3 days' average pay for the following reasons: refusal to transfer to another locality with the enterprise, the elimination of the enterprise, the reduction of the enterprise's work force, inadequate skills or poor health, and the return to work of the worker for whom someone was substituting. Severance pay is equal to 2 weeks' wages in the case of permanent workers.[53]

COSTS AND BENEFITS OF SEASONAL WORK

There are definite patterns that have emerged over the years which provide insights into the costs and benefits of seasonal work from the perspective of both individual workers and the state.

There do not seem to be any obvious benefits accruing to industrial workers who do obligatory seasonal work at peak times on collective farms. In fact, it is possible that workers suffer an income loss during the time they are away from their regular job. At a minimum the decision to work in the countryside is not voluntary. But from the perspective of the state, there is a gain in the higher level of agricultural output.

But there are several interrelated costs which are direct by-products of this annual seasonal migration of workers. The first is the opportunity cost of sending skilled non-agricultural workers to do largely unskilled field work. It is well-recognised by a number of commentators within the Soviet Union that the value of crops picked in the autumn may well be less than the output not produced in industrial enterprises, hospitals and universities.[54] Soviet calculations indicate that agricultural products picked by seasonal workers are twice as expensive as those picked by agricultural workers. Moreover, these workers are approximately four times more productive at their own work place than they are in agriculture. Transporting industrial workers and employees to work in rural areas involves a large loss of time. Many workers travel two days each way. It is estimated that the time lost from travel is the equivalent of 55–110 thousand year-round workers.[55] There are even times when there is really nothing for these workers to do. But the collective farm management does not send idle workers back to their enterprises for fear that their next request for seasonal workers will be denied. It is also argued that collective farmers reduce their own efforts because they know that seasonal workers will come from the city to assist them. Sometimes workers have to take sick leave after they have finished working in the countryside because they are not used to hard physical labour and it takes its toll on them.[56]

There is a basic conflict between the needs of an industrial enterprise and those of a farm for the right to use the same workers at the same time. In dealing with this problem industrial enterprises have responded to the situation in a variety of ways. Their first response was to acquiesce to the request for labour. This would occur simply because there was a legal obligation to be met. But a manager's generosity would be greatest when he did not feel that his own production plans were threatened. Since it has been common for industrial plants to maintain a redundant labour force to assist with their peak periods they could often lend out workers to farms without experiencing any significant declines in gross output. However, once the temporary loan of workers threatened the plant's success, it was quite a different story. There are at least two roads to escaping a part of the obligation to supply workers. One way was for managers to bribe collective farm managers with money, timber and paint so that workers would not have to be surrendered. Less common was the route chosen by a group of match producers. They hired unemployed students, housewives and pensioners as temporary workers, placed them on half salary and sent them to the rural area for 1–2 months.[57]

The use of *shabashniki* who freelance for high wages also imposes several economic costs on the state. The first cost is the high wages which these workers extract from collective farms. As we saw earlier, wage payments are in the neighborhood of two to three times what they would be if the state wage scale was used. From the point of view of planned expenditures there is an opportunity cost to the use of financial resources expended this way. Yet these high wages reflect real market conditions in the Soviet Union and state wage scales are well out of line with market realities. Indeed, from the state's perspective there are negative spillover effects when villages go to recruit collective farmers for construction work through state channels. Because of the scarcity of rural labour, even the state is sometimes forced to pay wages that violate their own pay scales. For example, the state organisation 'Spetsgazmontazh', in the Kiev region, was actually paid almost five times the amount it should have legally received to supply workers to a village gas pipeline project.[58] That is, an adequate number of workers could not be supplied at the below-equilibrium state wages and the project could only be carried out by paying much higher market prices.

The absence of workers from their regular jobs also imposes other costs. One is that they are either away from their regular jobs or they are devoting their energies at work to their more lucrative employment as rural construction workers. For example, several brigades of highly skilled Soviet intelligentsia spent 40–50 days away from their regular, white-collar jobs doing construction work in villages, earning up to 1000 roubles or more. For a period as long as 2 months before the start of their construction jobs these workers were involved during their work time in fabricating or buying tools and other materials associated with their rural assignment. Then after the work was done a number of the individuals were physically exhausted and stayed away from work to rest.[59] It is common knowledge that workers sometimes ask for a leave without pay for a month or two to go to remote areas like the Far North to make a lot of money quickly.

Agriculture also suffers from the moonlighting of village workers. Labour shortages at peak times cut into farm productivity.[60] One state farm claimed that although it planned to complete its 1979 grain harvest in 20 days it actually took more than a month because machine operators were moonlighting elsewhere.[61]

SOVIET ATTITUDES TOWARDS MOONLIGHTING SEASONAL WORKERS

The state's posture towards entrepreneurial seasonal workers is ambivalent. The vacillation in the official view is consistent with the Soviet attitude taken toward any form of internal behaviour which is officially frowned upon but is useful to the state. There is a righteousness which excoriates individuals and institutions who violate the rules of the game. But the condemnations exist side-by-side with occasional words of praise or resignation to the utility of seasonal work. Some of the ambivalence rests on empirical grounds; the productivity of seasonal workers is questioned. One writer claims that in real terms seasonal and temporary workers only worked about 5.8 hours a day instead of 8 hours and that their productivity was lower than permanent workers.[62] On the other hand, there are those who claim that the productivity of seasonal workers is high. Indeed, a high official in the RSFSR's State Committee for the Utilisation of Labour Resources describes Far East economic development as 'inconceivable' without seasonal and temporary workers.[63]

The other basic objection to the seasonal workers has a quasi-ideological cast. There is disapproval because the workers often come from outside official channels[64] or because they 'extort money from the management of state and collective farms and enterprises'.[65]

CONCLUSION

A large number of workers are involved in seasonal and temporary work, particularly on collective farms during the peak agricultural seasons. The recruitment of industrial workers involves coercion. There are also moonlighting workers who go to the countryside and reap handsome returns. There is a concern about the net effect of seasonal construction workers (and the official seasonal farm workers from the cities). There appears to be a consensus that output in other areas of the economy suffers when workers go to rural areas. With respect to moonlighters, from the perspective of a market model, this simply means that the opportunity cost of staying in non-agricultural employment during certain times of the year is too high and the reallocation of resources to areas of higher marginal returns is perfectly rational. In the world of taut Soviet planning, however, such temporary losses produce negative reverberations throughout the economy. The use of bribery and the maintenance of a surplus in the enterprise's labour force are two means by which management attempts to protect itself against plan failure.

One cannot help but wonder where all the money comes from to pay moonlighters. Some of the amounts paid to workers are staggering. Where do collective farms get such sizeable 'slush funds' to pay these workers? What kind of control or laxity is there in the banking system—farm enterprise relationship that allows this to persist with impunity?

Another major issue is why workers engage in freelance seasonal work. Apparently, the living conditions are often harsh, although some moonlighting construction brigades receive favourable treatment. More importantly, there has been a slowdown in the production of consumer goods which would tend to discourage people from accumulating roubles. However, one can speculate on why workers try to earn large sums of roubles. An article cited earlier suggested that workers, particularly collective farmers, come back with money to build a house.[66] This suggests access to building materials, not always an easy trick in the Soviet Union. It implies that money may matter in the second economy, if materials have to be bought from those who steal from the state. Part of the second economy is a cash economy where roubles have importance. There is also some suggestion that intellectual workers may find manual labour a relief from the tedium of perpetual desk work.[67] It therefore serves a therapeutic purpose for these normally sedentary workers. However, this is probably greatly outweighed by the desire for more income and the consumption that is ultimately gained from the effort.

In spite of periodic objections by Soviet authorities to enterprising moonlighters who go to the countryside, there is little doubt that the practice will continue. At bottom these workers serve a useful purpose to village authorities and collective farm management and thus, eventually, to state economic planners. As long as the demand remains strong and the shortages of this kind of labour persists in the countryside, moonlighters will emerge to reap the handsome returns they have experienced to date.

4 Overtime Work

Despite the possibilities for expanding the supply of labour which we have treated in the previous two chapters, it is clear that this is not sufficient. As a result, there is an incentive for policy makers to lean rather heavily on overtime, a system that is mainly coercive. In this instance a worker is forced to make the trade-off between work and leisure. In a real sense the conflict that exists between planners who want more hours of work and workers who want to enjoy time away from work finds expression in the use of overtime employment. Earlier we saw that the length of the work week has fallen throughout the Soviet period. Two implications can be drawn from this. The first consequence is a decrease in the amount of labour available to the economy. Given the demographic and systemic deficiencies which have led to a chronic labour shortage, a shortened work week creates difficulties for growth-minded planners. On the other hand, from the perspective of the individual, a declining work week means more leisure time, all other things being equal.

Whereas for planners overtime employment represents a mechanism through which they can increase the amount of labour in the economy, for the individual overtime employment represents an alternative to leisure time. Fundamentally, there are two ways that individuals can be persuaded to increase the amount of time they work: by offering financial inductments to them which raise the cost of leisure time or by coercing them to work. Although money is an attraction, there appears to be a substantial amount of coercion.

Overtime employment in the Soviet Union is defined as work done over and above the work day.[1] This refers to work done within the state realm of economic activity. While the focus is on this part of the Soviet economy, there is another 'overtime' alternative to leisure time: activity in the so-called 'second economy' where individuals engage in illegal economic activity for private gain. This is also treated later in the chapter, mostly for the purpose of understanding the existence of overtime work. In a brief section there is a discussion of that quintessential Soviet institution, the *subbotnik*, the contribution of one designated Saturday a year when everybody is supposed to work without pay.

Four main topics are explored in this chapter:
1. the legal basis for overtime employment and the nature of the law's violations
2. the incentives for overtime employment from the perspective of both the state and workers
3. the system of overtime compensation
4. an estimate of the extent of overtime employment.

THE LEGAL BASIS

In principle, there is a strong belief in a stable work week and much is made of the fact that under Soviet rule the length of the standard work week has steadily declined.[2] The law is quite straightforward. The only criterion governing legal overtime work is that the situation be 'exceptional and extraordinary'.[3] Moreover, overtime is not supposed to exceed 4 hours in each of 2 consecutive days, or 120 hours a year.[4] This means that if a worker works 1 hour of overtime on a given day, then he can work 3 hours the next day. There is no monthly norm of overtime hours,[5] although it is apparent that a person can work on the average no more than 10 hours, a figure to which we will later make reference.

There are two relatively minor exceptions to the general rule governing the amount of overtime work. First, in several branches of the economy, overtime work is established by special rules, e.g. railroad and water transportation, and organisations in the Ministry of Communication. The nature of the work is recognised as often obliging workers to be working for several days in a row. Second, while seasonal workers cannot be obliged to work over 4 hours during 2 consecutive days, under a monthly calculation of work time, they can be required to work up to 50 hours a month.[6]

Under the law, there are five major categories which constitute legal justification for overtime employment:

1. production associated with national defence and coping with natural disasters
2. to keep public utilities functioning
3. to complete work which for technical reasons could not be finished during the regular work time

4. to repair equipment if its damaged state would force a work stoppage for a significant number of workers
5. on assembly line work, if a worker's replacement on the next shift does not show up then the worker can be asked to stay. In this case, the management is supposed to find another worker to replace the one working overtime.[7]

Workers cannot refuse overtime unless specifically exempted.[8] Several groups are exempted from overtime work: anyone under 18 years of age, pregnant women, nursing mothers, mothers with children under 1 year, tuberculosis patients and anyone enrolled in a general secondary school or vocational school on the days when they are attending school.[9] Since 1971 women with children from 1 to 8 years old can be required to do overtime work only with their agreement.[10]

The trade unions are responsible for protecting the rights of workers when overtime is requested by management.[11] In principle the enterprise management must seek permission from the local trade union committee (FZMK) for overtime work. A series of resolutions emerging from the All-Union Central of Trade Unions during the 1960s and early 1970s have repeated the theme that the FZMK is only supposed to grant permission for overtime work in those cases provided by law and not because fulfilment of the output plan is endangered. The FZMK has the legal right to refuse permission to the management to use overtime work if the union thinks the work can be done during the work day.

The need at the all-union level constantly to reiterate the prerogatives of local unions vis-à-vis the enterprise management suggests that local labour unions either cannot or will not assert their authority. In fact there is evidence that both of these are true. An appropriate portrayal of the role played by trade unions in this matter ranges from characterising them as a rubber stamp, to instances where they are well aware of managerial violation of the overtime law and do nothing about it, to a case where the head of the enterprise trade-union committee intervened and was told by the enterprise management to mind his own business. The impotence or indifference of the union has to do with the overriding goal of fulfilling the output plan. Hence we will see below how enterprises routinely use overtime labour during the so-called 'storming' period when there is a concentration of economic activity during the last ten days of the month to meet the monthly production plan.

WHY SOVIET WORKERS DO OVERTIME WORK

There are two main reasons why Soviet workers do overtime work: to increase income, and fear of reprisals. An income maximisation model is consistent with the neoclassical view of how workers are persuaded to increase the amount of hours they work. However, as will be shown, there are a number of aspects of the Soviet case which are inconsistent with a reliance on income maximisation as an explanation of Soviet worker behaviour. In fact, the analysis must focus on the illegal and non-market aspects of the overtime system.

The neoclassical or market model of labour force behaviour assumes that people: (a) are currently working the preferred number of hours and therefore only offer more labour during a given time period exclusively because of higher wages, (b) are not coerced, i.e. make completely voluntary choices between work and leisure, and (c) can alter the number of hours worked from zero to overtime. The first assumption is not true of the Soviet Union and, in the case of women is patently false; due to their heavy burden of household responsibilities, women want to work fewer hours. The second assumption is also inapplicable to the Soviet Union. As we will show below, there are a number of instances where implicit coercion is a force that must be acknowledged in explaining behaviour in the Soviet labour market. The third assumption is also not true in the Soviet case. In fact, it isn't even a useful description of how workers in a market economy can behave. Overwhelmingly, Soviet workers must either work the standard work week or not work at all. The only workers who seem to have the capacity to alter their hours are those who work an unnormed day. These are people who do not work a standard work day, e.g. eight hours every day. Instead they have a daily assignment to complete.

COMPENSATION FOR OVERTIME WORK

The notion that overtime is considered to be the number of hours in excess of a given work day is deceptive. For the purpose of actually determining how much overtime pay has been earned, the accounting period is the month. The amount of overtime work is calculated in the following way. One takes the number of work days in a month, multiplies it by the number of hours in the normal work day of the individual and compares this figure with the number of hours actually worked. Anything above the first figure is considered overtime work.[12]

This provides a great deal more flexibility for the Soviet employer, i.e. the state, than the typical American model where for workers covered by Federal legislation and most union contracts, overtime is anything over a 40 hour week. In the Soviet case, however, a worker could in fact work 8 hours over the norm during one week of the month, but if for some reason there is a work stoppage during another week and he works 8 hours under the norm, then from the point of view of compensation, no overtime needs to be paid.

How much workers are paid for overtime can best be understood by going through a hypothetical example.[13] Suppose a worker has a calculated residual of 70 overtime hours for a given month. The number of work days, say 25, will be multiplied by 2 hours to determine the maximum number of hours for which a time worker will be paid time and a half. For the remaining 20 hours, the worker will receive 100 per cent above her hourly pay.

Where ordinary time workers receive 100 per cent above the hourly wage, piece workers would receive 75 per cent of the prescribed figure. The compensation of workers who are on a monthly salary is done by dividing their usual salary by the number of hours that should have been worked during a calendar month to find the hourly figure. They are then compensated in the same way as ordinary time workers.

There is no extra premium for doing overtime work at night. This means that either workers do not differentiate between night and day, or there is coercion to get the work done because there is indeed a difference in tastes as regards day and night work. Nor is there the possibility of overtime compensation for workers who do not have a fixed work day, e.g. chief accountants and department heads. As a rule, overtime work on a business trip is uncompensated. Nor is there compensation for voluntary overtime,[14] a notion contrary to the neoclassical assumption that workers are working the hours they want. Part-time workers are not paid for overtime work. Normally, part-timers work 4 hours a day. Thus, if they work 6 hours, which is above their normal day, this is still regarded as below the norm for working time for the typical worker and is therefore paid at the usual pay rate rather than with an overtime premium. The fact that the typical length of the part-time work day is fairly well established at 4 hours and that the criterion for overtime pay is work above the established length of the work day has not escaped notice.[15]

If a person works on a day off (either Saturday or Sunday), she is supposed to get the next work day off. For example, work on a Saturday entitles a worker to Monday off. The use of compensatory time offers no premium to induce workers to try a different distribution of work and leisure. It is simply a shift of time off from one day to another. Again, either workers have no differences in tastes between a weekend day off and a day off during the week or some form of coercion is operating to increase the labour supply. Only if it is impossible for the management to give workers the day off are they paid double time for the free day that they worked.[16] Having to work on a day off is not uncommon during the period of 'storming'. While it is not a legal obligation to work on a Saturday or Sunday, pressure is often exerted to do so.[17] From the planners' perspective there is no net increase in the labour supply if workers must come to the plant on a Saturday or Sunday and are then given Monday off; but it does redistribute the labour supply during a crucial period of time to make it easier to fulfil a production plan.

During the period immediately following the changeover from a 6 day to a 5 day work week, a number of firms had difficulty changing their production schedule from a 6 day schedule. As a result in a number of factories overtime work increased and workers were also obliged to come to the plant on what was supposed to be a day off.[18]

Soviet citizens are entitled to 8 designated paid holidays.[19] However, some tasks must be carried out every day, e.g. by telephone operators, transportation workers, dock workers and railroad workers loading and unloading goods. Hourly workers are paid double time and piece-rate workers are paid twice as much for each piece produced, but workers may opt for a day off instead of monetary compensation when they work on a holiday. This is a change from the system which persisted until at least the early 1960s when the worker could only be compensated by a day off within two weeks. The more usual overtime work cannot be compensated by time off.

Overtime pay enters into the calculation of fringe benefits. It is used in determining the average wages for vacation pay or the compensation for unused vacation. However, overtime pay is not included in the wages which form the basis for calculating the disability allowance of those temporarily unable to work[20] and is usually not considered in calculating the pension. In regard to pensions the exceptions are those workers for whom it is difficult to separate overtime from ordinary work time such as home workers, peddlers and certain workers who prepare agricultural products and food by-products.[21]

There are several exceptions to the general rules governing overtime work and each reflects the idiosyncratic nature of the industry.[22] The first exception is state agriculture. During the periods of the year when work demands are the greatest, e.g. sowing, harvesting, autumn ploughing, the state farm (*sovkhoz*) management can unilaterally increase the work day up to 10 hours. In the winter period of little work the work day is usually reduced to 5 hours and sometimes even less. If the management is not able to reduce the work day then overtime work is compensated by additional days off. Generally the workers get up to 5 more days a month and this number can be increased if climatic conditions make work impossible during the planting period. Neither the additional days off nor the unworked hours nor the reduced day are paid. The major departure from the norm is that the unit of time in the accounting process is the year rather than the month. That is, the Soviets have increased their flexibility by not paying agricultural workers for overtime work accumulated during the busy season.

Sometimes the farm is unable fully to compensate the workers with time off for all the overtime they have worked. In such cases the remaining time is compensated with money. The calculation is done in much the same way as the ordinary case, except that the year is the benchmark accounting period. The number of overtime hours up to 2 hours is multiplied by the number of calendar work days in the year and is paid at time and a half. The remaining hours are paid at double time. Suppose a worker has an uncompensated accumulation of 650 overtime hours. If there are 308 work days during the year, for 616 hours (2 hours × 308 days) the worker is paid an overtime wage premium equal to 50 per cent of the appropriate tariff rate and for the remaining 34 hours the premium is 100 per cent of the tariff rate.

A second model is found in certain seasonal, public catering enterprises, e.g. summer outdoor cafés and restaurants in tourist areas. During the height of the season workers in public catering establishments can be obliged to work 10 hours a day, in comparison with the average of 7 hours a day for such workers during the year. Overtime accumulated during the season is compensated by granting additional days off at the end of the season. Thus, if a waiter accumulates 210 overtime hours, he will receive 30 days off at the end of the season (210 hours ÷ 7 hours = 30 days). These additional days will be paid since, during the season, overtime hours are not paid.

In the fishing industry there is a separate set of rules regarding compensation for overtime work. They are also compensated by additional pay with a premium equal to 60 per cent of the official tariff rate.

AN ESTIMATE OF OVERTIME HOURS WORKED

In trying to estimate the average number of overtime hours performed by a Soviet worker, two helpful sources have been found, although unfortunately the data are about 20 years old. One of the sources was published in 1972 which suggests there may not be anything more recent.[23] This source presents data for the number of hours worked in a day, including overtime, in a number of areas. The most solid evidence of the extent of overtime work is the fact that in 1959, the average number of hours worked in the Krasnoiarsk Krai (RSFSR) was 8.42 for men and 8.36 for women.[24] This was associated with an 8 hour work day. If one assumes 25 work days a month, this means that men worked 10.5 overtime hours a month (0.42 × 25) and women worked 9 overtime hours a month (0.36 × 25). In other words, if the Krasnoiarsk data accurately reflect what goes on in the country, then workers perform overtime work at approximately the legal maximum of 120 hours a year. This is consistent with the assertion that management views the legal 120 hour maximum as a worker obligation.[25]

Therefore, it appears that a large number of individuals work many hours of overtime. Some Soviet citizens are not indifferent to the impact of overtime work on their lives. In a Leningrad survey of working women who were asked about difficulties connected with their jobs, 10 per cent of the women cited overtime work, the third most frequently mentioned factor.[26]

THE 'OTHER' OVERTIME SYSTEM

The traditional type of overtime employment, namely the unscheduled addition of hours to a worker's day, exists side-by-side with another system where the overtime is added beforehand to the normal shift schedule (*pererabotka po grafiku smennosti* – literally, 'working additional time according to the shift schedule' – hereafter called PGS).[27] It has been asserted that an average of 5 to 7 hours per month are added to the normal shift schedule.[28] However, the number of workers affected by PGS, or whether it exists in addition to unplanned overtime for a given worker, is unknown. What is known is that the PGS system and unplanned overtime can coexist in an enterprise or part of an enterprise during a given accounting period.

The PGS system is quite widespread. If the Soviets already have an overtime system (*sverkhurochnaia rabota*) why is it necessary to have another system? The formal reason for PGS' existence is that the system is applied in areas of the economy where it is necessary to provide for overtime work beforehand. For example, if technological conditions demand a full shift, workers will be scheduled to work their entire shift the day before a day off or a holiday rather than having the usual reduced work day. Thus, the seventh and eighth hours on such a day will be considered as falling under the PGS system rather than unplanned overtime. Other examples would be the need to accommodate longer watches on ships if there is a shortage in the crew. But it also seems that the PGS provides a safety valve for management in that PGS is not subject to the 'exceptional and extraordinary' criterion applied to unplanned overtime. Therefore, there is less concern about violating the law. A second difference between the two systems is that the factory management does not need the permission of the local trade union committee to implement PGS. However, given what is known about trade union impotence in their relationship with management, this may be of little importance. Third, the basic form of compensation of PGS is the granting of additional days off (*otgul*), in contrast to the increased wages of unplanned overtime. Moreover, these days off are allowed to be taken outside the given accounting period which means, depending on the particular circumstances of the work situation, that the days off can be taken the next month, in two months' time, during the internavigational period, at the end of the season, etc. These days off are paid according to the usual rate of pay. It is also possible for workers to add these days to their next paid holiday. If it is not possible for workers to get additional days off, the extra hours are treated as if they were ordinary overtime and compensated in the manner described earlier.[29]

SUBBOTNIK

One of the underpinnings of Soviet ideology has been the notion that state and worker interests merge in the ultimate goal of constructing communism. In theory one of the concomitants of communism is the so-called 'new communist man', a selfless creature who will represent the best that the human spirit can produce. While the world waits for the arrival of this new being, Soviet workers can demonstrate their selflessness through their voluntary participation in the annual *subbotnik*, which is a Saturday selected once a year during which people contribute a day's work without pay. The idea of the *subbotnik* has existed for a long time under Soviet rule. It was a part of Lenin's 1920 emergency recovery program during the period of the Civil War and War Communism.[30] In a more general way, it is an example of the idea that, in principle, overtime is voluntary and yet, in practice, is a duty. While the *subbotnik* may not be very important economically, it is symbolic of Soviet expectations about worker obligations.

On this day people generally work at their usual place of employment. The outcome of their productive activity is published in *Pravda* and *Izvestia*, announcing how many people participated, how many roubles worth of output was produced and where the proceeds from the day's efforts will be directed. Although these funds appear to enter the general budget, the announced intention is to spend the monies on social welfare facilities, such as preschool facilities, health care institutions such as hospitals and specialised clinical facilities.

The number of people participating in the *subbotnik* exceeds the number of people actually in the Soviet labour force. According to column 6 of Table 4.1, the number of people the Press reported as volunteering for work was about 16 to 20 per cent higher than the number in the labour force, including those in the non-*sovkhoz* labour force. This is due to the fact that high school and university students also participate. They will do such things as cleaning and maintenance around their school or plant trees and shrubbery. Thus, in 1978, we

TABLE 4.1 *Number of people participating in the* subbotnik, *selected years, in millions*

1	2	3	4	5	6
Year	Number participating	Number in state labour force	Number in non-sovkhoz Agricultural labour force	Total of columns 3 and 4	Ratio of columns 2 to 5
1971	120	92.8	17.1	109.9	121.1
1973	132	97.5	16.7	114.2	115.6
1975	140	102.2	16.1	118.3	118.3
1976	144	104.2	15.8	120.0	120.0
1977	144	106.4	15.5	121.9	118.1
1978	147	108.6	15.1	123.7	118.8

SOURCES *Trud*, 21 April 1974, p. 2; *Pravda*, 5 May 1975, p. 1, trans. in *Current Digest of the Soviet Press* (hereafter *CD*), vol. XXVII, no. 18, p. 19; *Pravda*, 13 May 1976, p. 1, trans. in *CD*, vol. XXVIII, no. 19, p. 21; *Pravda*, 30 April 1977, p. 1, trans. in *CD*, vol. XXIX, no. 17, p. 24; *Pravda*, 11 May 1978, p. 1, trans. in *CD*, vol. XXX, no. 19, p. 18; *Narkhoz 1973*, pp. 476 and 573; *Narkhoz 1978*, pp. 287 and 365.

estimate that a minimum of 24 million students were involved in the *subbotnik*.

ILLEGALITIES

We have already hinted at abuses of the Soviet overtime system by managers. These violations can be understood as a consequence of several key problems within the Soviet economic system. As indicated earlier, the major reason for the use of overtime is the intensification of production at the end of the month to fulfil planned output. There are numerous examples of workers having to work excessive hours during the last third of the month. The intense use of overtime at the end of the month appears to be associated with another chronic Soviet problem, the irregular delivery of supplies which prevents production scheduling and the use of labour evenly over the month.[31] It is not clear how much workers actually work during the storming period, but one source said that some workers put in about 5 overtime hours a day during the last 2 to 3 days of the period.[32] While this far exceeds the allowable limit, one way around the law is for the management to under-report overtime work or not report it at all.[33] In order to deal with the pay issue, workers are often paid bonuses or are given compensatory time off.[34] In the post–1965 period workers were sometimes quite willing to work illegal overtime hours because under the reforms, the bonuses they received from overfulfilling plans exceeded the pay they would have received from overtime compensation.[35] The willingness to work overtime for the additional income is highest among unskilled workers, who put in more overtime than other groups of workers.[36]

There are also instances when the management has illegally given workers short holidays (1 of 2 days off) without a corresponding reduction in wages, in exchange for an obligation to work overtime at a later date.[37] This should be distinguished from the high level of 'unplanned' absenteeism which averages about 18 days a year in the Soviet Union. For example, in one plant where more than 10 000 hours were lost during the year due to absenteeism, 15 000 overtime hours were worked, in exchange for which workers were (illegally) granted compensatory time off.[38]

The entitlement of workers to compensatory time off when they voluntarily work on a day off was discussed above. However, both the alleged voluntary nature of such work and the compensation have been inconsistently enforced. One manifestation of this is that workers who have not shown up on a day off during the storming period have been labelled absentees and either been fired or threatened with dismissal.[39] In addition, compensatory time off has not always been granted. As a result, in at least one case, workers have left their jobs.[40] In the past, workers have been threatened with the delay of passes they receive to state sanatoriums for their leave.[41]

THE SECOND ECONOMY AND OVERTIME WORK

The literature on the secondary economy in the Soviet Union suggests that illegal economic activity is widespread and may constitute a substantial proportion of total economic activity, especially in the consumer goods sector. It is not my intention to attempt an estimate of the extent of the second economy or to develop at length its many manifestations.[42] Rather, after briefly discussing some second economy activity, I want to suggest how its existence provides insight into overtime employment in the state sector.

Moonlighting in the Soviet Union is, strictly speaking, not illegal. Moreover, there is hardly an activity where moonlighting does not occur. Physicians practise medicine in their homes, dentists pull teeth in makeshift offices in their apartments, a music teacher gives lessons at home, a university teacher of English tutors struggling Leningraders, a car owner sees a line of people waiting for a taxi and 'helps out'. Moonlighters are also extremely important in doing home repairs. In a 1978 *Literaturnaia Gazeta* survey, 20 per cent said that even after they talked to a state repair person he did not come and another 5 per cent said that he came but did not do anything. Moreover, because of scheduling difficulties people often had to leave their jobs to receive the repairman, a phenomenon not without its personal or societal costs. For these reasons people turn to moonlighters or *shabashniki*.[43]

Moonlighters are also prominent in the finishing work done on new apartments. The work may be done by either a single individual or a team of workers. One such group working in Moscow was so well organised that when it received a work order it would immediately telephone one of its workmen who would take a taxi to where the job was to be done. It is estimated that of the 14.4 million roubles of finishing work that is done on new apartments in Moscow, about 10 million roubles or about 70 per cent goes to moonlighters rather than into state coffers.[44]

What makes this kind of work legal is whether the practitioners go through proper channels. A very high income tax is paid on the income earned from private activity and only private property may be used to earn the income. The fact is, people rarely inform the state that they are engaging in private economic activity, but on some occasions an individual or group may be intentionally quite public about their activity because it will make their business more lucrative, so they therefore go through the proper channels. For example, it is not uncommon for a group of teachers to form what amounts to a private school in the summer for the purpose of tutoring students in preparation for university entrance exams. However, they are likely to under-report their income. It is quite difficult for the state to prove the existence of more taxable income since there are no official records.

Therefore, we can say that most urban moonlighting is quite illegal either because income is not reported or because other legal violations are involved, such as using state equipment to earn private income.[45] There is no doubt that this form of moonlighting will clearly continue to be demanded as long as it continues to be useful to Soviet citizens. As one member of a freelancing brigade said in an anonymous letter: 'we don't have to get a thousand papers signed before we hammer in one nail.'[46] And these services will continue to be provided so long as high incomes can be earned.

Overtime work and illegal moonlighting are simultaneously available alternatives to leisure. If the individual pecuniary returns to second economy activity are so high, why do people engage in overtime work which, at state wage scales, appears to pay considerably less than can be earned from illegal, free market sources?

There are two possible answers. First, not everyone possesses a skill which can be marketed in the second economy or has access to goods which can be sold or bartered in the underground economy. Therefore, for these people, overtime work is the only viable alternative if they seek more income. A second explanation of why people do overtime work rather than participate in the second economy is that there is coercion in the Soviet enterprise. While available evidence is not conclusive, it is clear that people are confronted with threats if they do not work overtime.

CONCLUSION

It is not shocking that overtime work might be used illegally in the USSR. Soviet economic history is replete with examples of illegalities, many much more draconian in intent. What is interesting is to ask why Soviet authorities allow this to exist. Secondly, why has it existed for so long with no visible sign that it will end?

The answer to the first question is to be found in the Soviet priority for growth of output. The output plan should be fulfilled at all costs. As to the historical persistence of overtime, this may reflect two things. First, its use reflects the labour shortage from which the Soviets currently suffer. Yet overtime work has always existed even without a labour shortage. It has served another purpose; namely, to increase the likelihood of plan fulfilment in the face of the erratic behavior of the Soviet supply system. Additionally, within the Soviet system a great deal of power is held by the enterprise director vis-à-vis the trade unions, the chief accountant, the banking system, and higher-ups in the economic echelon. This is evidenced by his ability virtually to ignore the formal role of the trade unions, manipulate the internal budget and perhaps the local branch of *Gosbank* which is supposed to be exercising control over the use of enterprise funds. So long as chances for plan fulfilment are increased, the monitoring institutions of the Soviet system are likely to ignore violations of workers' rights.

Several questions go unanswered for lack of adequate data. For example, it would be interesting to know if the illegal use of overtime has recently increased. There is no evidence of a relaxation of rules and regulations that would permit an increase in legal overtime. It would also be interesting to know what has happened to the actual hours of overtime over the years. One might expect an increase in the amount of overtime used today as opposed to the early years of the industrialisation drive when there was a plentiful supply of labour to transfer from agriculture to industry. On the other hand, while the demand by enterprises for overtime might be greater, the higher level of discretionary income possessed by Soviet citizens might reduce the supply of overtime.

The lack of more evidence on the amount of overtime and its concentration over the production cycle adds more frustrations to the attempt to ascertain more precisely how widespread storming is in the Soviet system. We certainly have a great deal of fragmentary evidence that storming exists and that it is built into a system of economic planning which weds success so closely to plan fulfilment within a certain calendar period.[47] Better data on overtime could confirm the prevalence of storming as well as sharpen our knowledge of the real amount of overtime used in the Soviet economy.

If the Soviet situation is compared with that of the US one can see the use of overtime over a planning cycle. In the US overtime employment tends to fluctuate with the oscillations of the business cycle. In the Soviet Union, overtime employment fluctuates more predictably, i.e. basically at the end of each month, but in the US cyclical fluctuations are not readily forecast. Overtime employment results from the basic nature of the Soviet planning process and should be regarded as an undesired consequence of central planning. But without its role as a buffer and compensatory mechanism, the Soviet economy would not function as well as it does.

The last three chapters have all provided an overview of how planners deal with alternative short-run labour supply models in a labour-short economy. Chapters 5 and 6 confront the work–leisure trade-off directly. Chapter 5 is an overview of daily leisure activities and develops a sense of the options and limitations imposed by policy makers and the choices made by Soviet households. Chapter 6 analyses the holiday economy, which is a special variant of the work–leisure decision because of the concentrated nature of a holiday.

5 Leisure

The stereotypical view of the Soviet Union is that it is a society at work – in the workers' state people labour and there is no play. From a distance the view is of a people who live grey lives in a ponderous, unrelentingly morose world with no time for laughter or real respite. When not working they hunt for food, and when not hunting for food they are beseiged with boring lectures and newspaper exhortations on the glories of fulfilling the current five year plan. Life is endless tedium. While there is more than a grain of truth in this picture, the portrait is more caricature than photographic realism. There is leisure in the workers' state; not yet the workers' paradise but time for play nevertheless.

Leisure is perhaps the nexus of the axes of public policy and private choice. It is in the nature of economic planning that planners always want to have more control than they presently possess. Planners would like to control the way in which individuals divide their life between work and leisure and they would like to control the leisure activities people select. The days of overt coercion have long since disappeared from the Soviet Union. Planners no longer dispose of people's lives as they did during the Stalinist era; the combination of more freedom and higher incomes allows Soviet citizens to make choices they did not have before. These choices are not necessarily what planners would prefer and it will be seen that there are specific criticisms of certain types of activities. On the other hand, planners do limit the choices people make. As will be seen, the quantity and quality of Soviet leisure activities are constrained by the low priority accorded this sector of the society.

In this chapter we take a detailed look at the Soviet world of leisure: how much there is and what is done with free time. We analyse the major determinants of leisure time: sex, marital status, children, income, education and occupation. We also analyse the impact that the 5-day work week has had on leisure activities since 1967.

Two leisure activities receive special attention because they play such a prominent role in Soviet life: namely, television and reading. An analysis of the impact of television is absolutely essential to an understanding of what has happened to life after work in the USSR. Television has come to be a dominant leisure institution in the country and its presence has come to constitute the pre-eminent vehicle for daily respite from work and the extraordinary pressure of life in the Soviet Union. Reading is a leisure activity the regime supports through a high level of production, albeit selectively. On the other hand there is a substantial subsidy of book and newspaper prices. The leadership wants the population to read for two reasons; because it furthers the development of skills and because the printed word is a major force for the transmission of the system's values. The third leisure activity to which we give detailed consideration is the agricultural activity of urbanites. Many Soviet urbanites are either from farms or are the children or grandchildren of farmers and large and growing numbers of urbanites are engaged in gardening not only for pleasure, but also for income. In a real sense it is an activity which jointly maximises the desire for income and leisure.

Finally, we examine the phenomenon of going to school after work. It is a free-time activity which would certainly not ordinarily fall within a narrow definition of leisure. Strictly speaking, going to school should be considered as a substitute of work for leisure since it is directly tied to advancement at the workplace and hence maximisation of income rather than leisure time. In this regard we also look at the number of people who explicitly choose a second job and the groups from which multiple job holders are drawn.

LEISURE ACTIVITIES

In much the same way that Soviet social scientists have made innumerable studies of the basic time budget, so too have they produced a large number of studies of leisure time and its various constituent parts. The one major difference is that leisure studies have been done as recently as the early 1970s. Thus our knowledge of leisure activity is more up to date. Given the large number of studies available, I have selected those that are the most comprehensive. This means either they cover several different time periods or a large sample of individuals at a given period of time.

The data in Table 5.1 show the relative importance of the various activities during the non-working time of Soviet workers for a typical week over a 47 year period of time beginning with the early 1920s and ending with 1970. The data not only exclude work, but also sleeping and

TABLE 5.1 *Relative importance of several non-work time activities, large cities in European parts of the USSR, various years*

	1923–4	1936	1963	1965–8	1967–70
1. Housework and work in the private plot (excluding care of children)	35.0	24.0	21.2	19.5	18.5
2. Daily cultural life					
(a) leisure, including	6.7	5.5	12.4	16.0	17.3
reading books and magazines	2.1	1.0	2.3	2.1	3.3
Reading newspapers	2.9	1.8	1.4	1.6	2.5
TV, radio	—	1.0	5.1	6.2	7.5
Movies, theatre & other public performances	0.6	0.7	0.9	1.3	1.3
(b) Studying		1.0	2.6	4.0	2.3
(c) Amateur talent activities and other kinds of non-professional creative works	1.1	—	0.1	0.8	0.4
3. Physical culture, sports, hunting, fishing, going to the country	0.2	0.3	0.7	0.7	1.6
4. Meeting with friends, guests, dances	6.2	7.6	5.8	5.2	5.8
5. Occupied with children	5.6	4.3	3.0	5.0	3.1
caring for children	5.0	—	1.9	2.9	1.5
upbringing of children	0.6	—	1.1	3.0	1.6

SOURCE L. A. Gordon, E. V. Klopov and L. A. Onikov, *Cherty Sotsialisticheskogo Obraza Zhizni: Byt Gorodskikh Robochikh Vchera, Segodnia, Zavtra* (Moscow, 1977) p. 149.

eating. There are a number of observations to be made about the patterns of these results. First, the time devoted to housework and the private plot is now half of what it used to be. As we pointed out earlier, this is due more to the decrease in the time this generation of urbanites spends doing agricultural work than it is to the fall in housework. Second, there has been an enormous increase in the time devoted to 'daily cultural life'. This is broken down into leisure, studying, e.g. going to night school and amateur activities, e.g. singing in a local choir, playing in a band. In fact, many studies call all these activities leisure activities. Indeed, the next two major categories which deal with physical activity and social relationships with people are also often simply incorporated under the umbrella of leisure. Finally, the category dealing with children makes the distinction between caring for children (the Russian word is *ukhod*), which includes such things as feeding and dressing children, and the upbringing of children (the Russian word is *vospitanie*). The latter deals with such things as the inculcation of values and helping children with such creative activities as learning a musical instrument. We are therefore obliged to deal with definitional differences between studies.

Looking at the 1960s, the data show that reading (books, magazines, newspapers) increased in importance at the end of the decade, constituting about 5.8 per cent of the workers' time budget after falling from its peak in the 1920s. The decline after the 1920s was probably due to the fact that in the previous decade the literacy campaigns made it very fashionable to read as well as creating upward mobility. Moreover, it would not be unreasonable to believe that peasants would tell investigators what they wanted to hear. The increase in reading is at least partially caused by the higher level of education in the country. There was from 1963 a large increase in the number watching television and listening to radio, so much so that these are the most important of all the leisure activities.

The percentage of time devoted to going to school dipped according to the most recent research. This is probably due to having caught up with the needs of those who went without education because of World War II as well as the disappearance of the Red Universities and Rabfaks of the 1920s and the continuing education programmes of the 1930s. The second most important leisure activity is the time spent with other people. There is a high degree of consistency over the length of the Soviet period; whatever technological changes have taken place during these decades Soviet citizens still enjoy spending their time with friends and relatives. Finally, with some caution we may conclude that a smaller proportion of time is being spent with children. While this is most true for basic care, it may also hold for time spent in their upbringing. At least part of this phenomenon is due to the increased use of institutional child care.

Physical activity has made major gains in the Soviet Union, although it is not a major activity for Soviet workers.

In the early 1960s a study was carried out in 7 industrial cities with a total sample of 25 635 people. The data in Table 5.2 show both the average weekly time and the proportion of total free time spent on each activity. Total free time for the average worker was 21 hours and 42

TABLE 5.2 *Utilisation of free time of workers in seven cities, in hours and minutes per week and percentage of total*

	Per week in hours and minutes	Percentage of total free time
	hr min	
Study and increasing skills	1 59	9.1
Self-education	3 44	17.2
Social work	0 49	3.8
Athletics	0 28	2.2
Amusements:	7 49	36.0
dance, singing, playing musical instruments	0 14	1.1
cinema and theatre	2 13	10.2
listening to radio and watching television	1 24	6.5
visiting and receiving guests	1 52	8.6
domestic games	1 17	5.9
other	0 49	3.8
Raising children	2 06	9.7
Hobbies	1 31	7.0
Other expenditures	3 16	15.1
TOTAL	21 42	100.2

SOURCE G. S. Petrosian, *Vnerabochee Vremia Trudiashchikhsia v SSSR* (Moscow, 1965) p. 163. The seven cities are Yerevan, Novosibirsk, Novokuźnetsk, Kostroma, Sverdlovsk, Krasnoiarsk and Norilsk.

minutes per week. The largest portion of leisure time (36 per cent) comes under the heading of amusements. Within that category, going to the movies and the theatre (10.2 per cent) and visiting other people (8.6 per cent) were the most popular activities. Of all the free time possibilities people spent the most time in 'self-education'. This refers to reading books, magazines and newspapers as opposed to more formal academic and vocational education which took up 9.1 per cent of leisure time. People also spend about 10 per cent of their free time in the raising of children (*vospitanie*).

A 1960s study involving 10 000 workers looked at the question of how many people participated in the major leisure activities.[1] On a daily basis the five most popular leisure activities were: reading newspapers (82 per cent), listening to the radio (71 per cent), reading books (55 per cent), reading magazines (36 per cent) and spending time with children (35 per cent). Surprisingly, only 16 per cent said they watched television every day. This may reflect the absence of the geographic dispersion of Soviet television in the 1960s to the degree it exists today or a skewing of the sample towards areas where televisions were not very prevalent. Certainly the figure is very low compared with more recent data. The most popular activities on a several times a week basis were: going to the cinema (45 per cent), visiting relatives and friends (29 per cent), reading magazines (22 per cent), watching television (22 per cent) and participating in social work (22 per cent). On a day to day basis Soviet citizens depend upon resources within their own homes to sustain their leisure life. Less importance is attached to free time activities available outside the home.

In the period 1972–5, a study was done which covered highly skilled blue-collar workers whose job requires at least a high school education (see Table 5.3). The research, which was carried out in Moscow, Klin and Kstovo, points out the great differences in the lifestyle of different urban areas and the differential in the availability of facilities and consumer good between urban areas. Moscow, of course, is the largest city in the country with a population of 7 million. The population of Klin is about 81 000 and that of Kstovo 49 000.

If we arbitrarily choose to call differentials of 10 percentage points or less insignificant, then the only leisure activities where this holds are

TABLE 5.3 *Participation in various leisure activities by urban blue-collar workers, in percentages*

	Moscow	Klin	Kstovo
Walking and playing games with children	42	45	52
Watching television	76		
Listening to the radio	69	80	74
Reading newspapers, magazines, books	87	67	76
Studying, including self-education	29	16	10
Going to stadiums, parks	41	22	27
Going to theatres, concerts, exhibitions	49	22	18
Playing sports		16	19
Tourism, hiking in the country	40		
Hobbies	22	—	13
Having guests, visiting relatives, friends, acquaintances	45	17	43
Participation in amateur circles	3	1	1
Work on a private plot (or garden)	8	28	54

SOURCE A. M. Geliuta and V. I. Staroverov, *Sotsialnyi Oblik Rabochego-Intelligenta* (Moscow, 1977) p. 156.

playing with children, watching television and listening to radio (one of the two major leisure activities) and participating in amateur groups (e.g. singing, poetry, reading). Otherwise the differences between the three cities are substantial. For example, while 87 per cent of Muscovites read (the other major activity), only 67 per cent of those from Klin read. There is also a much higher percentage of workers who are studying in Moscow than in the other two cities and this probably reflects the existence of more schools in Moscow. The higher percentage of people who go to stadiums and to plays and concerts most certainly reflects the rich endowment of cultural facilities in Moscow. With respect to social relationships, Moscow and Kstovo are virtually the same and both have a high level of participation. But in Klin, not as many spend time with other people. The largest difference is in agriculture. While only 8 per cent of the Moscow workers have a garden, as we might expect, in the smaller cities 28 per cent and 54 per cent of the workers are involved in some kind of garden. As we will later show, it is likely that many of these workers are participants in a collective garden associated with their enterprise.

THE DETERMINANTS OF LEISURE I: SEX

We have already established the fact that men have more leisure time than women. In this section we will see that there are significant differences in the time devoted to various activities by sex. However, in terms of simple participation in a particular activity the similarities between men and women are more notable than the differences. For example, in a 1971–2 study in Gorky among both blue-collar workers and engineering–technical workers (ITR), out of twenty activities, in only 7 cases was there a 5 percentage point or greater difference in the percentage of each sex participating in a given activity.[2] Five were dominated by men: parties with alcohol, two involving indoor games (cards and dominoes), hunting and fishing, and gardening. The other 2 activities were dominated by women and involved going to the cinema, theatres, exhibitions and museums. Among the ITR there were significant differences between men and women in 12 of the 20 activities.

In an earlier mid-1960s study, there was a 5 point or greater spread between men and women in 10 out of 22 activities. Men were more likely to read newspapers and books, go touring and hike, attend sporting events and evening dances, participate in sports, be hobbyists and eat out. Women were the dominant television watchers and more women spent more time with friends than did men. Thus men were much more likely to be doing things outside the home while women were more likely to spend their free time indoors.

Finally, in Table 5.4 we present the relative importance of various leisure activities for men and women for the years 1924 and 1961. Some remarkable changes took place between these years. The most obvious one is that Soviet men and women actually began to do things, particularly women. In 1924 Soviet women spent half their leisure time doing nothing. The amount of time Soviet men and women spent without any focused purpose is highly suggestive of the absence of facilities and/or the ability or education to take part in certain leisure activities. For example, note that the share of leisure time women spent reading in 1971 increased by about 50 per cent (from 20.6 per cent to 30.5 per cent). Their reading time went up even as the time for cinema, theatre, radio and television became the dominant factor in their leisure time (as it is also for men). Women spend more time reading fiction than men, while the latter spend more time than women reading non-fiction material. The share of time involved in social work declined for both sexes; the activities here include going to party meetings and helping the militia. There is an increasing appetite for private rather than for collective consumption of leisure.

Men do much more reading which is geared to their professional lives and to their role as participants in the political life of the country. This is consistent with the fact that the share of free time devoted to education

TABLE 5.4 *Relative importance of leisure activities, by sex, 1924 and 1961, in percentages*

	1924		1961	
	M	W	M	W
Education	8.3	11.8	18.7	9.1
Cinema, theatre, radio, television	3.7	5.4	25.3	36.7
Amateur activity	0.9	0.7	4.0	3.9
Reading newspapers and magazines, political and technical literature	24.0	5.5	15.9	11.6
Reading fiction	16.0	15.1	12.7	18.9
Physical culture and sports	4.0	—	5.6	2.2
Social work	9.5	11.8	7.0	5.3
Doing nothing	33.5	49.6	10.8	12.3

SOURCE A. V. Mialkin, *Svobodnoe Vremia i Vsestoronnee Razvitie Lichnosti* (Moscow, 1962) p. 24.

has become relatively much more important for men than women; men spend about twice as much as their time studying than do women.

THE DETERMINANTS OF LEISURE II: INCOME

There is an unequal amount of free time available to people in different income groups. In the Soviet Union money buys leisure. In a 1953 Krasnoiarsk study, men in households with a per capita income of 50 roubles or less had 116 hours of free time a month; those in families with more than 50 roubles had 188 hours, or 62 per cent more free time. For women in households with more than 50 roubles per capita, free time was 111 hours, or 71 per cent more than the low income households.[3]

A Krasnoiarsk study broke down the relationship into 5 major categories of leisure time (see Table 5.5). The first 4 categories deal with specific activities. With one exception, the consumption of each leisure good rises with per capita household income. The exception is the decline in participation in sports and related activities for the 31–50 rouble group. The difference between the highest income group and lowest is quite staggering. The highest income group takes part in 3 times as many cultural activities, 1.5 times as much entertainment, almost that much of 'other entertainment' and a bit more physical activity than the lowest income group. There is also a significant difference in the time

TABLE 5.5 *Free time in Krasnoiarsk Krai by income class, 1959, in hours*

	Per capita monthly household income (roubles)			
	Up to 30	31–50	51–100	over 100
Physical development	120	83	104	135
Cultural activities: reading, artistic activity	255	385	546	785
Entertainment: cinema, theatre	260	322	385	390
Other entertainment, visiting	177	224	234	255
Doing nothing	234	208	130	94
Total Hours	1046	1222	1399	1659
Percentage of total possible time	12.1	14.2	16.1	19.2

SOURCE G. A. Prudenskii, *Problemy Rabochego i Vnerabochego Vremeni* (Moscow, 1972) p. 265.

spent 'doing nothing'. The poorest Soviet households spend a lot more time simply doing nothing with their free time than the better-off households. The poorest Soviet households are about 2.5 times more likely to be doing nothing with their leisure time than those with the highest per capita income.

THE DETERMINANTS OF LEISURE III: MARITAL STATUS AND CHILDREN

In the chapter dealing with time budgets we demonstrated that married couples, especially those with children, have less free time than single persons. We now expand on this to show the kinds of activities associated with different material situations and family sizes. A Kazan study looked at what people did after work and what they did on their day off.[4] The three most prominent activities of each group provide insight into the contour of their leisure time. For unmarried persons the most important activities after work are going to the cinema or a play or watching television (38 per cent), going for walks or working in the garden (18 per cent), resting at home (9 per cent) and doing housework (9 per cent). Married people without children also favour films, plays or television (44 per cent), walking and gardening (33 per cent) and housework (11 per cent). But for those with children, housework dominates their free time (44 per cent), followed by their occupation with children (13 per cent) and only then is there room for the respite of walking or garden work (10 per cent). After lunch on Sunday, single people go to the country or fish (18 per cent), read (12 per cent) or study (12 per cent). Childless couples sleep or rest (22 per cent), do housework (20 per cent) and read (13 per cent). Couples with children spend time with their offspring (25 per cent), sleep or rest (13 per cent) and study (12 per cent). People with children are much less likely to read. They are also much less likely to do things with friends (2 per cent) than married but childless couples (9 per cent).

Not surprisingly, the amount of free time declines for both men and women as the number of children increases (see Table 5.6). The first child makes the greatest impact on women while very large families (4 or more children) affect men the most. For childless women, who already have much less free time than their husbands, the first child reduces free time to only 1.5 hours a day. Even that limited free time decreases by small amounts as the number of children increases. In the unlikely event a fourth child arrives, men and women have about the same amount of

TABLE 5.6 *Influence of number of children on the length of free time, 1959, hours per work day*

	Hours of free time	
	Men	Women
Families without children	3.7	2.2
Families with one child	2.9	1.5
Families with two children	2.5	1.3
Families with three children	2.4	1.1
Families with four or more children	1.2	1.0

SOURCE V. A. Artemov *et al.*, *Statistika Biudzhetov Vremeni Trudiashchikhsia* (Moscow, 1967) p. 87.

free time, but in households with 1, 2 or 3 children, men have twice as much free time as women.

One of the great problems for women with small children is that they still receive little help from their husbands. Urban parents spend about 13 to 15 hours a week doing things like helping children with their homework. According to some studies up to 16 to 18 hours a week may be spent with preschool and elementary school children. In the case of teenagers in secondary school this time falls to about 2 hours a week.[5] It might also be noted that a number of studies show a positive correlation between the level of educational attainment of women and the time spent in raising children (*vospitanie*). One source reports that women who did not finish either elementary school or middle school spend 4.7 hours a day with their children, those who completed middle school spend 5.1 hours and for women with higher education it is 5.3 hours a day.[6] The number of hours reported in this study seems high in relation to other research. For example, while the findings of a Vil'nius study generally agree with the conclusion that better educated women spend more time with their children, the time involved is closer to 2 hours a day. This particular study showed that as the number of children in the family increased, holding the level of education constant, the amount of free time available to women declined in all but one instance.

THE DETERMINANTS OF LEISURE IV: EDUCATION

Several studies have been carried out looking at the relationship between leisure and the level of education. In general the results are remarkably consistent with one another and there are only a couple of instances where there are contradictions. A study in several Ural cities surveyed younger persons (aged 30 or under).[7] For some activities there were consistent relationships while for others the patterns were ambiguous. The unambiguous relationships were the inverse correlations between education and listening to the radio, watching television and playing dominoes and cards. On average those with a higher education read more fiction, go to more films and fewer dances, and are a little more likely to be involved in athletics than their less well educated compatriots.

A 1965-8 study showed a number of differences between the most educated workers (completed secondary education and higher education) and the least educated workers (four classes or less).[8] The most educated spent about three times as much time reading books and magazines, watched less television or listened less to the radio, and were also about three times more likely to go to the cinema, theatre and other public performances. The least educated spent a bit more time with friends and going to dances. For the poorly educated Soviet workers radio and television are the primary means of entertainment.

THE DETERMINANTS OF LEISURE V: OCCUPATION

There are also class differences in the consumption of leisure. The world of leisure inhabited by a Soviet blue-collar worker is much different from that of his boss in the upstairs office. In turn, the world of the Soviet intellectual is different from that of people involved in production. According to a 1973 study, engineers and specialists have 4.4 hours of free time on a work day and 9.1 hours on a day off. Blue-collar workers have 3.6 hours of free time on a work day and 8.9 hours on a day off.[9]

These differences show up in a differential rate of participation in free time activities (see Table 5.7). It should be noted that these data reflect access to leisure and not time spent, thereby demonstrating the income and class differences that exist in the Soviet Union. A much higher proportion of engineering-technical workers than blue-collar workers spend time advancing their job skill. They are also more likely to be TV watchers, go on their own to films, plays and museums, go to parties with friends, spend time with their family, go on their own to the country, spend time gardening and do social work. Indeed, there are only 2 activities out of 18 where a higher proportion of blue-collar

Leisure

TABLE 5.7 *Percentage of blue-collar and engineering–technical workers (ITR) participating in selected free time activities, Gorky and Gorky Oblast, 1971–2*

	Blue-collar workers	ITR
Doing nothing	5.7	4.4
Studying to increase general level of education	5.2	7.1
Studying to increase knowledge of special skill	3.0	11.5
Participation in amateur activities	2.8	1.1
Regular participation in athletics	5.2	5.8
Reading, listening to radio, watching TV	60.3	80.5
Unorganised trips to cinemas, theatres, exhibitions, museums	32.4	56.3
Organised trips to cinemas, theatres, exhibitions, museums	14.5	16.4
Parties with friends with alcohol	28.9	36.6
Unorganised trips to cafés, restaurants, clubs	3.3	6.4
Organised trips to cafés, restaurants, clubs	3.7	5.7
Playing dominoes/cards	17.3	10.7
Playing chess/draughts	17.4	21.1
Spending time at home with family, with children	48.1	61.4
Unorganised trips to country	21.9	33.9
Organised excursions to country	17.5	20.9
Hunting/fishing	15.1	16.7
Gardening	15.1	33.2
Social work	6.9	14.4

SOURCE G. M. Podorov, *Rabochee i Svobodnoe Vremia* (Moscow, 1975) pp. 134–5.

workers than ITR participate and more blue-collar workers than ITR 'do nothing'.

A somewhat earlier study compared four occupational groups: manual workers, technical intelligentsia, intelligentsia not employed in production, and white-collar workers. The data in Table 5.8 are for 10 leisure activities and covered over 10 000 workers. There is virtually no difference in the percentage of each group reading newspapers and in all cases there is only a small minority who do not read a newspaper. Manual workers do not read magazines as much as the other groups, but with the exception of the technical intelligentsia, there are as many readers of books in this group as the other two groups. All four groups have about the same participation rate with regard to listening to radio and playing with children. Many more of the technical intelligentsia watch television, go to plays and are tourists than the other three groups.

TABLE 5.8 *Participation in leisure activities, mid-1960s, in percentages of those surveyed*

	Blue-collar workers	Technical intelligentsia	Intelligentsia not employed in production	White-collar workers
Reading newspapers	90	94	93	92
Reading magazines	67	91	82	86
Reading books	75	87	74	76
Listening to radio	76	76	81	79
Watching television	45	54	43	39
Going to cinemas	76	80	81	72
Going to theatres	39	62	49	44
Tourism, hikes	33	45	36	33
Going for walks	44	43	36	38
Games, playing with children	44	39	38	45

SOURCE B. Grushin, *Svobodnoe Vremia: Aktual'nye Problemy* (Moscow, 1965) p. 81.

A 1971–2 study surveyed 1000 blue-collar workers in the city of Dubna. This is an academically-orientated city and this may account for the extraordinary amount of time workers spend reading. Sixty-four per cent of the free time of women is spent reading; among men the figure is 52 per cent. Ninety-four per cent subscribe to periodicals and 90 per cent read their periodicals regularly. Among the women, 83 per cent say they use radio and TV selectively, in contrast to 43 per cent of the men. They are also voracious theatregoers: 97 per cent of the women and 60 per cent of the men regularly attend plays.[10]

The occupational groups with the least amount of free time are intellectual workers, defined as persons working in scientific research institutes (NII). In 1925 these workers had 1 hour and 21 minutes of free time a day. Two studies in 1964 and 1968 said they had 2 hours and 30 minutes, and 2 hours respectively.[11] At best there was an increase of 1 hour of leisure over a period of about 40 years. Much the same is true of professors in higher education institutions (VUZy). Sixty-three per cent of the institute researchers and 69 per cent of the professors have no more than 2 hours of free time in a day. Ten per cent of the researchers and 7 per cent of the VUZy teachers have no free time at all. The data also show that the situation for women in both institutions is worse than it is for men.[12]

THE DETERMINANTS OF LEISURE VI: CITY SIZE

The final determinant of leisure in Soviet society is city size. The situation is no different in the Soviet Union from what it is in the United States: the richest cultural offerings are concentrated in the large cities. The smaller the city, the more difficult it is to find interesting things to do with free time, much less to find diversity in leisure. There is a larger difference between large cities and small cities than between middle-size and small cities, but in both of the latter the choice of activities is restricted. Research done in one small town (under 40 000 population) found that people with different levels of education came together to spend free time because there were no places to go. This is different from a big city where people with either a specialised education or higher education tend to take part in activities with people at their own level of education.[13]

In the small towns, free time, particularly at weekends, revolves around the Palace of Culture where dances are held or amateur groups meet.[14] But this bears inspection: one author cynically complained that the Palace of Culture is only heated once a week for a dance or when a second- or third-rate touring company comes with a ten year old performance.[15] People in small cities tend to have maintained stronger contact with their relatives than have those who live in big cities and consequently often visit relatives.[16] As a rule, small cities do not have a theatre.[17] One author claims that a consequence of the lack of cultural facilities in small cities is that the percentage of people who read magazines and newspapers on a daily basis is highest in small cities.[18]

The most systematic study of the relationship between city size and leisure activity was done in the mid-1960s. The results are shown in Table 5.9. Moscow, which at the time probably had a population of about 6 670 000, is compared with large cities (over 500 000), middle-size cities (100 000–500 000), small cities (10 000–100 000), and small towns and villages (0–10000). The city sizes of greatest interest are the three intermediate categories since Moscow, as the single largest city in the country, is an aberration and because such a small percentage of the total population lives in towns of less than 10 000. The data show the proportion of each city size consuming a given leisure activity. There is high degree of uniformity with respect to reading newspapers except for those in small cities, where the participation rate is lowest. There is a general tendency for magazine and book reading to decline with city size. The lowest level of radio listening is in large cities and this is probably due to the presence of television. Watching television in

TABLE 5.9 *Participation in leisure activities by city size, mid-1960s, in percentages of those surveyed*

	Moscow	Population			
		500 000 or more	100 000– 500 000	10 000– 100 000	0– 10 000
Reading newspapers	92	92	94	84	91
Reading magazines	81	75	76	68	66
Reading books	81	80	75	73	67
Listening to radio	81	71	83	81	83
Watching TV	77	79	47	25	18
Going to cinemas	72	64	79	76	69
Going to theatres	51	62	50	30	11
Tourism, hikes	55	39	32	28	20
Going for walks	50	50	45	46	21
Games, playing with children	31	44	39	38	45
Going to concerts	48	37	44	35	24
Sporting events	41	33	33	35	16
Evening dances	15	18	19	28	14
Amateur societies	10	16	9	17	12
Participation in sports	29	24	20	23	12

SOURCE B. Grushin, *Svobodnoe Vremia: Aktual'nye Problemy* (Moscow, 1967) pp. 81 and 88–9.

middle-size and small cities is much lower, no doubt because the absence of facilities to transmit television programs. Cinema-going is least important in the large cities, again probably due to the substitution of other leisure activities; it is the second most important activity in middle-size cities. The percentage of people going to plays is highest in the large cities and lowest in the two smallest categories of city size. Engaging in tourism is directly related to city size. This is associated with the rising percentage of big city inhabitants who have become a disproportionate part of the explosion in tourism and holiday making. Walking as a leisure activity is engaged in by about half of all Soviet citizens except in the very smallest towns where they probably walk all the time because they have no mass transit system. There is a large spread between the 31 per cent in Moscow who play with their children and the 45 per cent who do so in the smallest towns, but there is no consistent pattern by city size.

For those activities requiring facilities, the participation rate is extremely low, e.g. going to concerts and sports events. The high participation rates in these activities in Moscow suggest that Muscovites are blessed with more facilities than others. If this is so, then for at least some activities the differences in the availability of facilities between the large, middle and small cities are not so great. For example, a higher percentage go to concerts in middle-size cities, but there is virtually no difference in the proportion going to sporting events or participating in athletics.

If we could assume that participation reflects the relative availability of facilities it would be interesting to know the bases upon which the state decides to allocate resources to the various sized cities.

THE IMPACT OF THE FIVE DAY WEEK ON LEISURE

As we saw in Chapter 1, the 5 day work week increased the amount of leisure time. In general people do the same things they previously did; they simply spend more time doing them. This means Soviet citizens are watching more TV, reading a little more, and going to the cinema more often.[19] A study in a number of industrial enterprises in the Urals from 1968-71 looked at the question of how people responded to the change in the work week in terms of how many increased the time spent on a given activity, how many spent about the same amount of time and the number doing something less than before. As might be expected the proportion engaging less in an activity was quite small. The leisure activity with the highest proportion of people spending less time was the 6.5 per cent who said they spent less time with the family. However, this was also the activity with the highest proportion of people who increased their time (64.6 per cent). The other big gainers were reading (61.6 per cent), walking with friends (52.5 per cent), watching television (43 per cent), and going to the cinema (30.3 per cent).[20] A major study of the impact of the 5 day work week was done in the industrial city of Taganrog, situated on the Sea of Azov on the Black Sea. In spite of its location, few families used the beach even one day during the year. Only 5-10 per cent walked along by the sea or fished. About half watched television on their day off. In studies of Moscow, Penza and Leningrad, 80 per cent of the married women with families said they either watch television or do nothing at all on their day off.[21]

The 5 day work week also created the opportunity for weekends away from home. However, it appears that state accommodation for people who want comfortable facilities is in very short supply. Passes to guest houses are typically for 12 days, not weekends. What Leningraders do when they want a weekend in the country is to spend it at a *dacha*, about half of which are rented. Young people go camping at weekends.[22]

HOUSEHOLD EXPENDITURES ON LEISURE

We can estimate the amount of money that workers spend in what we will call the leisure economy. The definition of the goods that belong within this category is certainly sufficiently debatable to make it impossible to agree on any one concept and therefore on a single figure. A study of industrial workers said that the percentage of income going for 'daily cultural needs' (e.g. cinema, newspapers) was 11.7 per cent in 1958 and 12.3 per cent in 1961.[23] A 1975 publication set the figure for 'cultural services' at 10.7 per cent of household income for the urban population.[24]

The consumption of alcohol, notwithstanding its many pathological effects on Soviet society, is an important leisure time activity. In the 1958 and 1961 studies, tobacco and alcohol as a single category represented 5.4 per cent and 5.6 per cent of the total household budget or roughly half of what was spent on cultural goods.[25] In the United States, recreation expenditures were 5.5 per cent of total personal consumption expenditures in 1960 and 6.8 per cent in 1975. Over the same period tobacco purchases fell from 2.1 per cent to 1.5 per cent of total consumption expenditures and spending on alcohol fell from 3.3 per cent to 2.5 per cent of consumption.[26]

In a 1966–7 study in the city of Nikolaev, the typical blue-collar family annually spent 122 roubles for 'films, the theatre, newspapers and other cultural needs'. They spent 93 roubles on vodka, beer and other alcoholic beverages.[27] While expenditures on alcohol relative to cultural goods are high, at least the pattern has changed. In 1925 in Moscow, the annual per capita expenditures on alcohol was 8.15 roubles, while the expenditures on 'cultural needs' was 6.26 roubles.[28]

THE CULT OF THE TELEVISION

In this section we explore in detail four free time activities that are prominent in the lives of urbanites: television, going to school, reading and gardening. Television has become the primary leisure activity for the ordinary citizen. In this section we will see how it has affected their lives and how it has altered the relative structure of leisure consumed in the USSR. The sheer number of televisions has grown dramatically. In 1965, there were 24 televisions for every 100 families, in 1970, 51 per 100 families, and in 1975, 74 per 100 families, a virtual trebling in a period of 10 years.[29] As of 1978 there were 60 million television sets in the country, or one for every 4.3 people. Television broadcasts reach 80 per cent of the country's population.[30] In the US in 1978 there were 119 million television sets, or one for every 1.8 persons in the country.[31] We have earlier established that an extremely high percentage of the Soviet population watches television, especially in urban areas. For example, in 1968 95–98 per cent of the population of Leningrad and Kostroma said they watch at least some television.[32] In 1975 about 70 per cent in these two cities plus Odessa and Kazan said they watch television daily.[33]

Soviet citizens also spend a lot of time watching television. One study said that during a typical week people watch 7 to 10 hours.[34] Another study suggests that workers watch about 13 hours a week, about 1.7 hours on a week day and about 2.4 hours on a day off. Housewives and pensioners watch about 15 hours and 16 hours a week, respectively. Blue-collar workers watch more than any other work group – 14.5 hours, and intelligentsia who are involved in production watch the least – 12.1 hours per week.[35] Yet the Soviets do not hold a candle to the voracious viewing appetites of US families. The typical American household currently watches 6.5 hours *per day*.[36] This reflects the presence of many more American women at home during the day, the programmes directed at children, and the existence of more than one television (1.6 sets per US household) which increase the possibility that the interests of all family members can be met at the same time.

It is difficult to measure the qualitative effects television has on the individual and on society. One such study attempted to do this by asking blue-collar workers whether they participated more in a number of other common leisure activities since they began watching television (see Table 5.10). The results are absolutely consistent; they engage in every activity much less than before the entrance of television into their lives. It is particularly striking how many fewer people go to the cinema and to social clubs since the arrival of television. Reading of all kinds has suffered a setback. On a net basis there is also much less social contact with friends since television. Although 6 per cent spend more time with friends, 13 per cent spend less time. This suggests that to some extent people watch television with their friends. In fact a 1966 Kazan study indicates that 5 per cent watch TV with friends and another 7 per cent

TABLE 5.10 *How watching TV influences the participation in other cultural activities of blue-collar workers, 1968–71 (in percentages of total surveyed)*

	Participate less	Participate more
Listen to the radio	35.7	3.8
Read newspapers and magazines	12.1	3.5
Go to the cinema	39.0	2.8
Go to the theatre, museums, exhibitions	26.8	1.3
Read fiction	16.4	4.9
Go to a club	27.9	2.1
Go to lectures	26.5	2.1
Participate in amateur societies	12.7	3.5
Sports, tourism	9.9	4.8
Visit friends	13.2	6.2
Hobbies	11.3	6.0

SOURCE M. T. Iovchuk and L. N. Kogan (eds), *Dukhovnyi Mir Sovetskogo Rabochego* (Moscow, 1972) p. 367. (The numbers do not add up to 100 per cent because certain categories such as 'about the same' and 'no answer' have been omitted.)

with acquaintances.[37] Another source also attributes the decline in cinema and theatre attendance in large cities to television.[38]

GOING TO SCHOOL AFTER WORK

There are so many Soviet citizens who go to school after work that it has to be seriously considered as a free time activity. The data in Table 5.11 show the steady increase over the course of the Soviet period. There was an enormous increase in enrolment starting in the mid-1950s. From the period 1955 to 1965 the number of people going to school and working tripled and as a percentage of manual workers and employees doubled from 6 per cent to 12 per cent. The sharp increase was due to the fact that at the end of the 1950s and the beginning of the 1960s there were still a large number of people who did not have much education because of the war and the exigencies of the immediate postwar period.[39] While the proportion of workers going to school fell to 10 per cent in 1975, because they had caught up with the educational needs after World War II, the absolute number broke the 10 million mark. About 60 per cent are currently trying to finish high school and about 20 per cent are working towards a university degree.

TABLE 5.11 *Enrolment in correspondence courses and evening education in the USSR (in thousands)*

	1926/27	1940/41	1955/56	1965/66	1975/76
High school adult education	103	786	1853	4845	6199
Correspondence courses and special education institutions	—	187	491	1827	1708
Higher education	—	254	720	2276	2226
Total	103	1207	3064	8945	10133
As percent of all blue-collar and white-collar employees	1	4	6	12	10

SOURCE L. A. Gordon, E. V. Klopov and L. A. Onikov, *Cherty Sotsialisticheskogo Obraza Zhizni: Byt Gorodskikh Rabochikh Vchera, Segodnia, Zavtra* (Moscow, 1977) p. 158.

Several studies have demonstrated the importance of income, age and the existing level of education as determinants of people either attending school or studying on their own. In a mid-1960s study of the relationship between per capita household income and the number of hours blue-collar workers went to school, it was found that those with a per capita income of 30 roubles or less went to school just under 1 hour a week, those with an income from 30–100 roubles about 3 hours a week, and with an income over 100 roubles, 7.3 hours of school. In this same study it was found that after the age of 25 the time spent in school declined sharply. This was particularly true of women. Women under the age of 25 spent more time in school than men in the same group, but after age 25 men spent more time in school.[40] For women the period after age 25 corresponds to the years for childbearing and rearing. In 1965, 16.4 per cent of all women did not go to school because of their domestic obligations.[41]

Although the aggregate data show more students are trying to finish a high school education, two studies suggest that those who are already well-educated spend more time studying. Those who have four classes or less of education spend 0.6 per cent of their week studying, while well-educated workers with a minimum of a completed secondary education or better spend 9.4 per cent of their weekly free time studying.[42] In the city of Taganrog, 10 per cent of those with 4 to 6 classes of education and 36 per cent with a secondary specialised education said they would study if additional time became available.[43]

Given the large numbers that spend time studying, what are the reasons for workers not going to school? A study was done among Leningrad machine building workers in four different occupational groups ranging from unskilled manual workers to highly skilled workers whose job combined physical and intellectual functions. In a climate where the social ethos favours people finishing or continuing their education there would be pressure on an individual to say that they were not going to school for some reason other than their lack of interest. The main reason given by workers for not going to school is that they see themselves as either too young or too old for school. Roughly 35 per cent of the workers gave this reason (55 per cent among unskilled blue-collar workers). Some 7–12 per cent of the workers said housework and child care kept them from school; presumably these were mostly women. Of the most skilled workers and the skilled machine workers, 7–18 per cent said they did not want to go to school. Another 3–7 per cent said they had been out of school too long to return, and about 4 per cent said they were too tired after work. Only 4–5 per cent said the distance from work to school and school to home was a deterrent.[44]

PRIVATE PLOTS AND COLLECTIVE GARDENS

Earlier we showed that the percentage of time that urbanites devote to the private plot has declined during the Soviet period. Nevertheless, for a large number of urban families there are still strong ties to the land. This is evidenced by the large numbers engaged in collective gardening. There is a distinction between the private plot and the so-called collective garden. The private plot is literally a piece of land which is owned by the individual household. But collective gardening (*kollektivnoe sadovodstvo*) involves a piece of land which is subdivided among many families. The land is formally owned by an enterprise and while families nominally farm as a collective, in reality these small plots are private. Indeed, as we shall see, recent Soviet legislation has essentially conceded this fact. These pieces of land are generally located in the suburban areas of cities. The land cannot be sold by one individual to another, nor can one will it to his heirs. However, heirs can apply for the right to work the land and ordinarily the enterprise allows the family to continue to farm the piece of land once tended by their father or mother, even if they are not employed by the enterprise. Each collective elects a board and they define their own rules within the framework of regulations for collective gardens which have been established centrally. People chip in to buy certain items jointly, such as fertiliser; seeds are bought individually. Many people have built houses on their gardens and this is where they go for their summer holiday.[45]

Collective gardens are not a new phenomenon, but they have gained an enormous popularity in the post-Stalin period. It is also clear that recent policy sanctions their existence. In 1951 about 40 000 workers were involved in collective gardening. It has grown to the point where 2.6 million families were gardening in 1978. The Soviets claim that more than 10 million people spend days off and holidays at their plots.[46]

The participation in private plots and collective gardens (*sadovo-ogorodnye uchastki*) differs depending on city size. As Table 5.12 shows, those who live in large cities are the least likely to have gardens. This is confirmed by a 1965 study of Leningrad machine building workers which showed that 90.2 per cent did not have a *dacha*, garden or private plot. This figure dropped to 80 per cent in 1970.[47] Nor does the private plot play much of a role in the new cities of Siberia.[48] This is likely to be due to the fact that the younger group of people who move to the new cities are less attached to the traditions and life style of the village. It is in the suburbs of large cities and in the middle-size and small cities that collective gardens have their greatest importance. In the large and middle-size cities they are much more prominent than the private plot.[49]

The collective garden serves not only as a source of recreation but also as a source of income. Collective gardeners annually harvest about 450 000–500 000 tons of fruit and berries.[50] In 1976 the amount of fruit the collective gardens produced was estimated to be 15–20 per cent of the amount sold by co-operatives and the state.[51] Individuals are legally entitled to sell their produce in the market.[52] The existence of the garden

TABLE 5.12 *Percentage of people who own gardens* (sad) *and vegetable gardens* (ogorod) *by city size and sex, 1970*

Large cities		Suburbs of large cities		Small cities	
Men	Women	Men	Women	Men	Women
23	21	63	44	73	70

SOURCE L. A. Gordon and V. Klopov, *Chelovek Posle Raboty* (Moscow, 1972) p. 33.

as a potential source of output for the state and income for the individual household is demonstrated by the fact that members of the collective garden which belongs to the Moscow Car Building Plant annually harvest about 350–450 kilograms of fruit per family and in Zaporozhe a steel plant's collective garden yielded 630 kilograms of fruit and berries per family, certainly well above an individual family's needs.[53]

As is typical of all Soviet enterprises that involve private activity for personal gain there is ambiguity on the part of the authorities as to how to respond. As recently as 1976, a *Literaturnaia Gazeta* article obliquely criticised the garden plots because they were a source of private income. Much more direct was the criticism of gardeners who use building materials they obtain through illegal channels. Such channels are used because these materials are not available in state stores. Gardeners also have problems obtaining humus, sand, fertiliser, pesticides and garden tools.[54]

The latest wrinkle seems to be that collective gardens have won favour with the state. A new charter on gardening associations went into effect on 3 July 1978 in the RSFSR. It explicitly permits building guest houses, fruit storage space and other buildings which meet common needs. Permission has also been granted to build cottages with sizes ranging from 12–25 square metres. Members of collective garden associations may now also keep poultry, rabbits and bees. Finally, people may borrow up to 1000 roubles from *Gosbank* to finance construction.[55]

Soviet policy has therefore moved to *de jure* recognition of the collective garden, at one time conceived strictly as a gardening venture, as a phenomenon responding to the broad leisure goals of Soviet citizens. The newest policy initiative which encourages the expansion of the economic base of the collective garden implies that policy makers value the output that finds its way onto the market.

READING

It may well be that the most stable area of growth in the Soviet Union is the publishing industry. The country publishes millions of books, newspapers and magazines every year. Not all of it is traditional reading fare – there is a heavy emphasis on ideological and political literature. The collected works of Lenin, Marx and Brezhnev are produced in staggering numbers. Keith Bush says that these 'non-books' may constitute 80 per cent of all the books published in the Soviet Union. For example, up to 1977, 528 million volumes of Lenin's books have been published.[56] Yet we certainly get a feeling from the data that in Soviet society people read a great deal. Even a casual observer of day to day life in the Soviet Union will notice how many people on a bus or train will be reading a book. Moreover, book kiosks on the streets, rather than featuring magazines which explore the lives of show business personalities, offer books on such subjects as hydraulic engineering. The data in Table 5.13 show the steady increase in all categories of print materials. During the 25 year period 1950–75, per capita book production increased by about 1.5 times, magazine production by 12 times, newspapers by more than 3 times and library holdings of books and magazines by 4.5 times. There is obviously a high priority given to the production of print materials. In addition, low prices are charged for all such materials reflecting the substantial subsidy on books, etc. The subsidy exists because Soviet print material plays an important role in the socialisation process and in maintaining loyalty to Soviet goals, both long term and short term. It has long been social policy to encourage the reading of books. In the 1920s workers could buy books on credit; they were given a book of coupons which entitled them to buy 10–15 (old) roubles worth of books on credit (*kreditnaia knizhka*) and pay for them over a period of 3 months.[57] *Pravda*, the party daily, has the largest circulation of any newspaper in the world. It represents the principal means by which the party conveys its goals on a day to day basis. However, it is clear that this mountain of publications does not accord with the demands of the Soviet population. The existence of a thriving second economy in books in the Soviet Union reflects the shortages of a number of titles.

TABLE 5.13 *Indicators of the development of print and library material, USSR, various years (number per 100 persons)*

	1927	1940	1950	1960	1970	1975
Books	154	237	456	578	561	667
Magazines and other periodicals	156	126	101	363	1080	1193
Newspapers	6	20	20	32	58	66
Books and magazines in public urban libraries	47	95	134	391	536	603

SOURCE L. A. Gordon, E. V. Klopov and L. A. Onikov, *Cherty Sotsialisticheskogo Obraza Zhizni: Byt Gorodskikh Rabochikh Vchera, Segodnia, Zavtra* (Moscow, 1977) p. 153.

The presence of books is associated with several different characteristics of a Soviet household. A late-1960s Leningrad study showed that the higher the level of education and job skill the more likely there is to be a library in the home. At the extremes, a household with two parents having jobs which require higher education is about twice as likely to have a private library as one which is comprised of blue-collar workers and unskilled workers.[58] A study in a small city (Ostrogozhsk – population 35 000) confirms these findings. While 95 per cent of those classified as specialists have private libraries, 82 per cent of the manual workers do not.[59] Moreover, the size of the apartment determines whether there is a book collection in the house. Roughly speaking, about 65 per cent of the one-room apartments, 73 per cent of the two-room apartments and 79 per cent of the apartments with three or more rooms have libraries.[60]

The difference in the amount of time spent reading seems to be considerably less between broad occupational groups than it is between men and women. In a Leningrad study in the early 1970s among manual workers, engineering–technical workers, and white-collar employees, men spent about twice as much time as women reading. But the 5.5 hours a week that men spent reading was 14.4 per cent of their free time, just a bit more than the 13.4 per cent of women's free time devoted to reading. The fact that women have so much less free time accounts for a large part of the difference in the absolute amount of time men and women spend reading. Of the three occupational groups, the largest difference in the proportion of time spent reading is between male and female manual workers. Only 12 per cent of the blue-collar workers and 8 per cent of the white-collar workers do not read at all.[61] Reading is more important in the lives of Soviet urbanites than it is for collective farmers; one rural study found that one-third of the households did not own any books.[62] But reading is declining in relative importance as television encroaches more and more into the lives of the Soviet household. It is plausible to speculate that Soviet society in 25 years may be a nation much more influenced by a passive relationship with the television than an active exchange with the written word. One does not know if this represents a desideratum from the system's directors, but it is nevertheless a process that is under way.

WORK AS A 'FREE TIME' ACTIVITY

There is one activity that never appears in Soviet leisure studies – work. Obviously, it would be a contradiction in terms. Yet we already know that above and beyond the normal work day Soviet citizens work for income. We have seen this in the analysis of overtime, where people stay at their regular job. We also know that many people engage in the so-called 'second economy' for private gain. The sales of fruit by collective gardeners in the free market constitutes one such activity. However, no one is reporting how much time they spend in illegal activities.

But there is another category. There are some people who legally do additional work to increase their income (*dopolnitel'nyi trud*). This includes holding two jobs and working at home but does not include overtime work. Table 5.14 shows that slightly more than 5.3 per cent of the total population, most of whom were men, worked at an extra job in the mid-1960s. As can be seen, the definition of multiple job holders is somewhat generous since it includes students, pensioners and housewives, none of whom have a first job in the labour force. The group with the largest number holding two jobs is the intellegentsia not involved directly in production. This includes doctors who often hold more than one medical post, and lawyers who often work for more than one agency. In general, there appear to be more opportunities for the intellegentsia to hold more than one job voluntarily than for manual and white-collar workers.

TABLE 5.14 *Number of multiple job holders, by social and professional group and sex, mid-1960s, in percentages*

	Men	Women	Both sexes
Total	6.4	4.4	5.3
Manual workers	3.4	3.4	3.4
Technical intelligentsia	11.7	3.8	8.6
Intelligentsia not in production	28.7	19.3	23.2
White-collar employees	3.3	1.2	2.0
Students	14.2	4.9	10.7
Pensioners	2.5	3.3	3.0
Housewives	0.0	5.0	5.0

SOURCE B. Grushin, *Svobodnoe Vremia: Aktual'nye Problemy* (Moscow, 1967) p. 46.

DISSATISFACTION WITH LEISURE ACTIVITIES

There is a high level of dissatisfaction with leisure in the Soviet Union. In one study, 43 per cent said they 'do not have the possibility to spend free time as they wish'. The dissatisfaction is especially high among those in the labour force: 51 per cent of the specialists, 46 per cent of the manual workers, 68 per cent of the *kolkhozniki* and 49 per cent of the white-collar employees were unsatisfied. Only students and pensioners were happy with the existing situation.[63] Leisure offerings seem particularly inadequate in the new towns. In one study of young workers in the east Siberian town of Ust-Ilimsk, 73 per cent described the 'conditions for cultural rest' as unsatisfactory.[64] Finally, in a 1973 study 47 per cent were less than completely satisfied with the way they spend their free time.[65]

There are several explanations for this lack of contentment. One view is that there are inadequate facilities: restaurants are crowded, the ambience is unpleasant and waiters are obnoxious.[66] There are many major cities where there are complaints about the absence of evening entertainment.[67] Urban areas with high population densities lack recreational facilities.[68] The absence of these facilities probably accounts for about a quarter of worker complaints about how they can spend their free time.[69] This appears to be particularly true of people in their forties whose children have grown up; they do not know what to do with their newly found freedom.[70]

Therefore one view is that there are not enough things for people to do in urban areas. Those who view the unhappiness as springing from the lack of opportunities recognise the qualitative implications for individuals as well as the society. For example, one explanation for the high crime rate in the new cities is that people have money but no place to spend it and so they drink heavily, commit crimes, etc.[71]

Another explanation is that the free time available to workers has increased more rapidly than their ability to know what to do with it. This is regarded as an explanation for the 35 per cent of Gorky workers, engineers and technicians who said they prefer to spend their time drinking with friends and another 10–17 per cent who 'waste' their time playing dominoes and cards.[72] In this view there is a lot of aimless use of time which is a product of anti-culture (*antikultura*). It has three aspects:

1. reactionary bourgeois culture, e.g. trashy novels, commercial films, abstract art, modernism, pop art
2. drunkenness, hooliganism, playing cards
3. bad pieces of art which are only a fascimile of real culture.[73]

When all these rather amorphous activities were added up, it was ruefully claimed that 31.6 per cent of those surveyed in the central Urals spent their free time aimlessly and this explains antisocial behavior. This is a clear case of individuals making choices of which planners disapprove, rather than the individuals being unhappy.

Those within the Soviet Union who agree with this assessment generally also favour a much greater role for the state in organising the free time of individuals. This means having trade unions, local party or *Komsomol* committees, and neighborhood Soviets doing such things as organising excursions to the theatre, cinema, country, etc. However, most observers generally dismiss the notion that planned activities are a panacea for social ills.[74] Although most people do not want their enterprise or a social organisation to organise their free time, one study showed that an increasing proportion think they need assistance in this area of their lives. In 1970, in response to the question: do you need help in spending your free time?, 78.6 per cent said they did not want help, 19.5 per cent said they sometimes wanted help and only 1.9 per cent said they definitely wanted help. In a 1973 study there was a fairly substantial shift. This time only 64.1 per cent declined the use of help, 30.1 per cent said they sometimes wanted it and 5.8 per cent said they often or always wanted an organisation of some kind to help organise their leisure time.[75] The question is itself intriguing. It can be interpreted either as a way in which Soviet planners need to insinuate themselves in people's lives or as reflection of the lack of autonomy felt by many members of Soviet society.

The picture that emerges is of a society somewhat at sea about what to do with spare time. The evidence is solid for the general perception that not enough free time is available. Attitudinal surveys disclose the discontent. What then do Soviet citizens want from the system? What do people want to do with their free time?

HOW PEOPLE WOULD LIKE TO SPEND THEIR LEISURE TIME

The concept of asking people what they want to do with their time is surrounded by several defects. Responses which show a significant departure from what people are already doing implies that their present activity does not reflect their real preferences. It implicitly means that if the underlying conditions change, people will make a different set of choices. A change in the underlying determinants of demand may mean an increase in household incomes, which allows for a different consumption pattern, or it may mean a different composition of outputs. In addition, in survey research there is always the danger that the respondent will answer the question the way he or she thinks the interviewer wants the question answered. The problem is aggravated if people think that what they would like to do should accord with what they believe the state wants them to do. However, we will assume that the answers given by Soviet citizens reflect their preferences.

In comparing how people would like to spend free time with the present way free time is spent I have used a 10 per cent difference between the two as a rough measure of significance. In a 1971–2 study of manual workers and engineering–technical workers in Gorky, there were only a few activities where the differential exceeded this figure. They are listed in Table 5.15. What is remarkable is that in this study of 19 activities, there are few differences between what people are doing and what they want to do. Both groups want to spend a lot less time reading, listening to radio and watching television. Regrettably, one cannot tell if the desire to reduce this activity is heavily concentrated on one of these activities or is equally distributed. There is also a strong desire to spend less time with the family. It should be noted that I have violated my own criterion by including two activities for blue-collar workers where the spread is a bit less than the minimum 10 point spread. It is interesting to note that Soviet workers, who are otherwise usually

TABLE 5.15 *Actual and desired expenditure of free time, 1971–2, Gorky*

	Actual		Desired	
	Blue-collar workers	ITR	Blue-collar workers	ITR
Reading, listening to radio watching television	60.3	80.5	31.5	56.2
Cinema, theatre, exhibitions, museums	32.4	56.3	23.5	37.1
Regular participation in athletics	—	5.8	—	16.6
Parties with friends with alcohol	—	36.6	—	18.6
Spending time at home with family with children	48.1	61.4	33.9	46.4
Organised trips to the country	17.5	20.9	25.8	39.1
Activities inside the home	29.6	35.8	14.6	25.0
Activities outside the home	11.3	17.6	12.1	19.7

SOURCE G. M. Podorov, *Rabochee i Svobodnoe Vremia* (Moscow, 1975) pp. 134–5.

not disposed to planned activities, want more organised excursions outside of the city.

If we were to divide leisure time into activities ordinarily done inside the home and those done outside the home, there is a slight increase in the desire to do more things outside the home. However, there is a substantial desire to reduce indoor leisure activities, particularly among blue-collar workers. These outcomes conflict somewhat with other studies. In a late 1960s study in the Urals, young workers were asked what they would do if they had additional leisure time. About 65 per cent said they would do more reading, cinema and theatregoing. A bit more than half said they would spend more time with their families. About 42 per cent said they would rest, do nothing and watch television. It should be noted that in this study television is included with inactivity whereas in the Gorky study it is lumped in with reading. This supports the notion that there is ambiguity about the qualitative impact of television. In one study it is grouped with indolence, in another it is evaluated on the same plane with reading, an activity that has always been held in esteem. About 35 per cent would participate more in sports, tourism, hunting and fishing.[76]

A Taganrog study from the early 1970s demonstrated differences in leisure activity preferences between workers by level of education. One group with four to six classes of education and another with a middle specialised education were asked what they would do with additional time. For the poorly educated, in order, the activities in which they would like to spend more time are: rest and relaxation inside the home, watching TV (61 per cent), housework (52 per cent), amusements outside the home, cinema and theatre (50 per cent), raising and caring for children (48 per cent). For the better educated group the primary interests are in more time for reading (65 per cent), raising and caring for children (61 per cent), amusements outside the home, cinema and theatre (54 per cent), rest and relaxation inside the home, watching TV (50 per cent). There are two other startling differences. Only 1 per cent of the poorly educated want more sports and physical culture in their lives in contrast to 15 per cent of the better educated. Second, only 10 per cent of the former want more education in comparison with 36 per cent of those with a middle specialised education. It is also interesting to note that 9 per cent with 4–6 classes of schooling, but only 4 per cent of the other group, would work for additional pay if they had more time.[77] This suggests the correlation between income and education in the Soviet Union and the greater need that the low income groups have for more money.

CONCLUSION

The idea that Soviet citizens are without access to leisure has been thoroughly dispelled. Indeed, historically speaking, the amount of free time has increased significantly. There have also been substantial changes over the history of the Soviet period in the time devoted to individual activities. Television has altered the way of life of the typical Soviet citizen. We have also seen that the amount of leisure individuals have is by no means equally distributed. In addition to the significant difference between men and women, leisure is seen to be positively correlated with income, education and place on the occupational ladder. It also differs by marital status and is particularly less available for married persons with children. There is a substantial number of Soviet citizens who engage in free time activities that involve trading work for leisure. This is true for workers who go to school, in some fashion it is true of collective gardeners, and it is absolutely true for those who have chosen to hold a legal second job. This excludes the unknown operatives in the second economy.

In general there is dissatisfaction with what the state offers. It is clear that everybody wants more free time. Yet workers typically do not seem to have a clear idea of what specifically they want to do with their time, except that they want fewer indoor activities. It is possible that people feel constrained by the general shortage of facilities. Less speculative is the fact that the free time of workers has been given a low priority by Soviet planners: in both quantitative and qualitative terms there is a shortfall.

The unwillingness of Soviet planners to allocate more resources for leisure activities may have some negative consequences. The incentive to work is diminished by the absence of leisure goods. The most dramatic change in the leisure area for Soviet citizens in the last 15 years was the shift to the 5 day work week. Workers were rewarded with more time, but they have not been rewarded with more leisure goods to consume in that extra time. For example, there are not enough weekend facilities. Moreover, the new work week is an uneven blessing for women because the new schedule decreased the amount of time they had for their housework and child care without concomitant increases in the service sector to assist them.

In Chapter 6, on the holiday economy, many of the same issues arise, although the character is different because a holiday is not a daily event but a once a year occurrence, and in Chapter 7 the problems within the service sector are analysed.

6 Holidays

All over the industrialised world nothing is more sacred to a worker than his annual holiday – it is the symbol of leisure. Whether we are talking about eastern or western Europe, paid leave from work has almost been deified. One of the major goals of West European industrial workers in the postwar period has been to press for increased length of holidays. Holidays demand a different decision in the work–leisure calculus. We have seen that there are incentives and pressures for Soviet citizens to work, rather than take their holidays. But if a decision is made to give up holiday time, then Soviet workers sacrifice the only long period of leisure time available during the year. While there are workers who do give up their leave in order to earn income, the more dominant feature of the Soviet scene has been the dramatic increase in the number of urbanites who devote their holidays to leisure. This is in spite of the fact that state resources devoted to holiday facilities have been dispensed in a niggardly fashion. The increase in income and education has increased the demand for holidays, but at the present time Soviet citizens must go it on their own rather than depend on the state to provide them with holiday facilities.

Internationally, the Holidays with Pay Convention adopted at the 1970 International Labour Conference, sets a standard of 3 weeks' holiday for 1 year of work. In 1936 the recommended length was 1 week and in 1954, 2 weeks. The 1963 European Social Charter recommended a 2 week minimum paid holiday.[1]

The minimum paid leave that predominated in individual countries of the Organisation for Economic Co-operation and Development (OECD) as of 1973 can be seen in Table 6.1.

In the Soviet Union the legal minimum since 1968 has been 15 days, which is where it presently stands. However, the actual number of leave days exceeds the legal minimum in both the USSR and the OECD countries. In 1958 and 1964, when the legal minimum was 12 days, the average number of paid leave days in the Soviet Union was 18.5 days and 19.3 days respectively. In 1968 and 1977, the actual holiday length

TABLE 6.1 *Minimum length of holidays, OECD countries, 1973*

Holiday length	Countries
Four weeks	France (collective agreements), Norway, Sweden
Three weeks	Belgium, Denmark, Finland, France (legislation), Luxembourg, Switzerland (small cantons), United Kingdom (most collective agreements)
Fifteen days	West Germany, Netherlands (collective agreements)
Two weeks	Austria, Canada, Iceland, Italy (collective agreements), Netherlands (legislation), Spain, Switzerland (federal), the United States

SOURCE Archibald A. Evans, *Flexibility in Working Life* (Organisation for Economic Co-operation and Development: Paris, 1973) pp. 67–8.

was 20.9 days and 21.6 days respectively.[2] In the OECD countries collective bargaining agreements often contain provisions which lengthen holidays above the statutory minimum because of length of service, age or type of industry. The reasons for variations in the Soviet case are much the same and are discussed in detail here. In general, about half the OECD countries have vacations which are longer than the USSR, while the other half offer holidays which are roughly the same length.

Table 6.2 gives a more detailed picture of the length of leave for various branches of the Soviet economy. The data are from 1964, the most recent year for which detailed information is available. These leave days are paid at the worker's average daily pay. The data suggest several things about Soviet policy. First, the legal minimum is seldom the same as the actual length of a worker's holiday. In 1964, when the legal minimum was 12 days, the overall average for the economy was 19.3 days. Holiday time must be used every year; a worker cannot accumulate holiday time over several years unless there is a prior agreement with the management. Even with such an agreement holiday time cannot be accumulated beyond 2 years. If holiday time has been accumulated and a worker leaves her job she will receive monetary compensation in lieu of time off.[3]

Second, the length of holidays is substantially different between different areas of the economy, even if we dismiss the lengthy 33 day leave of teachers. At the low end, state farmer holidays averaged 13.8 days. The longest holidays belong to certain industrial workers, particularly coal miners (25.7 days), forestry workers (25.3 days) and workers in ferrous metallurgy (22.2 days). They are closely followed by

TABLE 6.2 *Average number of paid holiday days, USSR by branch of the economy, 31 March 1964*

	Holiday days
Economy as a whole	19.3
All industry	18.8
coal industry	25.7
ferrous metallurgy	22.2
machine building and metal fabricating industry	18.2
forestry industry	25.3
light industry	15.3
food industry	18.0
Construction	17.1
State farms	13.8
Transport	19.4
Communications	16.7
Trade, public catering, procurement and material–technical supply	16.1
Housing and utilities	16.1
Health	19.0
Education	33.0
Science and scientific services	20.8
Credit and insurance institutions	18.2
Administration	22.1

SOURCE *Strana Sovetov za 50 let* (Moscow, 1967) pp. 224–5.

the party and government administrative apparatus which averaged 22.1 days. Because the *de facto* holiday period was so much longer than the legal minimum, the 1968 change to a 15 day minimum only affected about 40 per cent of the labour force.[4]

THE HISTORY OF SOVIET HOLIDAY POLICY UP TO WORLD WAR II

In June 1918 the fledgling Soviet government issued its first decree on holidays.[5] While the chaos of the civil war years of 1918–20 surely upset the practical application of the terms of the decree, its main points remain the core of Soviet policy in this area. According to the decree, all workers are entitled to an annual paid holiday. The main eligibility requirement is the amount of time the individual has worked at the enterprise.

According to the first decree one had to have worked at least 6 months at the same enterprise to be eligible for leave. The first leave period under the new regime was set at 1 month. Decrees of 1919, 1920 and 1921 reduced holidays to 2 weeks because of the civil war. Due to the food shortages associated with the war, in the summer of 1919 people were forbidden to leave their place of residence for a holiday. Soviet authorities were trying to prevent urbanites from going to villages and either working there in exchange for food or trading non-food items for food. The policy continued through 1920 for most industrial workers. The roots of the decision to prohibit holidays for seasonal and temporary workers can be traced to this period. Seasonal workers were drawn from the peasantry and they had enough time to 'rest' when the peak agricultural periods were over. Temporary workers, who were originally recruited from among the unemployed, were seen as not working long enough to justify a holiday. In 1938 it was decided to ratify the prohibition against paid leave for these two groups.

Early in the period of the New Economic Policy (NEP), a 1922 decree confirmed the principles of the initial 1918 decree. The eligibility period was shortened to five and a half months. The minimum leave period was declared to be 2 weeks, with a small number of workers eligible for 1 month's leave.

Prior to 1930 eligibility was determined on the basis of a calendar year. A decree of 1930 liberalised the rule and eligibility was determined on the basis of when an individual began work. But the minimum length of continuous employment at the same enterprise was increased to eleven months, a requirement which still holds. When the eligibility period was five and a half months, some workers changed jobs frequently enough to get two holidays in one calendar year. The 1930 decree was also the first to differentiate the length of leave by the kind of work and geographic area, e.g. miners and workers in areas with severe climates were given longer holidays. It also introduced some variations of extra leave days for certain categories of workers, e.g. workers in scientific research institutions.

The exigencies of World War II brought a dramatic change in holiday policy. In 1941 holidays were eliminated and workers were awarded extra pay in lieu of leave time. Only in the case of illness was a worker entitled to a holiday. In April 1942, the additional monetary compensation which was paid directly to workers was also eliminated. The money was paid into the workers' savings accounts and could not be touched until after the war. In reality, the Soviet government retained the use of these funds during the war and held down some of the inflationary pressure that was building during this period. In June 1945, the pre-war leave policy was restored and there have only been minor changes since then.

THE POLICY OF DIFFERENTIAL LEAVE PERIODS

The policy of making distinctions between workers and supplementing the leave periods of certain groups began as early as 1938 when longer holidays for workers on the night shift were introduced. They received one extra leave day for every month on the night shift. In 1941, those working under harmful conditions were added to the list. In succeeding years additional categories were added and by 1955 the policy which is presently in place was essentially completed. In 1955 the pre-war policy of a one month minimum for workers aged 16–18 years was also restored.

Longer holidays of 24–48 days go to employees of scientific research institutes and educational institutions.[6] The length of the holiday depends on the type of institution, the person's job, level of education, etc. For example, the directors, deputy directors, heads of laboratories and researchers in scientific museums have a right to a 24 day holiday. All teachers have a right to 48 days' leave, but administrators in education only have the right to 24 days off.

Although the Soviets make a distinction between 'longer holidays' and 'additional holiday days', they resolve into the same thing. There are several reasons why people receive extra leave days: (a) because of harmful conditions, (b) because they work an unnormed day, (c) because of lengthy uninterrupted work at the same enterprise, or (d) because they work in the Far North. The extra leave days are simply tacked on to the normal holiday period. Those who work in harmful conditions include lithographers and offset printers who receive 6 extra days, smiths who get 12 extra days, radiologists, 18 extra days, and those who work with mercury, 36 extra days. Those who do not work a set number of hours per day, such as engineers and hospital doctors, get 12 extra days.

There is an incentive to stay at the same job; those who have been at the same enterprise for 2 years are entitled to 3 extra leave days. For people in the Far North and other remote areas the only ones eligible for extra leave days are those who have signed a contract to work at least 3 years in the area. Those who work a standard week receive 18 extra days and unnormed workers receive 30 days. If less than 11 months is worked in one of the remote areas the right to a paid holiday is lost.

Labour turnover is very high in the Soviet Union; on the average, approximately 20 per cent of the industrial labour force and 30 per cent in construction annually leave their job or are dismissed for disciplinary reasons. Soviet holiday policy is intended to discourage people from leaving their jobs by stipulating the 11 month eligibility requirement and the longevity bonus. It seems unlikely that matters work out so neatly for industrial workers that they are able to stay at a job for 11 months, take the leave to which they are entitled, leave that job, find another and then go through this every 5 years or so. In fact a great many Soviet workers must surrender their holidays because they move around so much. Yet the data show that in spite of constant turnover, the average length of holidays keeps increasing. At a minimum, Soviet leave policy has not deterred high turnover. There are three possible explanations for this apparent contradiction:

1. the value of a holiday is less than the incremental benefits at a new job
2. employers are able to manipulate personnel records and illegally give workers leave time
3. a chronically tight labour market creates the possibility for workers to use leave as a bargaining chip in going to work at a new enterprise.

WHEN DO HOLIDAYS TAKE PLACE?

By law the enterprise management decides when workers get leave.[7] In fact, workers can take their holiday any time during the year. In the Soviet planning system this has serious implications. It is a taut one which physically allocates all inputs needed to produce the targeted output and strains the productive capacity of enterprises. In the context of operational considerations the distribution of leave would have to be planned so that the plant would not experience a labour shortfall. One writer said about 25 years ago that during any given month no more than 8–9 per cent of the enterprise is supposed to be on leave, which would distribute the holiday burden evenly over the year.[8] There is no evidence that such a policy was ever implemented. It would impose enormous psychic costs on all those whose preference for warm weather holidays would be denied. In fact 85 per cent of blue-collar workers, 92 per cent of intellectuals and 100 per cent of white-collar women workers can choose their leave period.[9] Therefore, one reason why Soviet enterprises routinely maintain redundant labour may be to cope with the absence of holidaying workers. A study from the late 1960s showed that about two-thirds of all urbanites have their holiday in the 4 month period between May and August.[10] In a somewhat later study, 63 per cent of urbanites said they preferred their holiday during July and August[11] and in Lithuania, 90.5 per cent expressed a preference for a summer holiday.[12] Therefore, during the peak holiday period there would be a need for extra workers or a reduced monthly production plan.

ORGANISED AND UNORGANISED HOLIDAYS

Within the Soviet Union a distinction is made between organised and unorganised holidaymakers. Organised holidaymakers are those who spend their leave at state and trade union facilities. These are facilities for which passes are required, such as houses of rest, sanatoriums and pensions. Unorganised tourists, colloquially called 'savages' (*dikari*), by definition do everything else such as renting country *dachas*, hiking and going to the traditional resorts on their own.

The distinction between these two groups is not simply academic. Organised tourists are treated much better than those who operate on their own. For example, it is much more difficult to find hotel rooms or camping facilities if you are an unorganised tourist than if you have the official status associated with having a pass from your enterprise or local trade union. If you want to go camping in the Caucasus, it is next to impossible since there are really no places set aside for unorganised tourists in campsites. Some local tourist facility managers have developed services for unorganised tourists, all of which were *outside the plan*.[13]

The problem unorganised tourists have in finding hotel space is so bad that a lot of them take boats and trains at night so they have a place to sleep while travelling. Many will not go anywhere if they do not have friends or relatives to stay with because they cannot count on the availability of hotel rooms.[14] In part (but only in part) the shortage of hotel rooms is illusory. For example, there are a number of hotels in the RSFSR affiliated with a particular ministry. But they are not permitted to rent rooms to unorganised tourists, even though the hotels are almost empty at weekends.[15]

Unorganised tourists are further discouraged by having to pay an additional amount for the right to holiday in the Crimea and the Caucasus: in the Caucasus they must pay 6 roubles and 40 kopeks for a temporary residence permit (*propiska*) as well as a resort tax (*kurortnyi sbor*) of two roubles.[16]

The number of unorganised holidaymakers is much greater than those who are organised. One estimate is that in 1975, only 8 per cent of the population had 'organised' holidays.[17] This is confirmed by data which indicated that suburban *dachas* constitute 80 per cent of the holiday facilities for Leningraders, while unorganised facilities are about 90 per cent of the total holiday facilities used by Muscovites.[18] Moreover, the proportion of holidaymakers which is unorganised has continually increased. Before World War II it is estimated they were 17–18 per cent of the total, in 1960, 62 per cent and 1968, 75 per cent. The majority of them go to the Black Sea coast during the four summer months.[19] In July and August in the holiday cities of the northern Caucasus unorganised holidaymakers outnumber organised ones: by 11:1 in Anapa, 5:1 in Adler and even by 3:1 in the city of Essentuki, purely a medical resort requiring passes for admission to the facilities.[20]

There are two reasons for the increase in the number of unorganised holidaymakers. It has been largely propelled by increasing levels of personal discretionary income and particularly by personal savings. This has created what has been termed a 'recreation explosion'.[21] As a consequence one author conjectured that there is a new stereotype which says that people should go away for their holiday and not stay at home.[22] The second reason for the increase of unorganised holidaymakers is that there has been a more rapid increase in household income than in the construction of state facilities. There is little doubt that the demand for organised facilities is strong. In a 1970 study 80 per cent said they wanted to spend their holiday in an organised facility.[23] More recent data show that 60–75 per cent of the adult population want organised holiday facilities.[24]

In spite of the fact that the average length of the holiday period has increased and incomes have increased, an extremely high percentage of Soviet citizens spend their leave at home. According to a 1975 study, about half the adult population spent their holidays this way.[25] A 1969 publication estimated that about 40 per cent of all holidaymaking urbanites did not leave the city where they live the year round.[26]

There are a number of reasons why people do not go away on holiday. The primary reason is the shortage of facilities which exists in both the organised and unorganised sector. A basic implication of any shortage is that inflationary pressures are created. Prices have risen in the unregulated private holiday economy as owners of property hold control in a sellers' market. The power of landlords has increased as the distance between supply and demand has widened. Another reason is that the quality of holiday facilities is often quite poor, partly as a result of the overcrowding of existing facilities and partly because of the low priority of quality in the service sector of the Soviet economy.

In addition, holiday facilities are not orientated towards families. For example, it was not until 1972 that passes were given to married couples if they worked at the same enterprise.[27] This meant that the husband and wife often did not have a pass to the same place, i.e. they had to have separate holidays. If the family wants to have a holiday together, ordinarily they must do so on an unorganised basis or stay at home. Otherwise people must have a holiday without their spouse or children. In fact the majority of unorganised tourists are in the age group 30–39 years old and they are mostly married with children.[28] At least into the late 1960s organised tours which required passes excluded children under the age of 16 years. The rationale for this is that younger children are not considered physically capable of bearing up under the pressure of having to travel to different places and to move from hotel to hotel. In addition, puritanical authorities did not want teenagers exposed to negative adult values, like card playing, on holiday.[29]

Soviet urbanites place a high value on having their children leave the city during the summer. The network of Pioneer Camps (much like Boy Scout camps) meets this goal for part of the summer. About 70 per cent of the children in Leningrad and Moscow can go to the country for 26 days and about 40 per cent can go for 45 days.[30] But the summer holiday of school children is 3 months long. Therefore parents rent suburban *dachas* to be used as holiday facilities during the rest of the summer. Either a grandparent or a non-working parent stays with the child during the week.

Related to the question of whether people go away for holidays is that of with whom they go. Two major patterns emerge from Soviet studies on who people spend their holidays with: the first is the dominance of the family on holiday and the second is the fact that so many people holiday alone. In a study from about 1970, 23.1 per cent said they spent their holidays alone.[31]

The tendency to spend holidays with families is particularly true of married people. Single men are most likely to have a holiday with friends or by themselves. Overall, 10 per cent of the population holidayed alone. Men are twice as likely as women to go off on a holiday by themselves. But women are much likelier to spend their holiday with friends. Married people with children are more likely to have holidays alone than those without children. This does not reflect the desire of Soviet parents to get away from their children on holiday. Rather it reflects the presence of three barriers preventing families from having a holiday together. One barrier is the lack of facilities on the Black Sea to accommodate families. Another is the apparent bias in favour of issuing individual as opposed to family holiday vouchers. For example, in 1979, 180 family vouchers and 3700 individual vouchers were issued for Black Sea holiday facilities for workers in the Kuznetsk Basin. Finally, only 16 of the country's 260 tours on water, horse and foot trails are designed to accommodate families. These are geared to adults.[32]

HOLIDAY OPTIONS

What are the alternatives available to Soviet citizens? Where can they go on holiday? What kinds of facilities has the State built? What are the options in the private sector?

Holidays are largely spent in the Soviet Union itself. While the number of Soviet citizens travelling abroad has increased quite dramatically in the post-Stalin period, travel is overwhelmingly confined to eastern Europe and other socialist bloc countries. According to the data in Table 6.3, there was about a fourfold increase in the number of Soviet citizens going abroad, increasing from about half a million in 1956 to more than two million in 1974. (It is not clear whether this includes those doing business in foreign countries or only those who are simply holidaymakers.) The proportion travelling to socialist countries has fluctuated wildly. In 1956, 80 per cent stayed within the bloc. This dropped to 54 per cent in 1967 and climbed again to 68 per cent in 1970. In 1970 the five most frequently visited countries were Poland (269 000), Bulgaria (151 000), East Germany (135 000), Czechoslovakia (93 000) and Mongolia (89 000).[33] Since more than 100 million people spent their

TABLE 6.3 *Foreign travel by Soviet citizens*

	1956	1960	1965	1967	1970	1974
Number of Soviet citizens travelling abroad (thousands)	560	730	1150	1550	1850	2200
Percentage travelling to socialist countries	80	68	55	54	68	60

SOURCES 1956–70 Azar, p. 41; 1974 *Literaturnaia Gazeta*, 25 June 1975, p. 14.

leave away from home in 1970, less than 2 per cent of Soviet holidaymakers went abroad. If the figure for foreign travellers include persons doing business abroad, then the percentage who take holidays outside the Soviet Union is even lower. An estimated 16 per cent of the French annually take holidays abroad.[34]

The two main state institutions used by holidaymakers are the so-called houses of rest (*doma otdykha*) and the sanatoriums. A house of rest is an institution where workers, employees and others can spend their non-working time. There are many forms of such houses, some where people can spend a few hours each day, or a weekend, or most commonly an annual holiday. Such a house is not formally part of the health system, although there may be some medical supervision.

The first house of rest was opened in Petrograd in 1920 and its purpose then was somewhat different in scope than it is at present. While the house of rest was designed to provide a place for workers on leave, it also served as a place where a doctor could send a worker who was considered overtired. In the beginning, both the houses of rest and the daily regimen of the houses were under medical supervision. However, since May 1921 the houses of rest have been under the supervision of the trade unions.[35] Indeed, only trade union members can receive a pass to a house of rest.

A sanatorium, on the other hand, is formally a health institution, run under medical auspices, where rest is combined with some form of treatment. However, in many instances, a sanatorium is simply a holiday hotel that passes for a medical institution. People are sent there for a rest and a holiday, but on the strength of a medical certificate.[36] In fact, Soviet sources count its bed capacity as part of the country's holiday facilities.[37]

A pass is required in order to gain access to either a house of rest or a sanatorium. Passes are obtained at the individual's enterprise. As will be seen below, passes either have to be paid for by the worker or they can be subsidised by the state's social insurance programme. Moreover, there are a number of different categories of passes corresponding to different lengths of holiday and the level of comfort provided.

The house of rest provides a room, meals and entertainment in a highly structured environment. A pass is required to enter the house, for a maximum period of 12 days, although sometimes people buy two passes and stay for 24 days. The houses of rest are divided into three categories: ordinary, higher and highest. The differences in the quantity and quality of the three gradations shows up in substantial differences in prices, although all of them are extremely inexpensive relative to other forms of holiday. The total cost of a 12 day stay at a house of rest is 30 roubles for the ordinary category, 40 roubles for the higher category, and 60 roubles for the highest. Thus the daily rouble cost ranges between 2.5 and 5 roubles.[38]

Life is so regimented at the houses of rest that, at least at the end of 1968, there was an 11 pm curfew! There were complaints about people being asked by the house management where they had been and what they had been doing if they were late. Moreover, there were two punitive measures that the management could take: send a letter to the violator's family and their place of work, and oblige a person to leave the house of rest and write to the individual's enterprise about their misdeed. People have been known to climb through windows when they returned at night either because they wanted to escape unwanted questioning or because the management of the house locked the front door at 11 pm.[39]

There is another institution, the pension, which is similar to a house of rest, although apparently there is a good deal more freedom. Pensions provide a room and board, but beyond that holidaymakers are on their own. People can stay for periods of 12, 18 or 24 days. The daily cost at a pension is 6.67 roubles, which is higher than the top rated house of rest.[40]

Sanatoriums are supposed to be for individuals who require some kind of medical treatment. Nevertheless the Russian term, *sanatorno-kurortnoe lechenie*, literally a sanatorium resort facility, implies a usage that is beyond medical care. The sanatoriums are usually located at major Soviet resorts where there are mineral waters, facilities for mud treatments or special climatic conditions. For example, in Sochi, one of the premier resort areas on the Black Sea, there were about 230 sanatoriums and houses of rest at the end of 1972.[41] People can stay for much longer periods of time in the sanatoriums. Passes are for 20, 24, 26, 45, 48 and 56 days.[42]

A sanatorium physician estimated that the proportion of patients actually requiring medical treatment in his sanatorium during the summer was about half of what it was during the winter. The reason is that healthy people bribe someone to diagnose them as suffering from 'exhaustion' or 'nerves' so they can get a highly coveted place in a health resort. It is routinely accepted that this sort of holiday will take place.[43] Moreover, passes to these resorts constitute a real plum within the well-known Soviet system of bribery and corruption. There is evidence that province and city trade union committees sell sanatorium and rest home passes to province committees and never distribute them to local trade union committees. At the local levels passes have been issued to trade union chairmen instead of workers, or they are sold to people not in that particular trade union.[44]

Eighty per cent of the people who spend their holiday in a house of rest or sanatorium receive their pass free or have it partially paid for by the Soviet social insurance system. Social insurance pays completely for 20 per cent of all passes to sanatoriums and for 10 per cent of the passes to houses of rest and tourist camps. For the rest, social insurance picks up 30 per cent of the cost. Workers and employees who live far from sanatoriums and houses of rest can receive monetary compensation instead of going to one of these facilities to the extent of 70–100 per cent of the price of the pass, not to exceed 100 roubles for a sanatorium pass and 30 roubles for a pass to a house of rest.[45] In 1969 there were 3 839 000 passes to houses of rest and 2 830 000 were paid for by the social insurance system. The great growth in the system has been in the provision of passes to sanatoriums. In 1950, 1 362 000 passes paid for by social insurance were issued to the houses of rest but only 543 000 to the sanatoriums. Thus during this 20 year period the number of passes to houses of rest tripled, but there was more than a fivefold increase in the passes to sanatoriums paid for by social insurance.[46]

The price of a pass at a sanatorium varies depending on the length of stay and the quality of the facility, e.g. the number of people per room, furnishings, modern conveniences. As Table 6.4 shows there are 3 categories of sanatoriums with the most expensive costing about twice as much as the ordinary group. At the level of the ordinary group, the daily expense at a sanatorium is about 75 per cent greater than at the ordinary house of rest while the highest group sanatorium is 68 per cent more expensive.

TABLE 6.4 *Prices at sanatoriums, 1970, by type (in roubles)*

	Price of a pass	Daily cost
Ordinary group	90–115	4.17–4.50
Higher group	140–170	6.54–7.00
Highest group	200–220	8.33–8.46

SOURCE Azar, p. 30.

TOURISM

While the houses of rest and the sanatoriums are the most important state institutions used by holidaymakers, the most popular form of holiday is tourism. Tourism in the Soviet Union includes two groups: tourists and excursionists. The basic difference between the two groups is that excursions are always run by the state and involve a guide. Tourists include either people who are travelling on their own or are on state-sponsored trips, which may or may not involve a guide. We will refer to both groups as tourists.

The number of people who take holidays as tourists has mushroomed. In 1969 there were about 35.7 million tourists and in 1973 an estimated 107 million. About 80 per cent of the tourists are excursionists, meaning there is a guide present.[47] About half of all those taking a holiday away from home did so as tourists.[48] The increase in tourism can be attributed to an increase in income, an increase in the amount of free time and a transportation system which has made travel easier.[49] The introduction of the 5 day work week has given people weekends to travel, something they did not have when Sunday was the only day off. In addition, the failure routinely to provide passes to state facilities for families creates an incentive for tourism.

DACHAS

The summer house or *dacha* is an important holiday facility for Soviet urbanites. (There are also *sadovye domiki*, or garden houses, which are actually *dachas*.) A mid-1970s estimate was that 25 per cent of Leningraders and Muscovites rent *dachas* in the summer. *Dachas* in the suburbs of Leningrad and Moscow constitute about 80 per cent of all the available rest facilities. Leningraders who rent spend 25–30 million roubles a year in the private sector.[50] There is a preference for *dachas* because it allows people to stay together as a family, particularly when there are small children and old people.[51] The *dachas* are usually extremely modest in size and furnishing. Urbanites take beds, cooking facilities, etc., out to the country and haul them back to their city apartment at the end of the summer.

Individual enterprises own and operate more than 5000 recreational facilities.[52] They are maintained as if they were private facilities and access to their less crowded beaches or recreational activities is controlled by caretakers working for the enterprises.[53] The Minsk Motor Vehicle Plant, for example, had one holiday facility and in 1976 was building two others on the Black Sea. A 12 day stay costs only 30 roubles for husband, wife and one child.[54]

THE DETERMINANTS OF WHAT PEOPLE DO ON THEIR HOLIDAY

The first determinant of what people can do on their holidays is income. Soviet data show that a monthly household per capita income of 100 roubles or less allows a family to make one trip every other year while a per capita income of 120 roubles or more allows the family to take a trip every year.[55]

Two other determinants are marital status and sex. Unmarried people are much more likely to spend their holiday at a resort. In one study, 53.9 per cent of single people spent their holiday in the houses of rest, on tourist hikes and at resorts. Married people spent their holidays differently: 41 per cent at home, 30.8 per cent at a relative's home, and only 27.8 per cent at resorts.[56] During the summer, women have priority for passes to sanatoriums and rest homes in the Crimea. In 1969 they received 60 per cent of the passes.[57]

The 1966 Kazan study pointed out some notable differences between the sexes (see Table 6.5). A somewhat higher percentage of men stayed at

TABLE 6.5 *How Kazan residents spent their last holiday, by sex and marital status, 1966, in percentages*

	Sex		Marital status		
	Men	Women	Single	Married without children	Married with children
At home in the city of Kazan	30	25	6	33	36
Going to other cities	10	25	32	11	19
Going to the villages	24	11	15	11	13
In sanatoriums or houses of rest	16	7	12	10	6
In the country on the Volga	14	5	9	2	10
At the seashore	1	10	9	2	10
In other countries	0	3	7	0	0
Studying	4	2	0	9	3
Other	0	5	6	0	3
Worked for pay	0	3	3	9	0
No answer	1	4	1	13	0

SOURCE G. T. Zhuravlev, 'Svobodnoe Vremia i Kul'turnaia Zhizn' Rabotnikov Promyshlennogo Predpriiatiia', in G. V. Osipov and Ia. Shchepan'skii (eds), *Sotsial'nye Problemy Truda i Proizvodstva* (Moscow, 1969) p. 388.

home. But there was a large difference in a number of activities suggesting that husbands and wives did entirely different things on holiday. For example, while 25 per cent of the women went to other cities, only 10 per cent of the men did. The percentages were almost exactly reversed for travel to other villages. In addition, a much higher percentage of men than women went to the country. On the other hand, many more women went to the seashore. These differences are consistent with the generalisation that men use their leave to do things that are associated with their hobbies, e.g. hunting, fishing and sports, while women 'prefer more comfortable conditions'.[58] But the data also suggest a surprising degree of freedom for women in what is a predominantly Muslim city unless the sample contains an unrepresentative group of non-Muslim residents of Kazan. It also suggests the secularisation of the traditional Muslim society. Finally, there is evidence that the higher the level of educational attainment, the more likely it is that the person will go away on holiday. In Kazan about 44 per cent of the blue-collar workers spent their holiday at home, compared with about 25 per cent of those who do intellectual work.[59]

Finally, there is a difference between the type of holiday taken by those who do intellectual work and those doing manual labour. Intellectual workers are more likely to travel and engage in tourism, while those who do manual labour are more likely to go to a holiday spot and stay there.[60]

WHAT SOVIET HOLIDAYMAKERS WOULD PREFER

There is a difference between what Soviet citizens do on their holidays and what they would like to do or where they would prefer to go. The major finding of most studies is that Soviet citizens want to spend their holidays in some kind of organised facility. For example, a 1970 study showed that about 80 per cent of those surveyed expressed a preference for an organised facility such as a sanatorium (21 per cent), house of rest (19 per cent), pension for families (27 per cent) or tourist camp (11 per cent). Only 2 per cent said they preferred to rent a private facility.[61] Given the earlier data which showed that at best 25 per cent use organised facilities, it is clear that the demand for such facilities far exceeds supply.

THE CHRONIC SHORTAGE OF FACILITIES

We have suggested that the availability of time and money have created an increased demand for the use of holiday facilities. But there has been a general failure to increase the supply of state facilities at anything approaching a similar pace. One manifestation of the shortage is the overcrowding of facilities. The most notable example is the overcrowded beaches on the Black Sea. This has been a problem for at least the last 25 years. One author described the Black Sea beaches as a 'crowded closet'.[62] Based on the amount of bread produced in the area, it is estimated that one million people visited Yalta in 1965.[63] Jokes about the crowding of Black Sea facilities have become so banal that satirical magazines have virtually stopped printing them.[64] Unfortunately there is a serious side to the problem, as the overcrowding is the chief cause of infectious disease.[65] The overcrowding was compounded by the sanatorium building programme at the Black Sea. As these facilities were built, the amount of beach area available to the general public declined and the public beaches tend to be about 100 times more crowded than the sanatorium facilities.[66] In the mid-1960s people began to drift to the western Crimea where the beaches were less crowded, but there was an extreme shortage of cafeterias and grocery stores so that holidays turned into a constant search for food.[67] Only 9 per cent of holiday facilities are in the Crimea and 13 per cent on the Black Sea coast of the Caucasus, but according to a 1975 study, the two top choices of all organised tourists are the Crimea (21 per cent), followed by the 16 per cent who want to go to the Caucasus.[68]

The major complaint of tourists is that there are not enough hotels and motels in the country. This is true regardless of city size. For example, people dare not go into Moscow unless they have someone they can stay with because they cannot count on the availability of a hotel room. The same is true of a small, historically important town like Uglich which only 10 years ago had only 50 beds to let.[69]

The Soviets themselves recognise the problem and regard their standard of 3 to 5 hotel spaces for every 1000 urban residents as too low. One piece of evidence is the fact that in Moscow there were 6.2 hotel spaces per 1000 Moscovites, and it is often impossible to find a room.[70] My own estimate is that the Soviet hotel construction programme has not even met this norm. The RSFSR urban population in 1969 was roughly 83 500 000. Based on their own lower norm of 3 to 5 spaces per 1000 population, there should have been between 250 505 and 417 500 hotel spaces. In fact, there were only 206 000 beds in RSFSR hotels meaning a shortage of at least 44 000–213 000 beds in the Republic.[71] The motel situation is even worse, there being a miniscule number in the country.[72]

The reason for the constant lag in the supply of hotels is that construction is always behind schedule and the number of hotels scheduled to open is perpetually behind the planned level of construction. For the period 1961–8, the construction plan for new hotels was only 66 per cent fulfilled.[73] In 1972 the plan fulfilment was 70 per cent.[74] Moreover, the average time it takes to build a health resort is 5 years instead of the 2 years established by Soviet construction norms.[75]

The shortage of facilities has led to a thriving 'second economy' in the provision of tourist accommodation. This is particularly true of the rental of *dachas*. Sometimes *dacha* owners subdivide to squeeze in several families.[76] Owners of private homes in resort cities may place several cots in a single room and rent them.[77]

There is a state mechanism for the renting of private facilities, but the second economy also operates here. There are rental bureaus (*kvartirnoposrednicheskoe biuro*) which provide information on the availability of facilities to holidaymakers. When people list their rooms with the bureau they pay a tax on their income, the facility is supposed to meet state health standards, and the rental charge is regulated.[78] One square metre is supposed to cost one rouble and 32 kopeks, but in fact rents are determined by the strength of demand and neither the landlord nor the renter publicise the real price that is paid.[79] In the Black Sea city of Evpatoria in 1967 there were 480 000 unorganised holidaymakers, of which 81 100 or 17 per cent used the rental bureaux.[80] In the private sector, renting rooms is big business. In 1966 the 2 million people who went to the Crimea paid landlords an estimated 50 million roubles.[81] Some people take the problem into their own hands. In several places urbanites who have been given land for the purpose of cultivating a collective garden have instead built their own *dachas* on it. In Tbilisi most of the collective gardeners have built *dachas* and in the city of Tskhvarichamia two-thirds of the 1500 members have done so.[82] In several Black Sea resort cities people have illegally built houses for rental purposes with money they have previously earned in the second economy.[83]

THE QUALITY OF SERVICES

Soviet holidaymakers not only face a shortage of basic facilities, they must also endure a lack of, and often poor quality, services. The service most frequently criticised is public catering (cafés, restaurants and bars). About 80 per cent of all unorganised holidaymakers use public catering facilities because they do not want to cook while on holiday.[84] One complaint that has not changed in the last 25 years is that the food is monotonous.[85] Nor are foreign tourists the only ones who complain about the legendary long waits for food in Soviet restaurants; Soviet citizens register the same complaint.[86] There are also complaints that the restaurants are expensive and the entertainment is limited and boring. More than 80 per cent of Soviet holidaymakers said that they disliked the atmosphere in restaurants.[87]

In the early 1970s the number of public catering establishments in the Crimea was only adequate to meet the needs of 36 per cent of the holidaymakers who were travelling on their own. It is not surprising that in a Crimean survey 44 per cent of the holidaymakers said that long queues were the main drawback in public catering establishments. Depending on the particular spot in the Crimea, the demand for places in restaurants outruns supply by 4 to 10 times.[88] Moreover, people are unhappy with the mix of public catering establishments available. As Table 6.6 shows, holidaymakers want to see relatively fewer restaurants and many more cafés. The preference for cafés is due to the lower cost of meals.

Various other complaints deal with the shortage or absence of guides at appropriate places of interest,[89] state-built holiday facilities which are without basic conveniences,[90] and dirty facilities.[91] Finally, we close this section with a cynical 1976 tale of woe. A tourist went to a sanatorium where his presence was a surprise in spite of the fact that he had a pass. So he had to have his meals either an hour before or an hour after everyone else ate. While the sanatorium had its own beach there were an insufficient number of chaises-longues and as a newcomer he had difficulty getting one. Having come for rest and medical treatment,

TABLE 6.6 *Distribution of public catering facilities in resort areas, by type of facility, in percentages*

	Actual usage	Desired usage
Cafés	26	45
Restaurants	69	31
Bars	5	14

SOURCE *Literaturnaia Gazeta*, 15 September 1971, p. 12. (The numbers add up to 90 per cent for 'desired usage' in the original article.)

he had the misfortune of being in a sanatorium that was near a restaurant with a bar that was noisy every night.[92]

These experiences translate into widespread dissatisfaction with holiday facilities. In a recent study by the Laboratory of Tourism and Excursions, 45 per cent of organised tourists said they 'would not want to repeat their experience'.[93] In Abkhasia 49 per cent of the organised tourists were unsatisfied with the way they spent their holiday.[94]

CENTRAL PLANNING AS A PANACEA

It should come as no surprise that in a country whose economic system has been wedded to central planning for more than half a century that solutions to the problems in the holiday economy should be sought in greater centralisation. The problem, as it is generally conceived within the Soviet Union, is the absence of co-ordination that a central organisation could rectify.

The degree of centralisation argued for ranges from a single organisation of tourism within each republic, to a single organisation for the whole country.[95] One reason for the call for centralisation is that state responsibility for building facilities is split among many organisations. For example, about half the sanatoriums are run by the trade unions and the rest by a variety of ministries and departments. One alleged negative consequence is the duplication of facilities and the failure to capture certain economies in maintenance.[96] The diseconomies of scale show up mainly in the form of many small hotels, pensions, rest homes and sanatoriums in the same resort city.[97]

It is certainly possible that a better co-ordination in management would resolve some of the difficulties, but this avoids the central issue, which is the low priority of the holiday economy. Furthermore, part of the problem is the overly centralised management of tourism. If local authorities want to open a tourist facility they may have to go all the way to Moscow for permission. Moreover, since the profits from tourism go to superior organisations, the local soviets often have little interest in tourists.[98]

The relative unimportance of the holiday economy is reflected in the inadequate amounts of investment funds that have been provided for construction of holiday facilities. Resort construction on Lake Baikal exemplifies the problem. A document with the lengthy title, 'The Maximum Permissible Amounts of Per-Unit Capital Investments in Trade Union Health Resorts That Will Ensure Their Economic

Effectiveness' prescribed the amounts that could be spent per place in resort areas in various parts of the country. The document said that 5500–5900 roubles in construction costs could be expended per place in sanatoriums on the Caucasus, 5800–6200 roubles in the Crimea, but only 4400 in the area of Lake Baikal. In the latter case there was also the need to invest in the local infrastructure such as roads and electric power. It was not until the end of 1974 that this directive was rescinded and per-unit construction costs of Siberian health resorts and sanatoriums were raised to 10 000–12 000 roubles.[99]

CONCLUSION

Soviet urbanites have exhibited a strong demand for holidays, particularly in recent years. At a minimum it appears that whatever additional income is to be earned in the Soviet economy (legal or underground), it is not sufficiently attractive to lure many people away from their holidays. The opportunity cost of additional work effort is too high. Less certain is a conclusion about price and income effects of the increasing demand for holiday facilities. Due to the shortage of state facilities, prices have risen in the private sector, yet the demand for these facilities has remained high. If we assume the normal inverse relationship between price and quantity demanded, this implies that the demand for holidays has increased due to a combination of rising incomes and an increased taste for holidays. For an increasing number of Soviet urbanites, there appears to be little ambiguity about the desirability of taking their annual holiday.

Moreover, their holidays have been getting longer. There is a way in which this violates the preferences of planners. The actual length of holidays is about one week longer than the legal minimum; if the amount of holiday time above the statutory minimum was half of that, or 3.5 days, that would be the equivalent of adding about 1 million full-time workers to the labour force. Yet there are pressures for holidays to increase in length because enterprises which need workers cannot attract them if they enforce the law and impose the length of service stipulation. Indeed, they are likely to have to maintain if not increase the leave of workers as an attraction. The irony is that for economic planners, on the one hand longer holidays are a sign that the society is providing more leisure and therefore fulfilling its promise of the good life, but on the other hand, the labour shortage is aggravated even more by workers being away from their work place for longer periods of time.

7 Women and the Service Sector

In the chapters on the time budgets of Soviet households and the more detailed discussion of leisure, the data repeatedly showed that for women, time may be the scarcest commodity. The existence of the double burden (*dvoinaia nagruzka*) in the Soviet context has a curious configuration. Women are considered the equals of men in terms of their participation in the labour force and in many ways this reflects an enlightened view of the rights and capacities of both sexes to be fulfilled as workers. It is the realisation of the revolutionary goal that women should be equal participants in 'social production'. But we have demonstrated that women have dual employment in the labour force and at home. It might also be added that there are ways in which life has become more complex for Soviet women than it was 50 years ago. We have seen that women are primarily responsible for supervising children's homework and going to parent–teacher conferences.[1] In an educationally acquisitive society this is not a task taken lightly. In addition, the typical Soviet family has an increasing amount of leisure time and in 80 per cent of the families the woman takes chief responsibility for organising the family's free time.[2] The extraordinary number of hours women work, playing two roles, is not simply determined by traditional roles assigned through the centuries by biology and acculturation. It is also a result of the dual failure of Soviet policy to produce enough consumer durables to ease housework and to provide public responsibility for what have traditionally been private responsibilities. It will be shown that the supply of public services and appliances is inadequate both in quantity and quality. Soviet policy makers expect women to help produce in industry but do little to help them produce home work.

We will first explore some of the issues surrounding the phenomenon of women's dual roles and long hours. This discussion will involve an analysis of public services and the production of household appliances.

The underlying hypothesis is that women's choices between work and leisure are restricted. The discussion has two premises: the Soviet wage structure in essence obliges both men and women to work; and women consider their family role and professional role to be equally important.[3] Taking these factors as given, we show that the low priority given by planners to services and consumer goods limits rather than enhances the choices in women's lives.

The connection we have suggested between women's roles and the production of public services and consumer goods is important. When women were asked if it was difficult to combine housework and a job, 25 per cent said it is 'very hard' and 31 per cent said it is 'hard'. These women found housework and shopping the most tiring of their general household responsibilities. About 70 per cent said they wanted to see an increase in the number of appliances and semi-prepared foods, another 30 per cent wanted an increase in the number of laundries and other public services, 25 per cent wanted a redistribution of housework within their family and half wanted the best of all possible worlds – a shorter work day with the same pay.[4]

THE PROBLEM OF SHIFT WORK

The issue of tiredness at the end of a work day is a serious one among women workers. Depending on the shift, the proportion of women workers who said they feel extremely tired at the end of the day ranged from 37 to 59 per cent. There are three shifts in the Soviet Union: the morning (first) shift from 7 am to 4 pm, the evening (second) shift from 4 pm to 11 pm, and the night (third) shift from 11 pm to 7 am. Those women working the night shift complain of tiredness considerably more than women working the other two shifts. Marriage and children compound the problem. While 31 per cent of married women complain of being 'greatly tired' at the end of the work day, 49 per cent of married women with children feel this way. There is also a direct correlation between the degree of tiredness and the number of children. While 45 per cent of the childless women feel greatly tired at the end of the day, 48 per cent with one child, 56 per cent with two children, 60 per cent with three children and 70 per cent with four or more children express this complaint.[5]

The issue of the particular shift that is worked matters much more to women than it does to men.[6] This is reflected in a study where 82 per cent of the men, but only 59 per cent of the women, expressed satisfaction with their shift schedule. The highest level of satisfaction among women (83 per cent) is with the first shift and a 5 day work week, and the lowest level is with the third shift (13 per cent) with a 6 day work week.[7] The first shift is the most advantageous for women. When they work the morning shift not only do they have more free time, they also get more sleep.[8] In Vilnius, women who work the day shift sleep about 7 hours a night, 2–3 hours more than a woman who works the night shift.[9]

There is an increasing awareness of the problem of the night shift for women. Several alternative models of work schedules are being tried in the situation where there is a three-shift enterprise. One is the so-called Ivanovo schedule which reduces the number of night shifts that must be worked every month to two. However, while workers also still receive two consecutive days off, under this schedule they are not the same days off every week. Alternatively, in certain assembly line industries which do not employ a large proportion of women, men are replacing women at night. Finally, in industries where there is both a three-shift system and a high concentration of women workers, such as the textile industry, the number of shifts is being reduced. Most of these enterprises have gone over to the Ivanovo schedule. Other enterprises are compensating women for the inconvenience of night work with additional money and days off.[10]

HOUSEWORK

We have already looked at the division of household tasks by sex in detail in Chapter 1 and will not go through the litany of differences again. What was demonstrated was a persisting burden of housework and child care falling on women. For example, a Leningrad study showed that in 81.5 per cent of the households the woman worker does the housework herself.[11] In another study 70–75 per cent of the shopping, one of the most time consuming of all household responsibilities, is done by women alone.[12] Only a quarter of all women in another study reported that they received a great deal of help from other family members; 68 per cent said they received 'not much' or 'hardly any' help.[13] There are some slight generational differences. In a study of two groups of married women – one 25 years old and younger and the other at least 50 years old – the younger women were more likely to receive help from their husbands. For example, among the 25 year old group, 22 per cent of their husbands do not help at all and in 23 per cent of the cases the husband and wife share the housework equally. Among the older women 29 per cent of the husbands do not help at all and only 3 per cent share housework on an equal basis with their wives.[14] It is not as if women believe they alone should bear these responsibilities; 85 per cent think that their husband should share equally in the housework.[15]

There are several negative implications of the Soviet version of the double burden. There is no doubt that a great deal of tension exists in Soviet families because of the 'contradiction between the professional and family roles of a woman'.[16] While it is always difficult to pinpoint the causes of divorce in any society, it is reasonable to speculate that this tension has contributed to the Soviet Union having the second highest divorce rate in the world.[17]

A second implication is that in the broadest sense the professional life of women is adversely affected. Women in all occupational groups have to deal with the lack of time to go to school or take further vocational training. In a Krasnoiarsk study, while 15.2 per cent of the men went to night school, only 8.6 per cent of the women attended.[18] A recent article about the machine-building industry points to the fact that 67 per cent of the women in the industry are low-skilled and only 5 per cent are highly skilled. The continuing concentration of women in low level positions is partially attributed to the fact that they do not adapt to the technological changes in the industry. The principal reason for this is the absence of time to take courses, resulting from their household obligations. Some blame is also placed on the industry itself which does not provide well organised, daytime training courses.[19] A woman specialist is considered to be at her productive peak at the age of 35–40, yet her advancement is slowed because housework takes up 42 per cent of her non-working time.[20] In Lithuanian sewing enterprises 40.5 per cent of the women said they do not work at upgrading their skills because of housework and child rearing.[21] The impact of children on women going to school is clear: 28 per cent without children go to school, but when there is one child only 13 per cent take courses. This falls to 9 per cent with two children, 7 per cent with three and 0.6 per cent with four or more children. In the evening and extramural programmes of the VUZy married men comprise 35–50 per cent of the students and married women 2–8 per cent. Only a few of the latter group have children.[22]

The double burden may also be responsible for the fact that the morbidity rate for women is twice that of men. In one study 46.2 per cent of the men took sick leave at some point during the year, while 55.7 per cent of the women did so. In the age group 30–39 years, 55.5 per cent of the women took 4 or more sick leaves a year. This is the period in the lives of most Soviet women when the family burden is most onerous.[23] In 1965, for every 100 men there were 61.8 cases of temporary illness; for every 100 women, there were 106.1 cases of temporary incapacity for work, but the average sick leave of women is shorter than that of men.[24]

When there is job dissatisfaction among women it can be traced mainly to the long distance of their job from home in 29.3 per cent of the cases, and inconvenient shifts 25.4 per cent of the time. For only 15.1 per cent of the women is inadequate pay the issue.[25] For women, housework begins the minute they leave work, for example, shopping for groceries or going to a repair shop, and does not end until late in the evening.[26] Thus, complaints about certain conditions of employment which create added pressures are understandable.

The 5 day week is overwhelmingly favoured by all workers. But it is not an unblemished blessing for women. When the work week fell from 6 days to 5, the work day increased from 7 to 8 hours. This leaves women 1 hour less in the day to accomplish their chores, many of which cannot be postponed, such as cooking, child care and even shopping, which must be done on a daily basis.[27]

CHILD CARE – THE BRIDGE BETWEEN THE BURDEN AND THE PROMISE

No issue could possibly rivet our attention more on the central issue of time than child care. Realistically, Soviet parents have few alternatives for child care. The younger the child the narrower the range of choices. There are nurseries (*iasli*) for children of 3 years old and younger, and day care centres (*detskii sad*) for children aged 3 to 7 years old. Parents themselves can mind their children if one of them is unemployed or if they work different shifts. Grandparents are also a possibility and, as we will shortly see, their presence has altered the way Soviet couples live. Paid babysitters, neighbours, siblings, and leaving a child alone are also used.

But the dominant form of child care is the state operated facilities. This is particularly true in the case of children from 3 to 7 years old. Grandparents are the second most important form of care, although they are most important in the care of children under the age of three. Once children are of school age they are overwhelmingly left on their own while their parents are at work.[28]

The reasons for using state institutions are quite practical; for 67 per cent of the parents there is simply no one to take care of their child at home. Among the other parents 24 per cent think 'public upbringing is better' and 10 per cent said it is 'materially profitable'.[29] The overwhelming number of Soviet parents who use state facilities because of the lack of a more acceptable alternative suggests that many fewer would use the state if they had another option. But on the other hand they also appear to choose the option of child care by grandparents in a three generation family largely from necessity, not preference. In a Vilnius study 19 per cent said they had their parents living with them to look after grandchildren and another 26 per cent said the grandparents were needed to take care of the household. While 17 per cent of all the families questioned were three generation households, the results showed that if there were more day care centres or there were apartments for their parents only 5 per cent would remain a three generation family.[30]

The issue of the shortage of nursery and day care facilities is a perpetual complaint in the Soviet press.[31] In 1967 only 23 per cent of all preschool children were in day care centres and in 1974 the proportion was 37 per cent overall and 50 per cent in urban areas.[32]

The need for nurseries and day care centres is greater in the new cities of Siberia than in the RSFSR as a whole, in part because of the younger demographic groups which populate this area of the country. But another part of the problem is that constructing these facilities has a much lower priority than building industrial enterprises. As a result the gap between supply and demand for institutional child care widens in these areas.[33] Similar construction shortfalls exist in the older cities of the country. For example, some recent data from 6 cities showed that out of 10 855 places that were to be built, only 17.5 per cent of their construction plans had been fulfilled.[34] While these are extreme examples, they do reflect the general nature of the problem. The USSR Ministry of Light Industry fulfilled its construction plan for preschool facilities by only 52 per cent from 1966–71; the Food Industry Ministry to the extent of 47 per cent for the same period.[35]

The problem is worst for the mothers of infants. There is an even greater shortage of spaces in the nurseries than in the day care centres, especially for children under 1 year of age. The law says that when vacancies appear in nurseries, those in the 2–10 month old group must be taken first. But nurseries go out of their way to refuse the admission of infants in this age group. In 1971 in the whole country only 2 per cent of the children under the age of 1 year were in nursery–kindergartens,[36] and in 1970 there was a waiting list of 200 000 children for a place in a nursery in the RSFSR.[37] Conditions are best in the large cities where about 5 per cent of children in this age group are in nurseries,[38] but that means it is substantially worse in smaller population centres.

The reason why child care administrators do not want infants in their establishments is that they lack the capability to care properly for them. There is a great shortage of personnel: in 1969 there were 250 children per pediatrician in the nurseries, or approximately 1 for every 3 nurseries and there are about 20 children for every nurse.[39] Nurses' salaries are abysmally low and their working hours are even longer than those who work in the day care centres. As a result there is a high turnover of nursery workers.[40] One of the consequences is that infants are sick more often when they are in the nursery than when they are at home.[41] But the problem of institutionally related illness also exists in the kindergartens.[42] Another consequence, and one that is also intimately related to the shortage of day care centres, is that nurseries in all cities keep children beyond the legal age. For example, in 1970 in the urban areas of the RSFSR there were approximately 120 000 children over the age of 3 who were in nurseries.[43]

There is substantial dissatisfaction with child care facilities among parents. There is a greater dissatisfaction with nurseries than with day care centres: 89 per cent of the parents with children in the kindergartens, but only 70 per cent with children in nurseries are satisfied with the facilities. There is even greater dissatisfaction with the third variant of public child care, the extended day in school. This is generally for children in the first three years who stay after school until 5 o'clock and parents are able to pick them up after the day shift. Only 62 per cent of parents are satisfied with the extended day in school. In contrast, when the family or other people take care of the child the degree of parental satisfaction is 86 per cent with grandparents, 80 per cent with the parents themselves, 73 per cent with older siblings and 66 per cent with neighbours. Only 30 per cent are happy about having older children stay alone. The most highly favoured solution is the use of babysitters or so-called domestic workers (*domrabotnitsy*). They receive perfect marks from parents.[44] But it costs more to use them. One article says it costs at least 30 roubles a month for babysitting as opposed to the monthly nursery fee of 12 roubles.[45] I have been told by emigrés that the true figure for a babysitter is closer to 60 roubles a month. In many cases this could take the larger part of a month's salary.

The inadequacies of the Soviet child care system have at least three effects on the labour–leisure choices of women. The first is that working mothers have to take unpaid leave of absence from work to take care of children who have become ill in Soviet preschool institutions. For example, in Novosibirsk in 1965, women had an average of 6 days of unpaid leave and men 0.6 days for the year.[46] Second, women stay out of the labour force because of the child care problem. In a 1968 study 25 per cent of the women not in the labour force were at home because of a lack of nurseries and day care centres and another 28 per cent said they needed to be at home when their elementary-school children came home.[47] Finally, there is the problem of travelling with a baby on the mass transit system. Even if parents secure a place in a nursery, it may be in a different district of the city and may take an hour to reach and then another hour back home from the nursery.[48] Soviet law allows 15 per cent of the places in day care centres which are affiliated with an enterprise to go to children whose parents live near the enterprise but do not work there. But the enterprise management does not support this since they see their preschool facilities as a carrot to attract workers.[49]

PUBLIC SERVICES – SOME GENERAL ISSUES

The most obvious fact about public services is their exceptionally limited role in the life of the ordinary Soviet citizen. Around 1970, only 5 per cent of housework was taken care of by the service sector; the remaining 95 per cent was in the hands of the household.[50] One of the harshest criticisms was the description of services as 'the most backward branch of the national economy'.[51]

The utilisation rate of various services varies widely not only within a particular city but also between cities. Table 7.1 shows the range of these differences between three major urban areas. For example, let us take the case of the rental points, which are stores renting appliances to the public. While 20 per cent of the households in Leningrad used these facilities, only 3.7 per cent of those in Kostroma did. If we assume that the tastes of the populations in these two cities do not differ very significantly from each other, then there are two explanations for the differential utilisation rates: the differences in the availability of these services and substantial differences in the private ownership of appliances as a substitute for public services.

There is also a large difference in the utilisation of services between age groups. In the Leningrad and Kostroma study workers under the age of 30 use service facilities much more intensively than the older generation: 71 per cent of the younger generation use launderettes, 35 per cent use public catering and 32 per cent use rental points.[52] There are two reasons for this. First is the fact that they are less likely to be owners

TABLE 7.1 *Utilisation of services, Leningrad, Kostroma and Kiev, in percentages*

	Leningrad	Kostroma	Kiev
Dry cleaning	34.6	20.8	46
Rental points	20.0	3.7	15
Laundries	13.0	5.6	6
Public catering	3.2	15.4	—
Pre-packaged foods	8.2	11.7	—
Shoe repair	—	—	74
Clothing repair	—	—	28
Appliance repair	—	—	17

SOURCES A. G. Kharchev and S. I. Golod, *Professional'naia Rabota Zhenshchin i Sem'ia* (Leningrad, 1971) p. 82; S. Vainshtein and Ia. Evreinov, 'Puti Razvitiia Tipovykh Zhilykh i Obshchestvennykh Zdanii', *Problemy Byta, Braka i Sem'i* (Vilnius, 1970) p. 68.

of appliances. Typically, there is a much higher level of ownership of major appliances such as washing machines and refrigerators among those who are middle-aged and older.[53] The second reason is that the older generation is more likely to be tied to the tradition of doing things at home rather than be 'lazy' and take housework elsewhere to be done.[54]

The degree of satisfaction with the work done by service enterprises is rather low. In Leningrad 45 per cent thought the quality of the work was poor, 30 per cent thought it satisfactory and only 25 per cent said it was good. Among the reasons why people do not use public services are the lengthy period of time required (25 per cent), the poor organisation of work (20 per cent), low quality (19 per cent) and the rudeness of the personnel (15 per cent).[55]

Another Leningrad study focused on two particular services; laundries and public catering. Table 7.2 shows that the long delays in getting work done and poor quality work are equally responsible for keeping people from using laundries. About 14 per cent do not use them because it is too far to travel with their laundry. The general complaint is that service establishments are located away from residential areas.[56] The main issue for more than half of those who do not use public catering is that it costs too much to eat out and the rest find the food unappetising.

The service sector also creates enormous frustrations for customers. For example, a great deal of unproductive time is spent in a laundry because of all the forms that have to be filled out. There is a different

TABLE 7.2 *Reasons why Leningrad families do not use services, in percentages*

Laundries	
Unsatisfactory cleaning	43.7
Do not do the work on time	42.4
Distance from home	13.9
Public Catering	
Expensive	54.1
Not tasty	44.5
Like to cook at home	1.4

SOURCE A. G. Kharchev and S. I. Golod, 'Proizvodstvennaia Rabota Zhenshchin i Sem'ia' in G. V. Osipov and Ia. Shchepanskii (eds), *Sotsial'nye Problemy Truda i Proizvodstva* (Moscow, 1969) p. 449.

form for each category of clothing. It takes at least half an hour to fill out the forms which require a listing of the kind and number of items. Then the clerk counts and weighs the laundry, which takes another 15–20 minutes. If several mistakes are made then you can be asked to rewrite the forms. Time is also sometimes wasted in laundries because the wrong clothing is handed back or because laundry is lost.[57]

This frustration is aggravated by the infamous time-consuming distribution system. In Novosibirsk and Yerevan, of the total time spent shopping for non-food items, 42 per cent is spent just standing in line, another 24 per cent weighing and packing and 11–13 per cent waiting at the cashier and paying for the goods. Thus, only about 25 per cent of the time is actually spent shopping.[58]

When the 5-day work week was introduced in 1967 it inadvertently created a serious problem in the service sector: many shops were either closed for the entire weekend or at least stopped functioning on Sundays. As a result, what people could not get done on Saturday had to be taken care of during the week, and that meant being excused from work. In 1968 the problem of workers taking time off from work cost the country 1.1 billion roubles; during the year people were 'excused from work' an average of about 5 times.[59] A 1982 Moscow study found that 73 per cent of workers leave their enterprise to take care of private business such as going to service shops.[60] The magnitude of the problem has become so great that the USSR Council of Ministers adopted a resolution in January 1983 instructing the relevant agencies to carry out measures to rectify the situation. In particular, more service enterprises are to have extended hours. At present only 3 per cent of the non-food stores open as early as 7 am and only 1 per cent close as late as 9 pm. There is also to be an increased provision of services at places of employment. Enterprises, construction sites and farms are to set up reception centres for footwear and clothing repair as well as for laundry and dry cleaning.[61]

There are major geographical differences in the availability of service enterprises. For example, in 1969 there was an average of 9.6 service enterprises per 10 000 population, ranging from a low of 8.2 in the RSFSR to a high of 19.4 in Georgia. There is also a great gap between the availability of services in rural and urban areas. With the exception of the Baltic Republics, most of the services that the rural population uses are in cities. The rural–urban differential is demonstrated by the fact that laundries are 10 times more likely to appear in urban areas than in rural areas.[62] In the RSFSR rural areas have one-sixth of the services of urbanites; in Kazakhstan it is a quarter and in Turkmenistan, one-seventeenth.[63]

LAUNDRIES AND DRY CLEANERS

The issue of laundries and dry cleaners is an important one if only because cleaning clothes is generally regarded as the most tiresome household chore in the country.[64] Yet we have already seen that a relatively small percentage of women use laundries. In a 1964 study 94.1 per cent said they always do the laundry at home.[65] In a somewhat later study 88–94 per cent of the laundry was done at home, about three-quarters without a machine.[66] In 1977, only about 3.4 per cent of the wash was done by laundries.[67] Part of the continued low use of laundries is due to the fact that there are more washing machines in private homes. But washing machines still require women to do laundry, although it is a great deal easier than doing it by hand. However, there are more important reasons why so little laundry is done outside the home. Soviet laundries are at best only capable of serving 10–20 per cent of the population. Even this may be a generous estimate because enterprises (e.g. hospitals) use outside laundry facilities.[68] Another problem is that the construction of laundries is very slow. For example, a laundry in Gorky which began construction in 1966 had still not been completed in mid-1970. In one bizarre instance a newly built laundry in the Armenian city of Dilizhan was converted to lemonade production![69] Finally, there is the issue of the poor quality of work done by laundries, to which we have already alluded. In a Vilnius study 20 per cent said the quality of the cleaning was poor, and 14 per cent said they damage the linen.[70]

Many of the same problems are associated with the use of dry cleaning establishments. Two separate studies showed that at most people use dry cleaners perhaps 3 times a year. One reason is that they are not located near urban residential areas.[71] Another is that they are often unreliable: clothing is lost, or one is given the wrong clothing, or buttons are missing. These difficulties go a long way to explaining the severe underutilisation of capacity in certain places. In three RSFSR *oblasts* capacity utilisation stood at about 33 per cent.[72] In Kazakhstan, depending on the city, equipment was used from 16–30 per cent of its capacity. Service is apparently especially slow in that republic.[73]

PUBLIC CATERING

If doing laundry is the most tiring of the household responsibilities, then cooking is the most time consuming. Between shopping, actual meal preparation and the washing of dishes, women spend approximately half of their time at home involved with food.

Public catering, in principle, could provide relief for Soviet working women, but all the evidence is that it does not. A distinction has to be made between the two basic forms of public catering: one type is the network of canteens, cafeterias, buffets, etc., which are associated with enterprises, that is, eating facilities directly connected with the workplace. The other is the restaurants, cafés, cafeterias, etc., which we may refer to as dining facilities for pleasure. Some sense of the balance between the two can be seen in the Moscow data for 1963. In that year 82.3 per cent of all public catering facilities in the city were located in enterprises.[74]

Public catering has a chequered record in the USSR, though it has grown at a rather rapid pace since 1960. In 1940 sales per urban resident stood at 30 roubles, in 1950 it was 55 roubles, in 1960, 57 roubles and in 1974, 107 roubles. It is contended that public catering establishments can now meet the needs of 20–25 per cent of the urban workers and students.[75]

While there is no shortage of data on the level of utilisation of public catering facilities, the studies are all bunched in the early- to mid-1960s. In addition, the research does not always make explicit the difference between eating in enterprises and using restaurants for pleasure.

However, eating in enterprises increases the utilisation figure so much that it is relatively easy to distinguish a figure which includes eating at work from other numbers. In 1963 somewhat more than one-third of Leningrad female textile workers used public catering, which included eating at their enterprise.[76] In 1964 a general study of Leningraders found that 95.5 per cent always ate at home. This apparently relates to meals where eating at the enterprise is not an option. When workers can eat at work about 60 per cent used the opportunity. Only 4 per cent ever buy pre-cooked dinners from public catering establishments, which they take home.[77] The data from Kiev in 1965–6 generally confirm the Leningrad figures. Almost everyone ate breakfast at home, and 92.8 per cent had lunch at home. Ten per cent bought pre-cooked dinners, and only 26 per cent had dinner at the place of work or at an eating place near work.[78]

A 1965 Pskov study is more detailed about the use of public catering. Table 7.3 shows that very few individuals eat more than one meal a day at a public catering facility on a regular basis. The differences between men and women are quite small. The fact that there is a decline in the number regularly eating at public catering establishments on days off suggests that these are people who eat at enterprises. The increase in the number who periodically eat out indicates that people take advantage of their time off to use a restaurant or café. This is particularly true of women. Only 4.6 per cent never use a public catering establishment on a day off, compared with 9.5 per cent of the men. For women who have the responsibility for cooking, a day off is apparently also an opportunity occasionally to retreat from the kitchen.

There is also a generational difference in the utilisation of public catering. The data in Table 7.4 show that in general older Soviet citizens

TABLE 7.3 *Utilisation of public catering, Pskov, 1965 by sex and day of the week, in percentages*

Utilisation of public catering enterprises	Work days		Days off	
	Men	Women	Men	Women
Regularly, 2–3 times a day	2.0	1.5	2.0	1.0
Regularly, once a day	17.1	15.5	10.0	12.8
From time to time	70.5	71.0	78.5	81.6
Do not use	10.4	12.0	9.5	4.6

SOURCE B. T. Kolpakova and V. D. Patrusheva (eds), *Biudzhet Vremeni Gorodskogo Naseleniia* (Moscow, 1971) p. 132.

TABLE 7.4 *Where families eat suppers, by age group, 1966, in percentages*

	Percentage of families eating		
Age group	At home	At home and in public catering facilities	In public catering facilities
Up to 25 years	52	30	18
26–30 years	66	23	4
31–40 years	64	30	6
Over 40 years	82	15	3
	66	25	8

SOURCE G. A. Slesarev and Z. A. Iankova, 'Zhenshchina na Promyshlennom Predpriiatii i v Sem'e' in G. V. Osipov and Ia. Shchepanskii (eds), *Sotsial'nye Problemy Truda i Proizvodstva* (Moscow, 1969) p. 431.

are more likely to eat their supper at home and, as a corollary, are the less likely to use public catering. The difference is particularly striking between the youngest age group (those under 25 years), and the group at least 40 years old. While 52 per cent of the former always eat at home and 18 per cent always eat at a public catering facility, 82 per cent of the older generation eat at home and 3 per cent always eat out.

Some enterprises have a large number of catering facilities and serve meals which are relatively inexpensive. For example, the daily special at the Dushanbe Silk Factory was 35–40 kopeks (about $0.50). Other workers fare less well. In a case involving mine construction workers public catering facilities were closed down because there was not enough food for workers. The actual eating facility was so small that only 30 people out of the 220 workers could eat at the same time.[79]

In general, it is reasonable to conclude that public catering has yet to get near the point of substituting for household (i.e. female) responsibility for meals; it has certainly not been a vehicle for creating substantial amounts of free time for women.

PREPARED FOODS

One of the other ways that the state could reduce the amount of time women devote to meal preparation is by developing a manufacturing and distribution capability that would place more pre-packaged, prepared and semi-prepared foods in the hands of consumers.

In 1972 only 10–15 per cent of all foods were pre-packaged.[80] The potential saving in time for shoppers is great because they spend an average of 5 minutes in buying a pre-packaged item but 15–20 minutes to buy a bulk item.[81]

There are two types of institution selling semi-prepared and prepared foods. One is the home kitchens (*domovye kukhni*) and the other stores selling semi-prepared and prepared foods (*kulinaria*). The *domovye kukhni* is a store combined with a cafeteria where you can buy a complete dinner from soup to entrée to dessert and eat it there or take it home. The *kulinaria* very often is a store connected with a restaurant where you can buy salads, cooked meats, cakes, biscuits and pies. Often there is a small cafeteria with 4 or 5 tables. If you want to eat in a *kulinaria* you can have coffee or tea with cake or biscuits but not dinner.[82]

The Soviets have demonstrated that cooking with semi-prepared foods saves a great deal of time.[83] Why is it then that only 8.2 per cent of the women in Leningrad cook with semi-prepared foods, e.g. cutlets which have been cut and breaded?[84] The primary reason is the insufficient supply of such foods. In addition, only 16 per cent of all the purchased food is pre-cooked because the quality of the food is poor.[85]

THE ETERNAL QUEUE

Another aspect of the food situation is the enormous amount of time that is spent shopping. The Soviet system of retail distribution is a rather archaic mechanism apparently designed more to create frayed nerves than it is to serve a population weary after work or feeling pressure because they are trying to get their shopping completed before they have to go to work.

There are several problems connected with shopping. One is that self-service is limited. In 1964, 6 per cent of all food stores were self-service;[86] by 1970 this had only improved to 10 per cent.[87] The Soviets have known since the late 1950s (self-service stores opened in 1955) that shopping in a self-service store requires one-third to half the time it does to shop in a serviced store.[88] Partly, this is tied to the development of pre-packaged foods, which allow shoppers to make their own selections. Thus the continuing predominance of bulk foods which have to be handled by store personnel is a severe constraint on the development of self-service.

Another problem is that the retail trade is dominated by small stores.

This requires shoppers to go to many stores in order to accomplish all of their shopping. The small size of stores is shown by the fact that in the mid-1960s 84 per cent of them had 1–3 workers.[89] And in the context of the dominant Soviet *kassa* system it means queuing three different times in each store. Under the *kassa* system a customer stands in line to order merchandise, then proceeds with a chit to a cashier to pay for the goods, and finally returns to the first line to receive the goods upon presentation of the cashier receipt.

There are three comparatively new developments which make life easier for shoppers. One is the ability to order goods over the phone in advance (*po predvaritelnym zakazam*), a second is the use of home deliveries, and the third is shopping services within industrial enterprises. In 1974, 8 per cent of the stores took orders in advance and 7 per cent of the food stores, altogether about 10 000, made home deliveries.[90] An example of the third development can be seen in the Minsk Motor Vehicle Plant. It has a shopping service where order blanks are filled out in the morning (usually taking about 15–20 minutes) and groceries can be picked up at the end of the shift in the late afternoon. Clothing, shoes and rugs can also be ordered at the plant.[91] There is no evidence that this has been widely copied although, as we saw earlier, a variant has been encouraged by the recent Council of Ministers resolution on the service sector. The convenience of this service is reduced when workers have to travel home for long distances on a crowded mass transit system, but for those who live near their job the benefits are considerable.

REPAIR SERVICES

We have already pointed out that many workers have to leave their workplace to deal with repair problems. The cost to the state in lost output is but one aspect of a repair service system that confers great costs upon the individual and society. The fundamental issue is time. Great amounts of time are wasted year after year in a system that works so poorly that it has given rise to a thriving second economy in repair services. For example, at the shoe repair shops 60 per cent of all jobs take 5–20 days to complete.[92] Moreover, people simply cannot count on repairmen. In a recent survey 20 per cent said that the repairman did not come at all after promising to do so.[93] Part of the problem is that today there are many more demands on the repair sector. During the period of about 1965–75, the number of electrical appliances in urban areas doubled and the amount of repair work increased by 2.8 times. In rural areas, the population's stock of appliances during the same period increased 6.7 times while repairs rose 4.3 times.[94] As a result there is a combination of inferior repair services and the increasing pressure on these services brought on by the production of more major appliances that will break down.

In 1973, in the USSR as a whole, people spent 75.2 million hours involved in the repair of their radios and appliances, 12.4 per cent of which were at the expense of work time. In the RSFSR, 39.9 million hours were expended, 14.5 per cent of which should have been spent at work.[95]

PRIVATE OWNERSHIP OF ELECTRICAL APPLIANCES

Home appliances substitute capital for labour in the household as well as reducing the drudgery of housework. Home appliances are, however, a highly imperfect substitute for public production of a good or service since they continue to oblige the individual to produce the final good or service at home. A good example is washing machines, whose presence in a Soviet household saves roughly 2 months of washing by hand.[96] This is the equivalent of a 16 per cent savings in time over a year. In evaluating the role that appliances have played in easing the household burden of women, the focus is on the 4 major appliances the Soviets have produced: washing machines, refrigerators, vacuum cleaners and sewing machines. There is no Soviet domestic production of such western commonplaces as clothes dryers, blenders, food processors or microwave ovens.

Soviet production of major electrical appliances began about 1950. (Rental points to lease appliances did not open until the mid-1950s).[97] In 1960, only 3-4 per cent of the total population had household appliances, but ownership rapidly increased and by 1965 65 per cent of urban families had a washing machine, 62 per cent had a refrigerator and 19 per cent had a vacuum cleaner.[98]

Production levels since 1965 have been quite different for the 4 appliances (see Table 7.5). The annual output of washing machines peaked in 1970 when 5 243 000 were produced, an increase of 53 per cent over 1965. Thereafter production fell sharply to slightly under 3 million a year in 1973. Output has risen steadily since then although 1980 output was less than it was in 1966. Sewing machine production has been much smoother. After peaking at 1 439 000 in 1972, it has declined slightly every year and now stands at a level of just over 1.3 million. Vacuum

TABLE 7.5 *Production of major electrical appliances, 1965–80, in thousands*

	Washing machines	Sewing machines	Vacuum cleaners	Refrigerators
1965	3430	800	800	1675
1966	3869	1025	899	2205
1967	4324	1198	1097	2697
1968	4700	1300	1230	3155
1969	5153	1324	1359	3701
1970	5243	1400	1509	4140
1971	4052	1408	1738	4557
1972	3001	1439	2168	5030
1973	2987	1400	2658	5423
1974	3075	1366	3319	5426
1975	3286	1360	2920	5579
1976	3510	1358	2661	5827
1977	3647	1360	2748	5798
1978	3697	1355	2925	6069
1979	3661	1317	3098	5953
1980	3826	1323	3222	5925
Total	61 461	20 733	34 351	73 160

SOURCES *Narodnoe Khoziaistvo SSSR*, various years.

cleaner production has oscillated over the 15 year period but has moved in a generally upward direction; output in 1980 was four times the 1965 figure. The highest priority for Soviet planners since 1965 has been refrigerators. During this period more than 73 million refrigerators were produced, compared to 61.5 million washing machines. The Soviets are now producing about 6 million refrigerators a year.

The increases in output have not been matched by increases in quality. For example, in the early 1970s there were no fully automatic Soviet washing machines. In fact, in recent times 85 per cent of the machines which are produced have manually operated wringers; only 15 per cent are semi-automatic. Even with the most sophisticated model of basic machines half the time is spent on manual operations, yet over half the population would like to buy semi-automatic or automatic machines.[99] In addition, a number of washing machines are not suited to wash all materials. Some are only capable of washing cotton and linens but not silk, synthetic fabrics or knitted goods.[100] There is also a problem with durability; one author disparagingly described the brief life span of a refrigerator as 'no longer than a dog's'.[101]

Ownership of appliances not only differs by age, as we have seen earlier, but also by occupation, education, income and area of the country. These studies clearly demonstrate that there are fairly significant differences in the degree of ownership between the broad occupational groups. A gap between white-collar workers and manual workers can be documented from the early 1960s to the mid-1970s. As Table 7.6 shows, in 1962 white-collar workers owned roughly twice as many appliances as blue-collar workers. In a 1965 study among Leningrad machine building workers, 11 per cent of the 'unskilled workers who do physical labour' owned both a refrigerator and a washing machine. This was the smallest share of any group of workers. The two groups with the highest percentage of ownership of both appliances were 'administrators of production collectives' (19.8 per cent) and 'highly skilled workers who do scientific–technical work' (22.8 per cent).[102] Finally, in 1973–4 and 1974–5 in a study in two industrial plants in Klin and Kstovo, 68.8 per cent of the blue-collar workers and 79.6 per cent of the ITR owned at least one or more of the following: washing machine, sewing machine, refrigerator and vacuum cleaner.[103]

TABLE 7.6 *Number of electrical appliances per 100 families in the RSFSR, 1 June 1962*

	Industrial workers	Construction workers	White-collar workers
Refrigerators	2.9	4.4	8.1
Washing machines	10.1	10.0	18.5
Vacuum cleaners	2.3	1.9	6.8

SOURCE V. G. Baikova *et al.*, *Svobodnoe Vremia i Vsestoronnee Razvitie Lichnosti* (Moscow, 1965) p. 240.

Income and education are also closely related to the ownership of appliances. Since income and education are highly correlated with each other in the Soviet Union, we may think of them as one variable, although we will present data where each is measured as an independent variable.[104]

In Table 7.7 we see the enormous impact education above the elementary level has on ownership. The most striking thing is that in absolute terms poorly educated families had almost no relief from housework. There is one serious defect in this study: the sample size of 227 married women is quite small. More recent research, however,

TABLE 7.7 *Ownership of appliances by level of education, 1966, Moscow, Leningrad and Penza, in percentages*

	Families with elementary school education	Higher than elementary school education
Washing machines	0	13
Sewing machines	15	50
Vacuum cleaners	1	19
Refrigerators	4	34

SOURCE G. A. Slesarev and Z. A. Iankova, 'Zhenshchina na Promyshlennom Predpriiatii i v Sem'e' in G. V. Osipov and Ia. Shchepanskii (eds), *Sotsial'nye Problemy Truda i Proizvadstva* (Moscow, 1969) p. 428.

confirms earlier findings. Table 7.8 shows that at the margin a specialised education is associated with a substantial increase in the ownership of household appliances. The study breaks down ownership by sex and it is clear that a greater percentage of men than women own appliances. How can this differential between men and women be explained? A large part of the answer rests in the fact that men earn higher incomes than women.[105] Moreover, a higher percentage of women is unmarried and, given their lower incomes, they are less likely to be able to afford appliances since they will not have a husband's income to provide a higher financial base in the household.

There is direct evidence that income and appliance ownership are correlated. Again, we are using the study of 227 married women. The data in Table 7.9 show a substantial difference between two broad groups: those households with a 1966 per capita income of 80 roubles or below and those households where income is above 80 roubles. The high income families own about three times more appliances than the low income households.

A study in the Tatar ASSR showed that families are much more likely to own appliances than are single people. While this is partially attributable to the lesser need for appliances among unmarried people, the differences expressed in Table 7.10 also lend support to the notion that it ordinarily takes two incomes in a household to be able to afford appliances. The data also confirm that those who do intellectual work are more able to afford appliances than those who do physical labour.

There are also differences in ownership because of the factor of climate. For example, while there were 5.5 refrigerators for every 100 families in the RSFSR and 9.9 per 100 families in Leningrad, in the

TABLE 7.8 *Ownership of household appliances by sex and level of education, in percentages*

	Women				Men			
	4 classes or less	5–7 classes	8–10 classes	Specialised education	4 classes or less	5–7 classes	8–10 classes	Specialised education
Washing machines	9	11	18	42	12	10	32	60
Vacuum cleaners	2	8	8	18	—	10	15	34
Refrigerators	5	16	16	42	19	16	34	68

SOURCE L. A. Gordon and E. V. Klopov, *Chelovek Posle Raboty* (Moscow, 1972) p. 111.

TABLE 7.9 *Correlation between per capita household income and the average number of appliances in the family*

Monthly rouble income per family member	Number of appliances in the family
0–60	0.63
61–80	0.4
81–100	1.5
101–130	1.3

SOURCE Slesarev and Iankova, p. 429.

TABLE 7.10 *Ownership of appliances in different types of Tatar families, in percentages*

	Refrigerators, vacuum cleaners, washing machines
Workers doing intellectual labour	
Single	3
Family	91
Workers doing physical labour	
Single	2
Family	21

SOURCE *Sotsial'noe i Natsional'noe* (Moscow, 1973) p. 160.

Central Asian city of Ashkhabad there were 44 refrigerators for every 100 families.[106]

The benefit from the ownership of household appliances shows up in more free time. Families with appliances had about 50 minutes per day free time more than those without such conveniences.[107] The potential saving in time is enormous. A recent estimate is that the 275 billion hours a year are spent doing housework. About 20 per cent of that time involves responsibilities that are already carried out in the service sector.[108] We saw that actually only 5 per cent of housework is currently done in the service sector. In other words, in principle, the Soviet service sector could quadruple its output. However, this would involve a massive reallocation of resources. The gap between the actual and potential level of service output is a measure of failures in an area of Soviet society so crucial to the quality of life of women; the shortfall restricts the range of choices between work and leisure.

From the viewpoint of Soviet planners, an investment in the service sector would increase the labour input. For example, if repairs were efficiently done, workers would not have to leave their jobs so often. In addition, women would probably be more productive at work if they were less tired from their housework and the difficulties they experience dealing with the cumbersome and underdeveloped service sector.

8 The Rural Sector

Up to this point the analysis has taken place within the framework of the Soviets' largely urban environment, and in this chapter we treat the rural sector as a separate entity. There are several justifications for according special treatment to this part of Soviet society. At the time of the 1917 Revolution 85 per cent of the total population were peasants and the economy was overwhelmingly agricultural. Even though urbanisation and industrialisation have taken place at a pace that has dramatically changed the shape of the Soviet Union, 37 per cent of the population still lives in rural areas. Moreover, their standard of living is lower than that of urbanites; in 1980 monthly wages for the economy as a whole were 46 per cent higher than collective farm income earned in the socialist sector.[1] Rural inhabitants have fewer amenities such as electricity, indoor plumbing and central heating. Rural roads are often primitive and educational facilities not good. One of the major features of urban/rural differences is that many peasants have escaped from what they believe is the less rich life of the countryside for what is seen as the good life of Soviet cities. The great wave of peasant migration to urban areas, which during the period 1928–40 was one of the lynchpins of Soviet industrialisation, has now become a source of serious concern for Soviet planners. Not only are too many people leaving agriculture, but the rural population is also 'ageing' as the young leave for the cities.

In this chapter we examine the ways in which the conflict between Soviet planners and rural households expresses itself in the Soviet Union's villages, particularly on collective farms. Planners affect the supply of labour in the countryside through a variety of policy levers. The most important one is their incomes policy. Agricultural prices have historically been kept at low levels and this has translated into low incomes for collective farmers. As a result there has been a great incentive for farmers to produce and sell goods on the free market in order to supplement their incomes. The second policy lever is the availability of leisure and cultural facilities. It will be shown that peasants suffer relative to their urban counterparts because there are fewer leisure facilities and the quality of these is poorer. The third policy lever is the level of services such as day care and public catering facilities. A shortage of services exists in the countryside.

A separate study of the rural sector is justified by the presence of the well known private plot. Most rural households have a small plot of a quarter to a half of an acre on which they grow crops and raise animals. The proceeds from this plot belong to the household; they can consume their output or sell it in a free market at prices well above those offered by the state. The existence of the ubiquitous private plot in the countryside creates a major income, supply and recreation source that does not exist in urban settings. In urban areas the choice is between market work, home work and leisure. On a Soviet collective farm the additional choice is between work in the socialist (i.e. collective) sector and work on the private plot. As a result, it will be shown that the choices in the countryside are considerably different from those facing urbanites.

THE LENGTH OF THE WORK DAY

It is in the nature of agriculture that the length of a work day cannot be regulated by law. With the exception of the storming period which comes at the end of the month in industrial enterprises, workers in the non-agricultural sector can expect regularity in their day over the course of a year. Agricultural workers, on the other hand, experience work days that vary between seasons. Moreover, the seasonality of agriculture reduces the length of the work year. The average collective farmer works 195–200 days a year in the socialist sector.[2] In contrast, non-agricultural workers work an average of 234 days a year.[3] As Table 8.1 shows, there are enormous variations in the country.

The number of days worked in the Northwest part of the country was almost double the number of days worked in Georgia. In the Ukraine and Moldavia, collective farmers worked 10 days less than they did in 1959; in Georgia, 13 days less.[4]

One can only speculate about these differences. The Northwest is an area characterised by a labour deficiency in agriculture. Because some agricultural areas are close to Leningrad where jobs are available for commuters, the higher wages in the urban area increase the opportunity cost of work in agriculture. Those who are left on the collective farms must work intensively. A second possible explanation is that there are extreme differences in the level of mechanisation of farms in different

The Rural Sector

TABLE 8.1 *Number of days worked by collective farmers in the socialist sector, 1965*

Northwest	—261
Ukraine	—188
Armenia	—174
Tadzhikstan	—173
Azerbaidzhan	—163
Moldavia	—153
Georgia	—135

SOURCE *Literaturnaia Gazeta*, 17 December 1969, p. 10. (The Northwest is an economic region which includes the following six *oblasts*: Arkhangel, Vologod, Leningrad, Murmansk, Novgorod and Pskov, and the Karelia and Komi ASSRs.)

areas of the country. Where capital investment has been heavy we would expect the number of days worked to be lower than in areas where agriculture is still more labour intensive. Recent data grouping agricultural regions on the basis of indicators of returns from capital investment show substantial differences in labour productivity increases between various republics. Such productivity differences have led to both increases in output and a decline in the labour input.[5] The situation in Georgia can also be explained by the high opportunity cost of participation in the socialist sector. Fruit and vegetable farming on a private basis has become extremely profitable and Georgian farmers have been known to fly to different locations to sell their output. Finally, some climatic differences would cause differences in the number of days worked.

There are a substantial amount of data on the number of hours worked by collective farmers, although detailed studies appear to have stopped after the mid-1960s. For several reasons it is not possible to produce a single figure for the length of the work day or work week in the socialist sector. Hours of work vary by the type of work done and the level of mechanisation of farm operations. Finally, work on the private plot is a substitute for work in the socialist sector and time devoted to the plot will vary depending on its size and profitability. As a result, the data in Table 8.2 come from several geographical areas and are presented as a range. The truth about how much farmers work is not an average, but the range itself. This is due to the fact that time demands vary according

TABLE 8.2 *Hours of work per day for peasants in 1923 and collective farmers in the socialist sector, various places and years, by sex*

Year	Place	Average for the year		Summer		Winter	
		Men	Women	Men	Women	Men	Women
1923[1]	RSFSR	6.2	5.7	10.4	7.5	2.0	4.0
1934[1]	RSFSR	9.3	8.4	10.4	9.9	8.5	6.8
1954[2]	Moldavia	7.9	8.0	—	—	—	—
1960[2]	Moldavia	6.8	7.5	—	—	—	—
1963[3]	Gorky, Sverdlovsk, Rostov *Oblasts*	8.8	6.5	—	—	—	—
1964[1]	RSFSR (4 *kolkhozy*)	7.5	4.9	9.1	5.9	6.0	3.9

SOURCES 1. V. G. Baikova, A. S. Duchal and A. S. Zemtsov, *Svobodnoe Vremia i Vsestoronnee Razvitie Lichnosti* (Moscow, 1965) p. 224; 2. V. N. Shubkin, 'Opyt Sravnitel'skogo Sotsiologicheskogo Issledovaniia Moldavskoi Derevni (na materialakh sela Kopanki)', *Sotsiologiia v SSSR* (Moscow, 1965) p. 327; 3. V. A. Artemov *et al.*, *Statistika Biudzhetov Vremeni Trudiashchikhsia* (Moscow, 1965) p. 62.

to the kind of agricultural activity, the availability of agricultural equipment and the degree of difficulty involved in farming a given piece of land.

There are several observations to be made about the amount of work done by collective farmers. First, it should be noted that these data refer only to work in the socialist sector. An analysis of work on the private plot follows directly. Secondly, collective farmers work a 6 day week. Thus, in the summer of 1964 male *kolkhozniki* worked 54.5 hours a week and women worked 35.7 hours a week. In the winter the hours worked per week were 36.2 and 23.9 respectively. Second, there are some substantial variations between different collective farms and between the sexes. For example, in 1963, the male collective farmers in the RSFSR *oblasts* worked 2 hours a day (or 12 hours a week) more than those farming in Moldavia. In 1960, the Moldavian women worked more than 2.5 hours a day (15 hours a week) longer than the women in the RSFSR sample. The Moldavian women worked longer hours than their male counterparts. This is attributed to two factors: women's work is more labour intensive and their responsibilities on the farm are year-round jobs, e.g. milking cows and feeding livestock and poultry.[6] In the

RSFSR studies women worked less than men in the socialist sector. This probably results from the greater importance of the private plot in the Russian Republic.

The data for 1923, some 6 years before collectivisation, indicate that on a year-round basis peasants worked considerably less before they were collectivised; in 1934 the men worked more than 3 hours a day longer than they had in 1923 and the women worked 3 hours longer than in 1923. Collectivisation did not change the length of the work day during the summer but it had a major impact on hours worked in the winter. Peasants who worked only 2 hours a day in 1923 were working 8.5 hours a day after collectivisation. The impact of collectivisation on women was somewhat different. The work day of women increased by 2.4 hours during the agricultural season and by just under 3 hours in the winter. After collectivisation women worked almost as much as men during the agricultural season, but close to 2 hours a day less in the winter.

The only research I have seen on hours worked in the 1970s was done in the Kokchetag *Oblast* in Kazakhstan. In the summer 39.9 per cent of the collective farmers had a 7 hour work day. All the rest worked from 8 to 10 hours and more. In the winter 57 per cent of the collective farmers had a 7 hour work day; the others worked 8 to 9 hours and more.[7]

THE PRIVATE PLOT

The private plot was initially a concession by the Soviet leadership to assuage the enormous anger of the peasantry when they were collectivised and their private property was appropriated. Over the past 55 years Soviet policy towards the private plot has vacillated. The rights of collective farmers have been alternately liberalised and tightened as planners tried to reconcile their negative views of the plot as an ideological heterodoxy with the plot's positive practical uses as a major producer of certain key agricultural products. Moreover, the private plot has served to increase the labour input in the economy. Women who might not otherwise have worked as much in agriculture have long found private plot agriculture profitable. From the state's viewpoint this has an additional benefit. The millions of Soviet youths who have gone to the cities have drained agriculture of a group that is better trained and more productive than the agricultural labour force, which is rapidly becoming disproportionately comprised of unskilled women and is also ageing.

Through the years the private plot has remained an attractive outlet for the energies of collective farmers for two major reasons. First, the plot provided food for the farmers when the collective farm itself could not adequately feed them because of the onerous burden of compulsory deliveries to the state. Second, the private plot has always been a major source of income for many farmers, especially those living close to urban areas. Table 8.3 shows the relative importance of various sources of income.

The data suggest that a high but falling percentage of income comes from the private plot. In 1940 the private plot accounted for about half of *kolkhoz* family income; by 1974 its share had fallen to one-fourth of income. The fact that its relative importance has fallen in recent years is attributable to two factors: the shift from a low level of uncertain in-kind payments to more stable and higher money wage payments to collective farmers and the demographic phenomenon of an ageing rural population which increases the dependency on social insurance rather than earned income. In spite of the fact that private plot income has fallen, there is still official criticism of the large number of people who devote time to raising and selling farm products in the collective farm market at the expense of their obligation to the state. One district in the Ukraine claimed, for example, that 20 000 to 24 000 work days were lost on state farms from May to July because of private selling activity.[8]

Almost everyone in the rural areas has a private plot. However, the time devoted to tending the plot varies by sex, level of family income, time of the year and age. The most important difference in the commitment of time is that women spend a considerably greater proportion of their work day on the private plot than do men.

TABLE 8.3 *The structure of kolkhoz family income, 1940–74, in percentages*

	1940	1965	1970	1974
Income from the *kolkhoz*	39.7	40.0	40.3	44.2
Income from the private plot	48.3	36.5	31.9	26.6
Wages of the family	5.8	7.4	8.4	7.8
Pensions, stipends, severance pay and other payments from the social insurance fund	4.9	14.2	17.7	19.9
Income from other sources	1.3	1.9	1.7	1.5
Total	100.0	100.0	100.0	100.0

SOURCE P. I. Simush, *Sotsial'nyi Portret Sovetskogo Krest'ianstva* (Moscow, 1976) p. 106.

TABLE 8.4 *Percentage of work time spent on the private plot, by sex*

Year	Place	Men	Women
1954	Moldavia	11.1	30.3
1960	Moldavia	8.9	38.5
1964	Novisibirsk	9.5	34.6
1966	Unknown	12.8	37.9

SOURCES V. N. Shubkin, 'Opyt Sravnitel'skogo Sotsiologicheskogo Issledovaniia Moldavskoi Derevni (na materialakli sela Kopanki)', *Sotsiologiia v SSSR* (Moscow, 1965) pp. 327–8; Iu. V. Arutiunian, *Sotsial'naia Struktura Sel'skogo Naseleniia SSSR* (Moscow, 1971) pp. 126–7.

According to the data in Table 8.4, men spend 9–13 per cent of their work time on the private plot and women spend 30–39 per cent of their work time in this way. Roughly speaking, women are about 3 to 4 times more likely to be working on the private plot than men. In the only case where the same collective farm was observed over time (Moldavia, 1954 and 1960), there was a slight decline in men's participation and a fairly substantial rise in women's participation. Whether this is a general pattern could only be confirmed by additional data from this farm.

As might be expected, the greatest difference between men and women in hours worked on the private plot shows up during the summer. According to data from four RSFSR *kolkhozy* in the mid-1960s, men work 8.4 hours a week on the private plot and women 26 hours in the summer; in the winter, men work 1.9 hours and women 3.0 hours a week.[9] These data imply that collective farm women make a major commitment to the private plot during the summer. This is confirmed by the data of Table 8.5 which show that the greatest difference in the hours spent by men and women on the private plot comes when considering the proportion working 5 or more hours a day: about 6 per cent of the men and 22 per cent of the women fall into this category. On the average, about half the men work on the private plot 2 hours or less on a daily basis.

When work time in the *kolkhoz* is added to work on the private plot, the work week during the summer is virtually the same for both sexes: 62.9 hours for men and 61.7 hours for women. Men have the longer work week during the winter. They work 38.1 hours and women work

TABLE 8.5 *Distribution of hours spent on the private plot per day in the summer, by sex, circa 1970, in percentages*

Daily hours worked	Men	Women
Up to 2 hours	46.3	35.5
3 hours	22.3	24.8
4 hours	7.7	7.7
5 hours and more	5.6	21.6
No answer	18.1	10.4
Total	100.0	100.0

SOURCE *Selo, Plan, Chelovek* (Volgograd, 1975) p. 144.

26.9 hours. However, when hours spent on housework are added to farm work, the picture changes. For example, women do 25.5 hours of housework during the summer and 50.5 hours during the winter. Men spend only 6.1 hours a week on housework during the summer and 10.1 hours during the winter. When farm work and housework are combined, the work week of women in the summer (87.2 hours) turns out to be 18.2 hours longer than men's. In the winter the discrepancy is even greater. The 77.4 hours women work in the off-season is 29.2 hours longer than their male counterparts'.[10]

Large differences in hours worked in the socialist and private sectors of agriculture are not confined to young men and women. A comprehensive study in Novosibirsk shows different commitments of time between several groups. As Table 8.6 shows, pensioners and invalids have the highest participation rates on the private plot, spending close to two-thirds of their time away from the socialist sector. As we indicated earlier the 1971 pension reform in agriculture reduced old-age pensions by 15 per cent if retired farmers had a private plot over 0.15 of a hectare. The outcome has been some shift of pensioners to the socialist sector. To the extent that children are involved in farming they divide their time equally between the socialist and private sectors. Overall, slightly more than a quarter of the entire labour input of collective farms is devoted to private plot agriculture. In effect, the collective farm labour force spends about 50 days every year doing nothing but working on their private plots.

Skilled workers spend less time on the private plot than unskilled workers. For example, according to 1963 data from the Novosibirsk

TABLE 8.6 *Structure of work time of various groups of kolkhozniki, Novosibirsk Oblast, 1964, in percentages*

	Distribution of work time for the whole year	
Group	Socialist sector	Private plot
Youths up to 16 years old	49.4	50.6
Old-age and non-able-bodied workers	37.4	62.6
Total for able-bodied workers	77.9	22.1
Able-bodied men	90.5	9.5
Able-bodied women	65.4	34.6
Total	73.3	26.7

SOURCE Iu. V. Arutiunian, *Sotsial'naia Struktura Sel'skogo Naseleniia SSSR* (Moscow, 1971) p. 127.

oblast, male field workers spent an average of 8.3 per cent of their time on the private plot, livestock workers, 6.7 per cent, mechanics, 5.4 per cent, management, 4 per cent of their work day. However, this does not mean that the income of unskilled workers from private agriculture is higher. On the contrary, in this particular region there is a direct relationship between income earned from the collective sector and income earned from the private plot. This is explained by the fact that males who earn relatively high incomes in the socialist sector can implement two kinds of factor substitution. The first is that other family members, especially their wives, are free to leave the socialist sector of the labour force and take care of the private plot. The second is that people with high incomes can better afford capital inputs, e.g. fertiliser, as a substitute for their own labour.[11]

For unskilled workers it is profitable to work on the private plot because the rouble value of agricultural output per hour of work is higher than the hourly income they earn in the socialist sector.[12] In a study done in 1963 in the Krasnodarsk *krai*, 75 per cent of the entire sample and 80–85 per cent of groups with low incomes said that the private plot was necessary because it provided additional income. Seventy per cent of the low income earners said they would not reduce their effort on the private plot unless their income from the socialist sector increased. For *kolkhoz* intelligentsia and white collar workers, a more important precondition for decreasing their time on the private plot was a better supply of food in the countryside.[13] In other words, high income workers are more likely to grow food to eat and low income workers are more likely to grow food to sell on the market.

The importance of the private plot to collective farmers cannot be overestimated: it is a basic source of both financial and in-kind household income. Moreover, it is an important outlet for female labour. The existence of the private plot does not significantly alter the male labour input into collective agriculture, but it does dramatically alter female labour force participation in this sector of the economy. The number of hours worked on the private plot is suggestive of this. If there were farms with no private plots and if we had data on hours worked by women in the socialist sector, we could render a more definitive judgment about the impact of the private plot on female participation in agriculture.

Finally, in a major study conducted between 1967 and 1971 of persons 15 to 30 years old living on either a *kolkhoz* or a *sovkhoz*, it was found that the main reason why young people do not leave the village is that they do not want to give up their private plot. This is especially true of those aged 27–30.[14] While there is no doubt that the private plot acts as a deterrent to agricultural outmigration, it has obviously not been sufficient to keep most young people on the farm.

TIME BUDGETS OF RURAL HOUSEHOLDS

The amount of time that individuals work cannot help but affect the entire time budget of the individual and family. In the case of agriculture two factors make it difficult to estimate how Soviet farmers divide their time between work, leisure and the physiological necessities of life: the seasonality of work and the existence of the private plot. At a minimum it can be said that there is less stability during the year in the time budgets of rural families than those of urban families.

There are three major studies of time budgets within agriculture; two of collective farm households and one of state farm households, each dating from the 1960s. The two studies of collective farms differ from one another: one divides time into the summer and winter seasons, the other divides the week into work days, Saturdays and Sundays. Since each offers a different perspective, they will be analysed separately.

The data in Table 8.7 reveal several patterns within the *kolkhoz* and a number of differences between men and women. First, it should be noted that work on the private plot is placed in the same category as housework, which is true as well of the other study we present below.

TABLE 8.7 Time budgets of collective farm families, 1963, Gorky, Sverdlovsk, Rostov oblasts, by sex and day of the week, in hours and minutes

Type of expenditure of time	Men				Women			
	Work day	Saturday	Sunday	Total	Work day	Saturday	Sunday	Total
Work time	8:51	8:11	5:08	57:34	6:28	6:25	3:29	42:14
Non-work time connected with the job	1:06	1:04	0:36	7:10	0:58	0:52	0:31	6:13
Housework and work on the private plot	2:23	2:09	3:36	17:40	6:19	6:42	7:30	45:47
Satisfying physiological needs	8:48	8:59	9:26	62:25	8:17	8:05	8:46	58:16
Free time	2:15	2:32	4:09	17:56	1:25	1:29	2:53	11:27
Other expenditures of time	0:37	1:05	1:05	5:15	0:33	0:27	0:51	4:03
Total	24:00	24:00	24:00	168:00	24:00	24:00	24:00	168:00

SOURCE V. A. Artemov et al., *Statistika Biudzhetov Vremeni Trudiashchikhsia* (Moscow, 1967) p. 62.

While this is consistent with the fact that housework is primarily associated with women, it accords work on the private plot the same status as unpaid household labour. Not only is this empirically untrue, but is also creates the implicit impression that such work does not deserve the same status as 'real' work, i.e. work in the socialist sector. Second, men have a good deal more free time than women every day of the week. The greatest difference is on Sunday, when it is likely that women use their day off to do housework which often cannot be completed during the week. For the week as a whole, men have about 7.5 hours more free time than women. Third, collective farmers work 7 days a week in the socialist sector. The inclusion of private plot agriculture with housework makes it impossible to say with certainty whether collective farmers work in the private plot on Sundays as well. Fourth, men have about 7 per cent more time every day to meet their physiological needs (eating and sleeping). Finally, men spend more time travelling to their job on the farm. The nature of women's work on the collective farm keeps them closer to home than men. This fact, combined with women's overwhelming responsibility for housework, strengthens the argument that private plot agriculture increases the total hours women work in agriculture.

There is a slightly different perspective of collective farm time budgets when the data are examined on the basis of the two main seasons, winter and summer (see Table 8.8). These data are more detailed by activity and, as a consequence, more revealing about the nature of what collective farmers do with their time.

There is much more free time available to men, a result to be expected after calculating the hours worked by each sex. This has been true throughout the period of collectivisation, although over the long-term free time has risen for both sexes. In 1934 men had 2.7 hours and women 1.6 hours per day respectively. By 1964 leisure time had risen to 4.3 hours for men and 2.1 hours a day for women.[15] In the summer men had about 20 hours of free time every week, while women only had 8 hours. It is striking that women only had about 1 hour a day of free time during the busy season on the farm! In the winter free time increased for both sexes. Men had about 39 hours of free time a week, about twice that available to women. These differentials cannot be accounted for by the hours worked for income, but by the enormous differences in housework. Indeed, when hours on the private plot are subtracted from the category of 'housework', men do only 6.1 hours of housework and women 25.5 hours a week in the summer. This housework differential more than accounts for the difference in free time. Overall, there is little difference

TABLE 8.8 *Weekly time budget of collective farmers, 1964, four RSFSR collective farms, by sex and season, in hours per week*

	Summer		Winter	
	Men	Women	Men	Women
I Work time in the *kolkhoz*	54.5	35.7	36.2	23.9
II Non-work time	113.5	132.3	131.8	144.1
(i) Connected with work in the *kolkhoz* including:	16.8	11.9	9.6	3.8
Round trip to the work place	9.0	5.4	6.1	2.9
Getting assignment	0.7	0.4	0.2	0.2
Lunch time	7.2	6.0	3.3	0.7
(ii) Housework, including:	14.5	51.5	12.0	53.5
Meal preparation	0.8	16.4	0.8	18.6
Cleaning the house	1.9	2.2	3.1	6.3
Laundry	1.7	3.0	3.0	7.2
Child care	0.3	2.8	0.5	4.9
Work in the private plot	8.4	26.0	1.9	3.0
Other kinds of housework	1.5	1.1	2.8	13.6
(iii) Satisfying physiological needs, including:	61.8	61.0	70.9	65.2
Sleep	53.6	51.2	59.7	55.3
Eating	3.2	4.1	6.9	4.6
Caring for oneself	5.0	5.7	4.3	5.3
(iv) Free time, including:	20.4	7.9	39.2	21.6
Upbringing of children	0.3	0.7	0.2	2.0
Going to school and improving skills	0.3	0.2	1.2	0.5
Social work	0.5	0.3	1.5	0.5
Creative activity	0.3	0.0	0.5	0.1
Athletics	0.0	0.0	0.0	0.0
Rest and entertainment, including:	19.1	6.7	35.8	18.4
Reading newspapers, journals, books	3.1	1.2	6.4	1.5
Listening to radio and watching TV	3.2	1.3	6.4	2.4
Going to cinemas, clubs, houses of culture	1.2	0.9	2.7	1.6
Visiting friends	4.9	1.2	7.2	6.1
Playing house games	3.4	0.2	5.4	2.1
Religious activity	0.0	0.0	0.0	0.0
Doing nothing	3.2	1.9	7.7	5.0
Total	168.0	168.0	168.0	168.0

SOURCE V. G. Baikova *et al.*, *Svobodnoe Vremia i Vsestoronnee Razvitie Lichnosti* (Moscow, 1965) pp. 223–4.

allocated to physiological needs. Men also spend a good deal more time getting to and from work, travelling about 3.5 hours a week more than women. Even in the winter when the amount of work drops and travel time does as well, the differential between men and women remains about the same.

A major distinction between the summer and winter periods is that in the latter case about 11 hours of the 17.5-hour difference in free time between the sexes can be accounted for by the difference in work for income. This is not true of the summer. The 40-hour difference in time devoted to housework in the winter covers the rest of the free time difference with plenty to spare.

The life of those who live on collective farms but work for the state rather than doing agricultural work is much different from the life of the farmers with whom they live. From Table 8.9 it can be seen that the distribution of their time is much closer to that of urbanites; they certainly work fewer hours than do collective farmers. The average work week for all workers in the USSR in 1963 was 40 hours, which is less than the 43 hours male state workers on collective farms worked but essentially equal to the work week of their female counterparts. They also have more free time than farmers, although the difference is not very great in the case of women. Men have about 8 hours more a week, but the women only have about 3.5 hours more.

Table 8.9 gives the impression that these state workers do not work on private plots. This seems hard to imagine, given the historical import-

TABLE 8.9 *Weekly time budget of members of collective farm families employed in the state sector, 1963, Gorky, Sverdlovsk, Rostov Oblasts, by sex, hours and minutes*

Type of expenditure of time	Hours and minutes	
	Men	Women
Work time	43:08	39.18
Non-work time connected with the job	11:04	7:37
Housework	17:47	40:42
Satisfying physiological needs	67:06	61:46
Free time	25:41	15:07
Other expenditures of time	3:14	3:30
Total	168:00	168:00

SOURCE Artemov *et al.*, p. 64.

ance that this institution has had in the countryside. It is reasonable that state workers would not devote as much time to a private plot simply because they are not around the farm all day; its absolute absence seems unlikely. Table 8.8 treats work on the private plot as a separate category, and suggests that on the average women devote about 14.5 hours a week to this activity (26 hours in the summer and 3 hours in the winter). If we assume that the farm women of Table 8.9 spend the same amount of time on the private plot then working farm women do considerably less housework than state workers who live on farms. That is, working farm women only do 5 hours a week more housework than the state workers. If they work about 14–15 hours on a plot, then they are doing less meal preparation, house cleaning, etc. The women who work for the state are not getting any more help from their husbands than the women in agriculture. In both cases men contribute just under 18 hours a week at home.

The generally shorter work week of both male and female state workers not only affords more free time, it also permits more time for sleeping and eating; about 5 hours a week in the case of men and 3.5 hours for women.

TIME BUDGETS IN THE SOVKHOZ

The only time budget data I have seen for the *sovkhoz* are presented in Table 8.10. The pattern here is very different from either collective farm agricultural workers or state workers on collective farms. It must be remembered that while collective farmers apparently had a 7 day obligation in the socialist sector, state farmers have 1 day off. Men who work on state farms had a 42 hour work week, far less than the work week of male collective farmers but essentially the same as state workers on collective farms and non-agricultural workers in general. This is not true of women. Women on state farms worked only a 28 hour week in the state sector, considerably less than the work week of women on collective farms, whether the latter were agricultural or non-agricultural workers. Men on state farms spend about the same amount of time on housework and the private plot. Women spend considerably more time in these two activities. It is reasonable to estimate that women who live on state farms spend close to 60 hours a week doing housework and working on their private plot. During the 6 days accounted for in Table 8.10 this category comes to 48 hours. We know that on both collective farms and in urban areas Sunday is a day when women work

TABLE 8.10 *Time budget of sovkhoz family members, 1963, in hours and minutes*

Type of expenditure of time	Men			Women		
	Working day	Day before day off	Total for work week	Working day	Day before day off	Total for work week
Work time	7:05	6:44	42:09	4:32	5:05	27:45
Non-work time connected with work	0:57	0:44	5:29	0:36	0:43	3:43
Housework and the private plot	2:38	2:14	15:24	8:00	7:54	47:54
Satisfying physiological needs	9:18	9:49	56:19	8:38	8:45	51:55
Free time	3:31	3:59	21:34	1:52	1:14	10:34
Other expenditures of time	0:31	0:30	3:05	0:22	0:19	2:09
Total	24:00	24:00	144:00	24:00	24:00	144:00

SOURCE Artemov *et al.*, p. 65.

even longer. If we assume the same pattern holds for state farms then these women work about 60 hours a week outside the state sector. That implies about an 88 hour work week for women, which is almost the same as collective farm women. The difference between the two groups is the composition of work; collective farmers spend more time working for income than state farm women and the latter spend more time performing household labour. This must be so because of the smaller private plots and livestock holdings of state farms.[16]

Sovkhoz workers have more free time than collective farmers. This is particularly true of men. Again there is the problem in comparing the data of Table 8.10, which is only for 6 days, and the data of Table 8.7, which is for a 7 day work week. If we make a conservative estimate that state farmers have only 5 free hours on their day off, when these are added to 21 hours and 34 minutes for the work week they have about 27 free hours a week. This is 50 per cent more than the 18 hours of male collective farmers. If state farm women have 3 free hours on a Sunday (which is what collective farm women have), then their total weekly free time will be 13 hours and 34 minutes, or only about 2 hours more than collective farm women. In other words, working on a state farm under conditions of regulated work life makes a substantial difference in the leisure time available to men, but is of little apparent benefit to women, under the somewhat arbitrary assumptions we have made.

State farmers also have more time for eating and sleeping than do collective farmers. Collective farm men have 62 hours and 25 minutes available to themselves. If we assume the same hours on a Sunday as on Saturday for *sovkhoz* workers (9 hours and 49 minutes) their total time is 66 hours, or 3.5 hours more each week. If we assume Sunday is like Saturday for *sovkhoz* women then their 60 hours and 50 minutes for eating and sleeping is about 2.5 hours more than *kolkhoz* women. In sum, working on a *sovkhoz* rather than a *kolkhoz* has a higher payoff for men than for women in terms of shorter working hours, more free time, and time for eating and sleeping.

HOUSEWORK

While we have earlier provided an overview of how much time is devoted to housework, in this section we look at the issue in considerably greater detail and define the determinants of the hours spent on housework. Although estimates vary rather widely, the general conclusion is that collective farm women workers spend many more hours on housework than do urban women workers. Urban women do about 1080 hours of housework a year. Various studies provide a range for collective farm women from 1327 hours to 1976 hours a year. Thus, depending on the study, *kolkhoz* women do from 23 to 83 per cent more housework than urban women.[17]

The amount of housework women do is determined by a number of variables, including the availability of public services and appliances, marital status, the number and age of children and the husband's occupation. The relationship between marital status and hours of housework was measured in a 1963 Krasnoiarsk Krai study.[18] A defect of the study is the incompleteness of possible categories of family situations, particularly the absence of data on intact families with preschool children. There are data for only four groups of women. The least amount of housework was done by women without husbands and children, 16.5 hours a week. A single parent with children aged 6–11 years did 38.7 hours a week. The mother in a two parent household with 6–11 year old children spent 42.4 hours a week on housework, which was two hours more than the situation where there were children aged 12–15 years old. These data suggest that children add much more to the weekly burden of women's lives than does a husband. The presence of a husband added 3.7 hours to the woman's work week, whereas children add 22–26 hours a week to their responsibilities. The presence of young adolescent children decreases women's work by a couple of hours a week.

In a Belorussian study it was shown that the number of hours devoted to housework increased as the number of children in the family rose. This also held true for men. The data in Table 8.11 show that childless

TABLE 8.11 *Time spent on housework by collective farmers in Belorussia, by sex and number of children, hours per week, 1969*

Number of children	Hours of housework	
	Men	Women
0	13.3	19.6
1	18.9	25.2
2	21.0	26.6
3	21.7	28.0
4+	28.0	32.9

SOURCE V. N. Shkurko, *Problemy Formirovaniia Vsestoronne Razvitoi Lichnosti Kolkhoznika* (Minsk, 1971) p. 139.

women do the least amount of housework, about 20 hours a week, and that women's responsibilities increase until they do about 33 hours where there are 4 or more children. Ignoring the category of 4 or more children because of its indefiniteness, at the margin the presence of 1 child has the greatest impact on women (and men), adding almost 6 hours to the women's work. The third child adds the least amount to housework. It should be noted that, relative to earlier studies, there is a smaller difference in the hours devoted to housework by men and women in Belorussia.

The occupation of the husband has a substantial bearing on the degree to which women shoulder household responsibilities. According to a study done in three Moscow Oblast villages (see Table 8.12), in households where the husband is a manager or specialist, women do most of the housework in 72 per cent of the cases; men either do most of the housework or share the work equally with their wives in 23 per cent of the cases. This is in striking contrast to the experience of the wives of unskilled manual workers. In 59 per cent of the households the wife does most of the housework, while work is either divided equally or done mostly by men in 34 per cent of the households. Indeed, the pattern for the four groups of husbands is that the more skilled the husband and the higher his income, the more likely it is that women will do most of the housework and as a corollary, the less likely is it that help will be forthcoming from the husband.

The time women devote to different household tasks can be seen by looking back at the data in Table 8.8. Housework in the summer was 'only' 25.5 hours a week because women were putting in 62 hours a week

TABLE 8.12 *Distribution of housework by husband's occupation, Moscow Oblast, 1960s, in percentages*

Husband's occupation	Responsibilities distributed equally	Mostly men	Mostly women	Mostly grand-mothers	Mostly minor children under 16 years
Managers and specialists	18	5	72	5	—
Mechanics	23	7	67	3	—
White-collar workers	23	9	61	6	—
Unskilled manual workers	29	5	59	6	0.9

SOURCE Iu. V. Arutiunian, *Sotsial'naia Struktura Sel'skogo Naseleniia SSSR* (Moscow, 1971) p. 216.

working for income. In fact the only household task that was accorded a major commitment of time was cooking; women spent 16.4 hours a week preparing meals in the summer.

During the winter, when the amount of time in the socialist sector and private plot dropped to 27 hours a week, housework literally doubled to 50.5 hours a week. In the winter women spent about three times as much time cleaning the house, more than twice as much time doing laundry and about twice as much time taking care of their children as in summer. The amount of time spent preparing meals increased only slightly. There is a fairly substantial catch-all category of 'other kinds of housework' in which is located about a quarter of all the time for housework. Given the relatively underdeveloped level of mass produced clothing in the rural areas, a problem discussed below, it is likely that some of this unaccounted for time involves making clothing. It should also be noted that there is no category for daily shopping in studies of collective farms, although it exists in survey research involving urban areas. This may reflect the relative underdevelopment of a retail network in the villages. As a consequence farmers are heavily dependent upon the productivity of their private plots for many basic food items.

Work on collective farms, particularly housework, can be summarised as comprising a labour-intensive production process dominated by women and containing many of the features of the primitive production model where households are simultaneously units of both production and consumption. Frequently women express dissatisfaction because they are obliged to work especially hard in the peak season in both the socialist sector and the private plot, but then do not earn enough money in the winter because they lack a permanent job.[19]

It is clear at this point that the lives of Soviet farmers are much different than those of urban workers. As a result, the decisions households make about how they will divide their time between work and leisure is governed by a different set of factors than exists in cities. There are 5 reasons for the work-leisure trade-off that prevails in rural areas:

1. the relatively low income of collective farmers
2. the existence of the private plot
3. the impact of traditional values
4. the relative shortage of public provision of services
5. the inadequate supply of home appliances.

The well entrenched traditionalism of the countryside is reflected first by the attitudes of husbands towards the wife's role. A high proportion of men think their wives should 'stay at home and take care of the household and the children'. Even among men 30 years old and younger, 14 per cent thought this was correct. There was also agreement by 25 per cent of the men aged 31–35 years, 28 per cent of those 36–40 years, 42 per cent of men aged 41–50 years and 26 per cent among men 51–60 years old. These attitudes hold among women as well. In a survey of collective farm women, 28 per cent of the unskilled farmers said they would prefer not to be in the labour force, a goal shared by 17 per cent of the white-collar workers and 5 per cent of the specialists and managers.[20] Even if the concept of women 'staying at home' means just working on the private plot, women would still be substantial participants in agriculture, since they average about 15 hours a week work over the year in private agriculture.

The attitudes towards women working are difficult to interpret. Do women mean that they do not wish to work at all or do they mean that they do not want to work in the socialist sector? The fact that private plot agriculture is voluntary and the fact that it constitutes such an important part of the income of collective farm families suggests that a great many women do not want to work in the socialist sector. They would apparently prefer to concentrate their efforts on the more profitable private plot. Male attitudes represent a contradiction. Their responses may represent a conservative view, but the fact is that their wives are substantial contributors to family income and there is no evidence that female participation in agriculture, particularly on the private plot, is on the decline.

THE DEFICIENCY OF LABOUR-SAVING PUBLIC INSTITUTIONS AND PRIVATE APPLIANCES IN RURAL AREAS

In this section we show that a major cause of the enormous number of hours devoted to housework on collective farms is the inadequate supply of collectivised public institutions and household appliances. An analysis of urban–rural differences gives perspective to the problem of free time in rural areas. A 1969 study of the entire country found that state enterprises supplied 60–90 per cent of all urbanites with their clothing, while only 10–50 per cent of those living in villages had their clothing needs met by the state. Among urban blue-collar families 60 per cent of all children's clothing was made in the home, while in rural areas the comparable figure was 80 per cent. In urban areas 85 per cent of the households mend their children's clothing; in the villages 99 per cent of the families do it at home. The figures for shoe repair are: 20 per cent of urban households do their own while 60 per cent of the rural households do this work at home.

Villagers use private services much more than urbanites. While 20 per cent of blue-collar households in urban areas hire private parties to make and repair clothing and shoes, 60 per cent of rural families hire outside sources. The major reason is that state repair facilities are much more available in cities than in the countryside. The absence of laundry facilities in villages marks the largest discrepancy in the provisioning of public facilities between the two areas; public laundries are 10 times more likely to appear in urban areas. In general, the differences are so great that, with the exception of the Baltic republics, most services that rural people use are in cities.[21]

There is not only a difference between rural and urban areas, there is also a difference between Muslim and non-Muslim areas of the country. The data in Table 8.13 show striking differences between Tatar and Russian-speaking regions of the country. Urban areas offer more services than rural areas in both cases. The meaning of the Tatar-Russian differences is weakened because the data are 8 years apart. Nevertheless, it appears that unless service areas increased at a very rapid pace in Tatar areas, Russian areas had more services. There are two possible explanations for this. One is that Russians are more willing to use services than the more traditional Muslim Tatars. Another explanation is that the Russian-dominated party and government has favoured fellow Russians with more services than the minority Tatars.

We have seen that preparing meals is the dominant activity of

TABLE 8.13 *Amount of daily services in Tatar and Russian-speaking regions, by type of area, in roubles per capita*

	Tatar regions 1958	Russian regions 1966
Services of an industrial character		
City	5.6	10.2
Village	0.6	2.9
Services of a non-industrial character		
City	2.7	5.0
Village	0.2	0.9

SOURCE Iu. V. Arutiunian, *Sotsial'naia Struktura Sel'skogo Naseleniia SSSR* (Moscow, 1971) p. 166.

collective farm women. A Ukrainian study states that if rural women were to use semi-prepared foods (*domovaia kukhnia*), they would save 25 hours a month in shopping and cooking.[22] *Domovaia kukhnia* includes salads, roast beef, pies, cakes and cooked liver. A time consuming cooking activity that has apparently been replaced by state activity on many collective farms is the baking of bread.[23] Some limited data from the late 1960s suggest that on collective farms without a bakery, women spend 2–4 hours a week baking bread, in addition to the time they already spend preparing meals.[24]

Public catering facilities are a potential substitute for cooking at home. But the rural population does not eat out, for several reasons. No doubt travel time, a lack of restaurants and poor service affects their decision. It is also generally considered impractical to spend money in restaurants, and Muslims are afraid there will be pork in the dishes that restaurants serve. In those areas where Muslims are predominant, fewer public catering facilities are built.[25]

There is a consistent complaint about the lack of adequate child care facilities in the countryside.[26] The complaints are borne out by the fact that in 1967, only 8 per cent of all children up to the age of 7 years were in the nurseries (*iasli*) and kindergartens (*detskie sady*) in rural areas; in urban areas the comparable figure was 40 per cent.[27] The data in Table 8.14 show that a more rapid growth of preschool facilities took place in rural areas than in urban areas in the post-Stalin period. In spite of that, the supply of rural preschool facilities lags way behind those in urban areas. Thus in 1975 only 18 per cent of those eligible were enrolled in preschool programmes in rural areas.[28] In part the gap between urban and rural usage may reflect inadequate demand rather than a supply problem. An unspecified number of rural families do not want to use the facilities because they believe children receive inadequate care there. The staff, largely comprised of 'semiliterate old grannies', are untrained and

TABLE 8.14 *Number of children in preschool facilities, urban and rural areas, per 10 000 population*

	1928	1940	1953	1966
City	41	219	202	496
Village	1	40	42	138

SOURCE Iu. V. Arutiuinian, *Sotsial'naia Struktura Sel'skogo Naseleniia SSSR* (Moscow, 1971) p. 136.

have been accused of only caring about feeding the children and putting them down for their naps. It is claimed as of 1975 that of the 430 900 places recently made available for children in rural areas only 211 500 were regularly taken.[29]

In general there is a great deal of dissatisfaction with services in the countryside. One study of the Volgograd Oblast, which appears to have taken place in 1970, had an unusually high percentage of respondents who 'didn't know' whether they were satisfied with various services (see Table 8.15). Of those with definite views, opinions were always negative, sometimes overwhelmingly so. The negative attitude towards the preschool institutions is not as extreme, but the views towards the food supplied in the fields and other services are all overwhelmingly so. These attitudes are confirmed by a 1974 study done in several Belorussian Kolkhozy. Thirty per cent of the villagers said they were dissatisfied with everyday services. They complained about the lack of day care centres, public baths, laundries, the supply of firewood, the fact that there was no place to get a radio or television repaired, and no tailor's shop.[30] In many districts one shop is designed to serve 25–40 villages.[31] Because villages are often far apart, shops intended to serve many small collective farms serve few of them well.[32]

Rural areas are therefore characterised by a chronic deprivation of adequate collective goods and services. Until the 1970s the same could be said about the existence of privately owned household appliances. In recent years there have been definite increases in the supply of certain appliances. As of the early 1960s, in absolute terms, all RSFSR households were without appliances (Table 8.16). For example, only 1 family in 10 among industrial and construction workers had a washing machine; only 3–4 per cent of these same households had refrigerators. But relatively speaking, these households were twenty times better off than *kolkhozniki* in the case of washing machines. Refrigerators hardly even existed among collective farmers. On state farms, the white-collar workers (obviously the minority on these farms) were better off than industrial and construction workers. Only 3 per cent of the state farm labourers had washing machines, although this was six times more than collective farmers.

By the late 1960s, the ownership of appliances had increased on both collective and state farms. In general, state farmers had more household appliances than collective farmers. Moreover, in the case of both types of farms, field workers were considerably less well off than mechanics, white-collar workers or specialists and managers (Table 8.17). The data also reveal rather large differences in the ownership of appliances by

TABLE 8.15 *Proportion of collective farmers satisfied with enterprise services, Volgograd Oblast, circa 1970*

	Yes	No	Don't know
Children's preschool institutions	19.4	21.8	58.8
Central public catering*	32.3	58.4	9.3
Stores	16.5	42.3	41.2
Public baths	12.1	41.2	46.7
Daily services	9.1	40.9	50.0

* This is the food that farmers take to the fields.

SOURCE *Selo, Plan, Chelovek* (Volgograd, 1975) p. 146.

TABLE 8.16 *Number of electric appliances per 1000 families in the RSFSR, 1 June 1962*

	Industrial workers	Construction workers	Sovkhoz Manual workers	White-collar workers	Kolkhozniki
Refrigerators	2.9	4.4	—	8.1	0.03
Washing machines	10.1	10.0	2.9	18.5	0.5
Floor polishers	0.1	0.6	—	0.7	0.001
Vacuum cleaners	2.3	1.9	—	6.8	0.04

SOURCE Baikova *et al.*, p. 240.

TABLE 8.17 *Household appliances owned by the rural population by professional group, late 1960s, Kalinin oblast and Krasnodarsk krai, in percentages*

	Manual workers		Mechanics		White-collar workers		Middle level specialists and managers	
	Kolkhoz	Sovkhoz	Kolkhoz	Sovkhoz	Kolkhoz	Sovkhoz	Kolkhoz	Sovkhoz
Washing machines								
Kalinin	4	11	28	39	23	36	30	57
Krasnodarsk	30	33	42	36	47	31	61	41
Refrigerators								
Kalinin	1	1	4	—	—	9	—	4
Krasnodarsk	2	4	5	7	4	—	26	7
Sewing machines								
Kalinin	54	62	80	57	92	73	75	61
Krasnodarsk	67	65	76	73	79	69	74	70

SOURCE Arutiunian, p. 210.

geographic area, a pattern confirmed by data from the Volgograd Oblast for the early 1970s. The latter show that among all state farm families, 60.4 per cent own gas ranges, 32.5 per cent refrigerators, 78.1 per cent washing machines, 10.4 per cent vacuum cleaners, and 78.7 per cent sewing machines.[33] Data from other parts of the country indicate that washing machines were a commonplace on many collective farms by the mid-1970s.[34] However, it is less clear that gas ranges were so widespread. A 1967 Novgorod study reported that stoves were only just beginning to appear in homes.[35] What is suggested by the data is a mixed picture. Some appliances appear to be in plentiful supply while other remain in short supply. Similarly there appears to be an uneven geographical distribution of appliances.

LEISURE ACTIVITIES

The participation in leisure activities by the rural population is determined by several factors. Low income limits the demand for leisure activities. Until the 1970s the disparity between agricultural and non-agricultural incomes was so great that the income difference must be regarded as a major factor in determining demand. On the supply side the major factor is the provision of facilities; there is no doubt that in the past rural areas were supplied with fewer cultural and leisure facilities than urban areas. This is true to a lesser degree today. A third factor is the distinctly lower amount of free time available to farmers relative to urbanites. Not only is this true in general, but there still exists the extreme problem for certain collective farm workers of not getting any days off, especially livestock workers.[36] Finally, where the rural infrastructure is underdeveloped, cultural facilities are lacking. There cannot be a cinema without electricity and it is difficult to travel if the roads are primitive. In the Ukraine the improvement in the quality of the roads has been directly linked to an increase in the number of amateur societies, from 127 in 1960 to 280 in 1974.[37]

The size of a village affects the availability of cultural and service institutions. The smaller the village, the less likely is it to have access to such facilities. As one Soviet writer put it, the smaller the village, the 'thicker is the filter through which culture comes from the city'.[38] A good measure of the impact of village size is the presence of a club in the village. The club is the central point of leisure activity and cultural life in rural areas. It is a facility for film shows, concerts, dances and lectures, as well as housing the village library. In the late 1960s all of the 'large' villages of the Kalinin Oblast, Krasnodarsk Krai, and Tatar ASSR had clubs, but only 81 per cent of the 'small' villages in the Kalinin area had clubs, as did 85 per cent of the small villages in the other two areas.[39] In a more detailed study of the Tatar ASSR of the 1960s, 31 per cent of the villages with a population of up to 200 had a club, 75 per cent of those with a population of 201–500 and 100 per cent of those with a population of over 500 people.[40]

When a number of small villages make up a large collective farm it is highly unlikely that each village will have its own cultural or service facilities. If such a farm has a club, library and film projector, they will be located in the main village and all the peripheral villages will have nothing. Sometimes even economically well-off villages are without clubs.[41] This reflects the fact that the building of clubs and other cultural facilities has a low priority. For example, in 1962 only 11 per cent of the plan for the building of clubs on *kolkhozy* in the RSFSR was fulfilled.[42] From an individual village's perspective the demand for these facilities is much more likely to be met when a smaller number of large villages forms a collective farm.[43]

The attractiveness of programmes that clubs provide are crucial because villagers do not have the kinds of choices urbanites enjoy. If the club has scheduled a boring political lecture or film on Saturday night (as often happens), farmers do not have much in the way of alternatives.

Attendance at the clubs is indicative of their importance in village life. In a 1972 study of several villages in central Russia, 74.5 per cent said they go to the club not less than 2 or 3 times a month and 10 per cent go every day.[44] Similarly, in a nationwide study of rural youth (ages 15–30), 48 per cent went to clubs, the most important leisure activity after reading, watching television and listening to the radio.[45]

There are several criticisms levelled at the clubs. The first is that they are inadequately furnished with supplies. In 1967 in the Tatar ASSR, 53 per cent of the villages had clubs. But 61 per cent of the clubs were without a film projector and 71 per cent had no library. Only 6 per cent of the clubs had television sets and 19 per cent had tape recorders.[46] Complaints about supplies can be traced until at least the mid-1970s. For example, in the RSFSR in 1973, orders for library shelves were only 44 per cent filled.[47] In Belorussia it was found that farmers did not go to clubs because the facilities were inadequate.[48] In addition, the low salary offered to those who work in the clubs attracts people without a specialised education.[49] In Belorussia in 1969 there were almost no club administrators with some higher education and only 10 per cent even had a secondary school education. Ten per cent of all rural librarians lacked even a secondary school education.[50]

The main reason for the existence of fewer cultural and leisure options for farmers is the failure of the Soviet system adequately to provide the countryside with these kinds of goods and services. This can be argued on the basis of the data in Table 8.18 which shows the share of the household budget which goes for the purchase of cultural goods and services. (The data for 1953, 1958 and 1961 are from the same source and presumably reflect the same definition of cultural goods. The 1975 data are from a different source and might be based on a different definition since 'urbanites' is a more inclusive concept than 'industrial workers'.) The share of expenditures by industrial workers for this category is roughly twice as high for industrial workers and urbanites as it is for state farm workers. The latter group in turn spends twice as much as collective farmers. In part the difference between the three groups can be explained by general differences in incomes. However, during the period from 1958 to 1975 there was a significant narrowing of the gap between industrial worker incomes and farm incomes. Yet there has been a fairly constant relative difference between collective farm expenditures on cultural goods and industrial worker expenditures. It may be argued that the differential is due to an inadequate supply of such goods and services to rural areas. The much higher rate of savings on collective farms is consistent with the view. Thus, for example, in 1958, collective farmers saved 11 per cent of their income, whereas the savings rate among *sovkhoz* workers and industrial workers was 5.5 per cent and 3.8 per cent respectively. By 1961, when relative spending among all three groups had risen, the savings rate remained highest among collective farmers at 9.1 per cent, in contrast to 4.1 per cent and 2.4 per cent of the other two groups.[51]

The differences which have been shown to exist between rural and urban areas in the general decision on how to trade off work and leisure

TABLE 8.18 *Percentage of yearly expenditures by different groups on cultural goods and services*

Collective farmers				State farm workers			Industrial workers		Urbanites
1953	1958	1961	1975	1958	1961	1975	1958	1961	1975
1.5	2.2	2.6	3.1	5.4	6.4	6.4	11.7	12.3	10.7

SOURCES Arutiunian, p. 63; M. T. Iovchuk and A. S. Kulagin, 'Nekotorye Aktual'nye Problemy Razvitiia Sotsialisticheskoi Kul'tury na Sele', *Sotsiologicheskie Issledovaniia*, no. 40, pp. 8–36.

also appear when we examine daily leisure activities and holidays in the countryside.

RADIO, TELEVISION AND NEWSPAPERS

The mass media (radio, television, newspapers), play a significant role in the leisure time of Soviet villages. According to one study, rural men and women spend 70.6 per cent and 62.8 per cent respectively of their free time with the mass media. In the city the corresponding figures are 42.8 per cent and 40 per cent.[52]

Television is not as dominant a factor in rural life as it has been shown to be in urban life, but it is still significant. Two factors seem to have played the major role in restricting the presence of televisions: low incomes and the absence of electricity in many rural households. As a consequence, in rural areas during the mid-1960s, the number of television sets and radios per capita was about half of what it was in urban areas.[53] However, those who do own televisions share their good fortune with others. As recently as the mid-1970s, in both Siberian and Belorussian villages, every television set was watched by 5 to 8 and sometimes 10 viewers.[54] Indications are that television is watched with an intensity out of proportion to its presence in the villages. Thus in the Stavropol *krai*, 75 per cent of all the collective farmers watch television daily and another 9 per cent watch 3 to 4 times a week.[55] In another study of rural youth, 48 per cent said they watched television 'regularly' and 37 per cent watched 'from time to time'.[56]

As might be expected, the ownership of television sets varies quite substantially between different areas of the country. The data in Table 8.19 date from roughly the middle to late 1960s. Ownership ranged from a low of 27 per cent in Krasnodarsk Krai villages to a high of 50 per cent in one Novgorod collective farm. While the figure of 32 per cent applies only to people 15–30 years old, it is probably a good reflection of the situation for households in general. There is inadequate information to determine if state farms have more television sets. On the basis of the higher incomes of state farms and the better treatment they have received as recipients of funds from the general state budget, one would expect a higher degree of ownership of televisions. However, in the Krasnodarsk and Kalinin samples *sovkhozy* had about the same proportion of households owning televisions as the *kolkhozy*. The only other state farm data were for the Volgograd Oblast in about 1970, when 73.5 per cent of the state farm households had televisions.[57]

TABLE 8.19 *Percentages of collective farm households owning television sets*

Place	Year	Ownership (%)
Krasnodarsk Krai (1)	Mid-1960s	27.0
Several republics (2)	1967–71	32.0
Kalinin Oblast (1)	Mid-1960s	36.0
Novgorod Oblast (one collective farm) (3)	Circa 1966	50.0

SOURCES (1) Arutiunian, p. 175; (2) I. M. Slepenkov and B. V. Kniazev, *Molodezh' Sela Segodnia* (Moscow, 1972) pp. 52–3; (3) *Pravda*, 2 January 1967, p. 2.

The radio is of even greater importance to the life of the village than television. It is very often the sole source of information about politics, sport and the weather. Since newspaper delivery is still erratic in rural areas, people depend on the radio.[58] There are two types of radio technology present in Soviet villages: cable radio and wireless radio. Cable radio means that a cable runs from a local point of broadcasting to a household to carry the signal. The wireless system transmits signals through the air from a broadcasting point which could be a substantial distance from the house into which the signal is sent. The latter system is, of course, a much more sophisticated technology while the former is a relatively primitive form of broadcasting. Cable radio constricts the variety of programmes since only programmes which are locally produced can be received on a local radio. Cable radio still exists in many Soviet villages. For example, in Moldavian villages in the mid-1960s, there were twice as many cable radios as wireless radios per 100 persons. In contrast, there are one a half times as many wireless radios as cable radios in Moldavian cities.[59] In one Belorussian *kolkhoz* almost 100 per cent of the village households had a cable radio. The percentage of households owning radio was 65 per cent in the Krasnodarsk Krai and 59 per cent in the Kalinin Oblast.[60]

An extremely high percentage of villagers listen to radio. In a survey of several republics 82 per cent listened daily, 14 per cent from time to time and only 4 per cent did not listen to radio.[61] In the Stavropol' Krai study 70 per cent said they listened daily; 12 per cent 3–4 times a week; 8 per cent 1–2 times a week; 8 per cent 1–2 times a month and 8 per cent practically never listen.[62] In this area television was actually watched with slightly more frequency. A study distinguishing between small and large villages in three areas showed that the intensity of radio listening was roughly the same regardless of village size. In the Tatar ASSR about three-quarters of all villagers 'constantly' listen to the radio, as do two-thirds of all villagers in the Krasnodarsk Krai. Only in the Kalinin Oblast is there a difference. In small villages 61 per cent listen constantly and in large villages the comparable figure is 71 per cent.[63]

Access to both television and wireless radio is partly related to the professional group to which one belongs. In one study it was found that about one-third of the manual workers and white-collar non-specialists owned a wireless radio or television set. But 60 per cent of the specialists owned one or the other.[64] A second study asked what villagers did with their spare time. The percentage of each group watching television and listening to the radio can be regarded as indirect evidence of ownership. There is a direct correlation between the share of a group who use radio and television and their place on the professional scale. At one extreme in the Krasnodarsk Krai, 42 per cent of the 'management and high level specialists' group watched television and listened to the radio; at the other extreme only 17 per cent of the manual workers did so. The same relationship held in the Kalinin Oblast: 51 per cent of the farm's elite group and 24 per cent of the manual workers engaged in these two activities.[65] A Moldavian study from the early 1970s confirms this pattern.[66]

Newspapers are intensively read in the villages. In the early 1970s in collective farm families 70 per cent read a newspaper every day, 12 per cent 3–4 times a week and 7 per cent 1–2 times a week.[67] The most popular newspapers are the local paper, read by 90 per cent of the population, *Sel'skaia Zhizn'* (the USSR's chief agricultural newspaper), read by 65 per cent of the villagers and *Pravda*, which is read by 24 per cent. Newspaper popularity is confirmed by a 1969 survey of young people in rural areas, 72.7 per cent of whom said they read a newspaper every day, while 24.6 per cent said they read one from time to time. The 97 per cent of this group who say they read newspapers is up from a figure of 70.3 per cent in 1938.[68]

READING

As we saw earlier, Soviet urbanites are avid readers and the evidence indicates that although villagers do not read as much as city people, they still read a great deal. In the Voronezh *raion* the average collective farmer reads 23 books a year, or about 2 books a month.[69] Of course, we do not know if this is Tolstoy or a World War II pulp novel about a heroic Red Army spy stealing German codes. Among male state farm workers reading was almost as important as radio and television as a leisure activity. However, it was somewhat less important among women.[70] Among young collective farmers, reading ranked as the number one leisure activity. Seventy-one per cent listed reading as a leisure activity compared to 56 per cent who named radio and television as their second favourite activity.[71] In a 1965 study of collective farmers (Maruskai ASSR) reading ranked third behind visiting friends and doing nothing.[72]

Differences in the importance of reading in the leisure life of farmers can be attributed to five factors: the availability of bookstores, the age structure of the population, occupation, sex and access to libraries. There is an apparent lack of bookstores in the countryside. Collective farm bookstores in the RSFSR rural areas receive about 20 per cent of the books produced in the Russian republic. Rural bookstores tend to receive only a fraction of what they order. For these reasons villagers go to the city to buy books.[73]

A study in the Tatar ASSR examined reading habits by age and found that the older the group involved, the smaller was the proportion which 'constantly reads fiction'. Consistent with this finding, the proportion which 'does not read fiction' increases with age. For example, 54 per cent of those 18–22 years old said they are 'constant' readers compared with 6 per cent of those over 60 years. Only 14 per cent of the 18–22 year olds do not read fiction, compared with 61 per cent of the over 60 age group.[74]

Two different studies show substantial differences in reading habits for different occupations. For example, on the collective farms of two RSFSR *krais*, 62 per cent and 53 per cent of the management and high level specialists read during their free time, while only 23 per cent and 17 per cent of skilled manual workers do so.[75] In the study of rural youth, 76 per cent of the male specialists, 84 per cent of the female specialists and 69 per cent of the administrators read more than 10 books a year; this is true of only 49 per cent and 41 per cent of the unskilled male and female workers, respectively.[76] According to the data in Table 8.8, men read a good deal more than women; about 2 hours a week more in the summer and 5 hours a week in the winter. The large difference in hours of work between urban and rural women at least partially explains their different reading habits. In the cities women spend approximately 594 hours a year reading, collective farm women about 234 hours a year.[77] It should be noted that the latter figure is considerably more than the number of hours suggested by Table 8.8.

Public libraries are a major source of reading materials (books and magazines) for villagers but they have had a chequered career in Soviet rural areas. Table 8.20 indicates the cyclical waves of commitment to providing libraries. First, over the past 25 years rural areas have had one library for about every 1000 population and urban areas one library per 3000 population. The need for more libraries in rural areas is dictated by the lower concentrations of population. While there are many more libraries in the countryside (about 70–75 per cent of the total number), on the average their holdings are considerably smaller than urban libraries. In the past 25 years there appears to have been a change in the direction of resources directed toward rural libraries. In 1955, the average urban library had 4.1 times as many books as a rural library. A decade later the gap had declined to a ratio of 3:1. Thereafter, urban libraries grew more rapidly than rural libraries and by 1980, the ratio had climbed back to 4:1. In 1955 about half the books and magazines were in rural libraries; at present the figure is about 40 per cent. Partly, this is rational because the population in rural areas is a declining share of the total Soviet population. But given the fact that there must be so many more libraries to cover sparsely populated areas, there would need to be a good deal of duplication in all these small libraries to provide the same composition of holdings as there are in urban libraries. The declining share of rural libraries in the total collections therefore suggests a less rich offering of books and magazines.

Two problems exist in rural libraries that appear to be peculiar to their location. The first is that libraries are distant from each other, usually about 7 miles apart. The severity of winters and the inadequacy (or absence) of roads sometimes makes this distance prohibitive.[78] The second problem is the absence of professional training of rural librarians. For example, in Kirgizia, where there are about 1220 libraries, only 58 rural librarians have a higher or middle special education. Librarians with real professional training are almost impossible to keep because rural income is so low and day to day living is so difficult.[79]

The growth of the role of libraries as a cultural and leisure vehicle for farmers is reflected in the data for the village of Kopanka which was first studied in 1937 and then again in 1963. In 1937 the number of books taken out annually per person was 1.1; in 1963 the number had risen to 15.

TABLE 8.20 Public libraries in Soviet rural areas

Year	Number of libraries in rural areas (thousands)	Number of books and magazines in rural libraries (millions)	Number of rural libraries as percentage of total in the USSR	Number of books and magazines per library (thousands)		Number of books and magazines in rural libraries as percentage of total in USSR
				Urban	Rural	
1945	37.9	31.1	80.0	8211	820	28.5
1955	119.6	301.9	81.1	10392	2524	51.1
1960	100.4	413.2	74.0	13312	4116	48.9
1965	90.1	487.2	70.9	16500	5407	46.3
1970	90.7	588.2	70.9	20786	6485	45.0
1975	95.3	673.6	72.5	25878	7068	41.9
1980	96.1	744.0	72.8	35077	7742	40.8

SOURCES *Narkhoz* (1972) p. 657; (1980) p. 473.

HOLIDAYS

Holiday time is used differently by farmers than it is by urbanites. Not only do relatively more city people actually take leave, but in increasing numbers they are using this time to get away from home. This is not true of farmers. In a study of state farm workers from the early 1970s, a quarter of the men and women said they had not taken a holiday in the previous year.[80] As Table 8.21 shows, about three-quarters of both sexes did not leave the farm. The categories are somewhat confusing because the distinction between 'staying at home' and work on the private plot and the house really disappear and they all amount to a decision not to go away on holiday. Men were almost twice as likely to get away as women. The same stay-at-home syndrome prevails among collective farmers. In a West Siberian study 60 per cent of the collective farmers spent their leave at home, and 20 per cent of them worked on their private plot.[81] On one of the collective farms in the Stavropol' Krai about 10 per cent of the collective farmers have the opportunity of going to a sanatorium for their holiday. The farm pays the total fee for 30 passes to sanatoriums. In a survey of 4000 collective farmers about 2.5 per cent went abroad.[82]

There are intercollective farm sanatoriums built co-operatively by several collective farms exclusively for collective farmers. In 1973, about 120 large sanatoriums had been built exclusively for farmers. However, it is relatively difficult for farmers to get passes to sanatoriums even if they have all the proper medical certification. The sanatoriums, which are presumably only for collective farmers from a certain region, are often occupied by individuals who are neither from that region nor are collective farmers. The reason for this problem is that the sanatorium

TABLE 8.21 *How state farm workers and employees spent their holiday, Volgograd Oblast, circa 1976, in percentages*

	Men	Women
In a sanatorium or resort	5.3	3.9
In a house of rest	9.4	5.5
Either building or repairing their own home or facilities in the yard	6.4	3.1
Working on the private plot	6.4	12.9
Stayed at home	63.4	62.2
Other	9.1	12.9

SOURCE   *Selo, Plan, Chelovek* (Volgograd, 1975) p. 148.

management trades passes for things they need for their institution, such as furniture. Sanatoriums for collective farmers are not included in the state budget. They depend on the generosity of a variety of agencies such as the local party committee, the local soviet, and sometimes the Ministry of Agriculture. The *quid pro quo* often includes trading passes for materials.[83]

SATISFACTION WITH LEISURE ACTIVITIES

Not surprisingly, there is a good deal of dissatisfaction with the leisure and cultural activities available in rural areas. Unfortunately, there are no longitudinal studies among the same population or area to give a sense of whether these activities are viewed as having improved. The issue is of importance because it relates to the inability of Soviet planners to stem the outflow of people from the villages, especially young people. In a 1972 study in central Russian villages, it was found that 20 per cent wanted to leave. Thirty-five per cent said it was difficult or impossible to continue either their own or their children's education, 35 per cent said there were not enough services and 22 per cent said they could not get their cultural needs met.[84] In a large study of people under the age of 30, the issue of leisure activities loomed large. Fifty-six per cent thought they saw the underdeveloped nature of cultural and leisure activities as the main problem of rural life. They complained about the lack of clubs and sports facilities and the unsatisfactory way in which existing clubs and houses of culture functioned.[85] In a Siberian study, much less dissatisfaction was expressed by collective farmers. Only 22 per cent said they were 'unsatisfied', 30 per cent said they were 'somewhat satisfied' and 49 per cent said they were 'satisfied'.[86]

The Tatar ASSR study which we cited earlier presents a comparison of Tatar and Russian views by village size. The larger the size of the village, the higher the percentage of people who are satisfied with cultural institutions (cinemas, clubs, libraries). While the same pattern prevailed in evaluating 'daily cultural conditions in the village as a whole' they received low marks. Russians gave a lower evaluation to cultural availabilities than Tatars.[87] This suggests that Russians have a higher expectation level, perhaps because they are more urban-oriented.

WHAT IS THE GOOD LIFE?

If farmers are unhappy with their current lot in the village what would make them happy? In a Moscow Oblast study villagers were asked:

'What do you think the good life is?' Of the 11 choices, the most frequently mentioned had to do with having interesting work, having a happy family life and having material security. Meaningful work was of highest importance to the management and high level specialists while income was the most important to manual workers.[88] When collective farmers were asked how many suits they would like to have the majority (undefined) said they wanted 2 or 3 suits. When asked what they wanted to buy in the store their preferences, in order, were: car, motorcycle, television set, refrigerator, good furniture, and washing machine.[89]

The desired market basket of goods reflects rising expectations in the countryside, not dissimilar to those of rural people everywhere. Such expectations have long been manifested in the migration of villagers to the cities. The demand for leisure is not only a function of rising collective farm incomes, but is determined by an urban demonstration effect. About two-thirds of the rural population has 'constant' contact with the urban population.[90] This contact has been made possible by improved transportation networks between cities and villages. In the 1970s collective farm families averaged about 2 trips a month to the nearest city. In places where train and bus routes connect rural and urban areas some people make 10–15 trips a month to a city.[91]

How can the conflict between public and private decision-making in rural areas be best summed up? The two most glaring features are the documented shortcomings of leisure goods and services and the short shrift received by women. Beyond these, it can be said that there is much more communal consumption of leisure in the country than in cities. For example, people routinely watch television at someone else's house. The centrality of the club's role collectivises leisure. Table 8.22 lists the main

TABLE 8.22 *Collective forms of leisure in the village, 1967–71, several republics, in percentages*

	Go regularly	Go occasionally	Do not go at all
Harvest festivals	65	15	10
Lectures, debates	28	39	17
Parties	23	36	32
Unpaid work on Sunday (*voskresniki*)	21	54	24
Sporting events	20	27	31
Meeting with famous people	19	40	34

SOURCE I. M. Slepenkov and B. V. Kniazev, *Molodezh' Sela Segodnia* (Moscow, 1972) p. 162.

collective leisure activities in village life (the numbers do not add up to 100 per cent for unexplained reasons). Overall, the data indicate that collective leisure is very important in the village. This is particularly true of the harvest festivals, although it also applies to other activities. However, it seems somewhat perverse to list unpaid Sunday work (*voskresnik*) as a leisure activity. It is more typically an obligation during rush periods or a type of *subbotnik* to honour Lenin. The meetings with famous people relates to well-known actors, painters, journalists, etc., who go to villages to give a reading and socialise with the local residents.

More importantly, the evidence is conclusive that the range of choices is much more limited in the countryside than in urban areas. The opportunity cost of additional work in rural areas is less than in the city because of the relative deprivation farmers experience in leisure facilities.

While it may be a cynical thing to suggest, the persistence of the private plot implies something about Soviet policy makers' world view. The ideological contradiction inherent in the private plot is accepted by the Party for a number of reasons. The main reason is that the private plot is an important contributor to agricultural output, particularly for many non-grain products. The income that farmers earn provides a strong incentive to stay in agriculture. In the absence of the private plot, probably many more would leave the farms, Soviet agriculture would be in even greater difficulty and the queues outside the Soviet food stores would be even longer. We may therefore consider the private plot partially as a labour market policy designed to increase the food supply and keep urban citizens tolerant of their meagre food stocks.

Conclusion

A summary perspective on the issue of the conflict between public and private decision-making where there is a shortage of labour in a planned economy is confounded by a number of considerations. There are really two broad perspectives which must be taken into account in evaluating what has happened in the Soviet Union historically and what is likely to happen in the future. One view of the problem comes at the level of the household where individual decisions are made. The other view of the problem focuses on the Party, where both short-term and long-term decisions are made.

Soviet citizens are acquisitive. Whatever else the data may reveal, at bottom, there is the desire for more: more income, more leisure, more time, more consumer goods, and so on. Thus an understanding of household behaviour proceeds from the view that there are really several goals which are held by households. There is a way in which these goals conflict. The goal of maximising income conflicts with the goal of maximising leisure. But the answer to a complex question (what are Soviet citizens trying to maximise?), does not call forth a simplistic answer. In fact we are witness to conflicting data.

On the one hand, we have good evidence that Soviet citizens, when faced with more time, as in the case of the onset of the 5 day work week, have chosen leisure, not market work. To some extent, of course, the nature of the Soviet labour market does not make it easy for people to make a choice between work and leisure. The absence of a large private sector in which workers can legally work places some constraints on individual mobility between work and leisure. We know there is a large substantial second economy and, outside the collective farm market where farmers can legally sell output they have produced on their private plots, most of the economic activity is either illegal or quasi-legal. Thus what is not reported as market activity may reflect the underground nature of work.

This decision is different for urban and rural households. The existence of the private plot creates the major difference between the two sectors. Farmers have a built-in potential for more income, and this does not exist in the cities. It is interesting to note the growth of collective gardens among urban workers, and their popularity cannot simply be chalked up to the leisure they offer. The garden contributes in-kind and cash income to urbanites and I suspect that their growth reflects a joint maximisation of work and leisure.

The desire for part-time work by women also suggests that we cannot always understand household behaviour as an attempt to maximise income. On the contrary, women want part-time work so they can meet the dual roles of worker and mother. In this case they are trying to find the optimal trade-off between market work, home work and leisure. This is an excellent example of the conflict between the goals of the household and the goals of the Party. The latter wants to maximise economic growth. This requires the largest possible labour input, which in turn requires that as many people as possible work full-time. It is a zero sum game for economic planners; gains to individuals are losses to the state. Since the planners are in charge, they minimise access to voluntary part-time work.

The data on overtime and seasonal employment are limited but they also suggest the dual perspective on work and leisure. For the individual, overtime employment is both a blessing and a curse. For certain groups of workers overtime employment provides additional income or compensatory time off. But for many, the compulsory nature of overtime and the inconvenience it imposes is not justified by any additional benefits. Overtime employment is, however, consistent with the goals of economic planners who want to maximise output. This creates a potential conflict between the household and the system. Seasonal employment is a bit different because there is more than a measure of voluntarism involved. Rural construction projects are very attractive sources of income because wages are well above those paid by the state. It is not clear, however, how many people are engaged in this activity. There is also a mixture of those who leave their regular job to do this kind of work and others who use their leisure time to moonlight on construction crews in the countryside. Some of these construction brigades are manned by collective farmers who either go to work in the off-season or leave the farm during the busy season to seek their fortunes in temporary construction work.

The trade-off between work and leisure is confused by the ambiguous policies of Soviet decision makers. At the most basic level more leisure has been made possible by simple virtue of the decrease in the work week, which is itself a policy decision. But there is a strong argument for saying that there has not been a concomitant increase in the production of leisure facilities. There are at least two views that can be taken of this phenomenon. One is to argue that there is inadequate household demand for leisure goods in the Soviet Union. But evidence shows quite the opposite. The rising cost of holidays in the private sector testify to the strength of demand. In addition, the accumulation of evidence about complaints over shortages in the provision of recreation facilities supports this notion. There is also systematic empirical evidence that people in both the rural and urban sectors of the economy are dissatisfied with the quantity and quality of leisure time.

Thus, we are left with the explanation that economic policy makers have not produced enough goods to meet the demand generated by increased incomes and changing tastes and preferences. The most likely explanation is that the leisure time of Soviet citizens is of low priority when it comes to dispensing resources in the Soviet economy. There is something of an inconsistency here because, in principle, Soviet planners prefer to have people consuming state produced recreation, rather than having them demand goods in the private sector. In point of fact, on both a day to day basis and with respect to annual leave, leisure is privately consumed. A more cynical view would suggest that the shortage of leisure is designed to lower the opportunity cost of additional work. After all, if there is not enough to enjoy when one is free from work, then perhaps people will be willing to work more. But there is a hitch. The economy must produce enough consumer goods to make it worthwhile to earn additional income. The decline in the growth of per capita consumption that was experienced in the 1970s and the likelihood that the growth of consumption may decline even more is a clear disincentive for households to consider additional work.

We return to the fundamental issue of policy makers having to deal with the dilemma of increasing the amount of labour in the economy at the same time that they try to honour the desire of citizens for both more income and more leisure. At the moment, there does not appear to be a solution. The state of suspended animation in which the issue now resides can perhaps be understood with a Soviet joke: Stalin, Khrushchev and Brezhnev are riding on a train which suddenly comes to a standstill. Stalin summons the engineer and orders him to move the train. He fails and Stalin has half the crew shot. Stalin leaves the scene and Khrushchev inherits the immobile train. Khrushchev orders the remaining railroad workers rehabilitated. Still the train does not move. Khrushchev is replaced and Brezhnev comes to power. He immediately and authoritatively issues an order: 'Pull the curtains and we'll make believe the train is moving.'

At the moment the train is still frozen in place.

Endnotes

INTRODUCTION

1. G. A. Prudenskii, *Problemy Rabochego i Vnerabochego Vremeni* (Moscow, 1972) p. 237.
2. G. S. Petrosian, *Vnerabochee Vremia Trudiashchikhsia v SSSR* (Moscow, 1965) pp. 94–5.
3. *Pravda*, 26 March 1972, p. 3, translated in *Current Digest of the Soviet Press*, (hereafter trans. in *CD*), vol. xxiv, no. 12, p. 28.
4. G. E. Zborovskii and G. P. Orlov, *Dosugi Deistvitel'nost' i Illuzii* (Sverdolvsk, 1970) p. 102.
5. *Izvestia*, 16 December 1973, p. 5, trans. in *CD*, vol. xxiv, no. 50, p. 17.
6. *Komsomolskaia Pravda*, 27 March 1963, p. 2, trans. in *CD*, vol. xv, no. 15, p. 22.
7. *Literaturnaia Gazeta*, 27 March 1968, p. 12.
8. *Izvestia*, 16 December 1973.
9. Cited in A. V. Netsenko, *Sotsial'no-Ekonomicheskie Problemy Svobodnogo Vremeni Pri Sotsializme* (Leningrad, 1975) p. 43.
10. L. A. Aza et al., *Tsennostnye Orientatsii Rabochei Molodezhi* (Kiev, 1978) pp. 153 and 158.

1 HOUSEHOLD TIME BUDGETS

1. V. A. Artemov et al., *Statistika Biudzhetov Vremeni Trudiashchikhsia* (Moscow, 1967) pp. 7–14.
2. G. S. Petrosian, *Vnerabochee Vremia Trudiashchikhsia v SSSR* (Moscow, 1965) p. 21.
3. Artemov et al., p. 49.
4. S. Vainshtein and Iu. Evreinov, 'Puti Razvitiia Tipovykh Zhilykh i Obshchestvennykh Zdanii', *Problemy Byta, Braka i Sem'i* (Vilnius, 1970) p. 71.
5. V. G. Kriazhev, *Vnerabochee Vremia i Sfera Obsluzhivaniia* (Moscow, 1966) p. 99.
6. *Ekonomicheskaia Gazeta*, no. 17 (April 1967) p. 12, trans. in *CD*, vol. xix, no. 20, pp. 11–13.
7. V. B. Mikhailok, *Ispol'zovanie Zhenskogo Truda v Narodnom Khoziaistve* (Moscow, 1970) p. 124.
8. Kriazhev, p. 106.
9. Petrosian, p. 109.

10. Ibid.
11. Mikhailok, p. 125.
12. B. T. Kolpakova and V. D. Patrusheva (eds), *Biudzhet Vremeni Gorodskogo Naseleniia* (Moscow, 1971) p. 211.
13. E. Z. Danilova, *Sotsial'nye Problemy Truda Zhenshchiny-Rabotnitsy* (Moscow, 1968) p. 56.
14. M. I. Zvarskii, *Sotsial'no-Ekonomicheskie Problemy Rabochego Dnia Pri Sotsializme* (Moscow, 1976) pp. 203–4.
15. *Ekonomika i Organizatsia Promyshlennogo Proizvodstva*, no. 3, 1978, pp. 5–18, trans. in *CD*, vol. xxx, no. 30, pp. 3–4.
16. I. I. Tsofnas and N. F. Kornienko, 'Struktura i Osobennosti Ispol'zovaniia Svobodnogo Vremeni Stroitelei', *Tezisy Dokladov: Nauchno Prakticheskoi Konferentsii "Vnerabochee Vremia i Sotsial'noe Planirovanie"* (Sverdlovsk, 1975) p. 146.
17. *Pravda*, 26 March 1972, p. 3, trans. in *CD*, vol. xxiv, no. 12, p. 28.
18. *Zhurnalist*, (January 1977) pp. 54–6, trans. in *CD*, vol. xxix, no. 8, p. 14.
19. G. P. Chufarova, 'Osnovnye Napravleniia Vzaimovliianiia Rabochego i Svobodnogo Vremeni v Sovremennyi Period', *Tezisy Dokladov*, p. 48.
20. *Izvestia*, 22 April 1966, p. 4, trans. in *CD*, vol. xviii, no. 16, p. 46; *Ekonomika i Organizatsiia Promyshlennogo Proizvodstva*, pp. 5–18.
21. *Trud*, 18 June 1966, p. 1, trans. in *CD*, vol. xviii, no. 24, p. 26.
22. Artemov *et al.*, p. 30.
23. *Ekonomicheskaia Gazeta*, no. 17, pp. 6–7, trans. in *CD*, vol. xix, no. 20, p. 12.
24. *Trud*, 27 April 1965, p. 2, trans. in *CD*, vol. xvii, no. 19, p. 31.
25. Artemov *et al.*, p. 30.
26. A. I. Ivan'kov, 'Biudzhet Vremeni Trudiashchikhsia i Plan Sotsial'nogo Razvitiia Predpriiatiia', *Sotsial'nye Problemy Novykh Gorodov Vostochnoi Sibiri*, vol. 2 (Irkutsk, 1974) p. 87.
27. G. T. Zhuravlev, 'Svobodnoe Vremia i Kul'turnaia Zhizn' Rabotnikov Promyshlennogo Predpriiatiia', G. V. Osipov and Ia. Shchepan'skii, (eds), *Sotsial'nye Problemy Truda i Proizvodstva* (Moscow, 1969) p. 372.
28. Kolpakova and Patrusheva, pp. 110 and 112.
29. Ibid., p. 113.
30. V. G. Baikova *et al.*, *Svobodnoe Vremia i Vsetoronee Razvitie Leihnosti*, p. 55.

2 NON-TRADITIONAL SOURCES OF LABOUR: WOMEN, PENSIONERS AND STUDENTS

1. 'O Metodicheskikh Rekomendatsiiakh po Izucheniiu Istochnikov i Vozmozhnostei Privlecheniia Naseleniia na Rabotu s Nepolnym Rabochim Vremenem', *Normativnie Akty po Ispol'zovaniiu Trudovykh Resursov* (Moscow, 1972) p. 578.
2. A. I. Protsevsky, *Rabochee Vremia i Rabochii Den' po Sovetskomu Trudovomu Pravu* (Moscow, 1963) pp. 111 and 125; *Trud*, 19 May 1976, p. 4.
3. *Trud*, 30 May 1974, p. 4.

4. 'O Metodicheskikh etc.', p. 579.
5. L. Ya. Gintsburg, *Regulirovanie Rabochego Vremeni v SSSR* (Moscow, 1966) p. 298.
6. Ibid., p. 299.
7. *Sovetskoe Gosudarstvo i Pravo* (October 1970) pp. 54–61, trans. in *CD*, vol. xxvii, no. 45, p. 22.
8. *Literaturnaia Gazeta*, 15 March 1972, p. 10.
9. Gintsburg, p. 300.
10. Ibid.
11. 'O Metodicheskikh, etc.', p. 578.
12. T. Skal'berg, E. Martirosian and L. Kuleshova, 'Rabota s Nepolnym Rabochim Dnem Vazhnoe Sredstvo Privlecheniia Trudovykh Resursov', *Sotsialisticheskii Trud*, no. 2 (1977) p. 103.
13. Gintsburg, p. 302.
14. Skal'berg *et al.*, p. 105.
15. *Izvestia*, 13 April 1972, p. 5, trans. in *CD*, vol. xxiv, no. 15, pp. 19–20.
16. *Sovetskoe Gosudarstvo i Pravo*, p. 22.
17. Skal'berg *et al.*, pp. 103–9.
18. I. Golubeva and L. Kuleshova, 'Ispol'zovanie Rezhimov Nepolnogo Rabochego Vremeni i Optimizatsiia Uchastiia Zhenshchin v Proizvodstve', *Sotsialisticheskii Trud*, no. 4 (1978) p. 106; Skal'berg *et al.*, p. 105.
19. *Employment and Training Report of the President*, 1978, p. 85.
20. Skal'berg *et al.*, p. 108.
21. A. E. Kotliar and S. Ya. Turchaninova, *Zaniatost' Zhenshchin v Proizvodstve* (Moscow, 1975) p. 102.
22. Skal'berg *et al.*, p. 105.
23. *Narodnoe Khoziaistvo SSSR v 1975*, p. 543. For example, they are 68 per cent of the labour force in communications, 75 per cent in trade and public catering and 85 per cent in the health area.
24. Z. M. Yuk, *Trud Zhenshchiny i Sem'ia* (Minsk, 1975) p. 123.
25. *Izvestia*, 13 April 1972, p. 19.
26. *Izvestia*, 25 December 1972.
27. 'O Metodicheskikh etc.', p. 579.
28. Kotliar and Turchaninova, p. 101.
29. *Izvestia*, 13 April 1972, p. 19; Skal'berg *et al.*, p. 106.
30. Golubeva and Kuleshova, p. 110.
31. *Izvestia*, 25 December 1972, p. 2, trans. in *CD*, vol. xxiii, no. 52, p. 21.
32. *Sovetskoe Gosudarstvo i Pravo*, p. 22.
33. Golubeva and Kuleshova, p. 107.
34. *Ekonomika i Organizatsiia Promyshlennogo Proizvodstva* (May–June 1978) pp. 57–64, trans. in *CD*, vol. xxx, no. 31, p. 9.
35. Skal'berg *et al.*, p. 107.
36. *Sovetskoe Gosudarstvo i Pravo*, p. 22.
37. Z. A. Iankova, *Gorodskaia Sem'a* (Moscow, 1979) pp. 50–51; A. G. Kharchev and S. I. Golod, *Professional'naia Rabota Zhenshchin i Sem'ia* (Leningrad, 1971) p. 42.
38. A. Novitsky and M. Babkina, 'Part-time Work and Employment', *Problems of Economics*, vol. xvi, no. 9, (January 1974), p. 45.

39. Kotliar and Turchaninova, p. 99.
40. Golubeva and Kuleshova, p. 106.
41. For example, see *Pravda*, 31 January 1975, p. 3, trans. in *CD*, vol. xxvii, no. 5, pp. 23–4.
42. Golubeva and Kuleshova, p. 107.
43. *Nedelia*, 8–14 August 1977, p. 11, trans. in *CD*, vol. xxix, no. 32, pp. 5–6.
44. Skal'berg *et al.*, p. 105.
45. Novitsky and Babkina, p. 45; Kotliar and Turchaninova, p. 99; Golubeva and Kuleshova, p. 106.
46. Twelve per cent of Hungarian working women work part-time. *Literaturnaia Gazeta*, 16 May 1979, p. 13.
47. Kotliar and Turchaninova, p. 98.
48. N. Shishkan, 'The Participation of Women in Social Production', *Problems of Economics*, vol. xx, no. 3 (July 1977) p. 29.
49. Kotliar and Turchaninova, p. 99.
50. Ibid.
51. L. Anikeeva and L. Shokhina, *'Zhenshchiny s Det'mi i Nadomnyi Trud'*, *Zhenshchiniy na Rabote i Doma* (Moscow, 1978) p. 49.
52. Golubeva and Kuleshova, p. 106.
53. Ibid.
54. Golubeva and Kuleshova, pp. 107–8.
55. N. V. Panova, 'Voprosy Truda i Byta Zhenshchin', *Problemy Byta, Braka i Sem'i* (Vilnius, 1970) p. 91.
56. Ibid.
57. *Nedelia*, p. 5.
58. Anikeeva and Shokhina, p. 47.
59. Ibid., pp. 53–4.
60. Ibid., p. 53.
61. Gintsburg, p. 300.
62. Anikeeva and Shokhina, p. 53.
63. Golubeva and Kuleshova, p. 106.
64. Kotliar and Turchaninova, p. 102.
65. *Literaturnaia Gazeta*, 16 May 1979, p. 13.
66. *Literaturnaia Gazeta*, 24 October 1979, p. 10.
67. *Literaturnaia Gazeta*, 16 May 1979, p. 13.
68. Anikeeva and Shokhina, p. 53.
69. *Literaturnaia Gazeta*, 16 May 1979, p. 13.
70. Ibid.
71. *Literaturnaia Gazeta*, 24 October 1979, p. 10.
72. Ibid.
73. *Literaturnaia Gazeta*, 16 May 1979, p. 13.
74. *Literaturnaia Gazeta*, 19 December 1979, p. 10.
75. A. A. Kartskhiia, *Pensionnoe Obespechenie Po Starosti* (Moscow, 1978) pp. 6–9.
76. Murray Feshbach and Stephen Rapawy, 'Soviet Population and Manpower Trends and Policies', *Soviet Economy in a New Perspective* (Joint Economic Committee, 14 October 1976) p. 115.
77. *Izvestia*, 6 January 1976, p. 5, trans. in *CD*, vol. xxvii, no. 1, p. 18.
78. Lantsev, p. 133.

79. Kogan, p. 84.
80. M. S. Lantsev, *Sotsial'noe Obespechenie v SSSR* (Moscow, 1976) pp. 127–40, unless otherwise indicated.
81. *Pravda* and *Izvestia*, 6 March 1964, p. 1, trans. in *CD*, vol. xvi, no. 10, p. 29.
82. Novitsky and Babkina, p. 43.
83. *Izvestia*, 26 July 1977, p. 2, trans. in *CD*, vol. xxix, no. 3, p. 16.
84. *Izvestia*, 25 December 1971.
85. *Nedelia*, 9–15 April 1979, p. 11, trans. in *CD*, vol. xxxi, no. 21, p. 10; V. Kogan, 'Pozhilye Liudi na Rabote', *Zdorov'e Pozhilykh Liudei* (Moscow, 1978) p. 87.
86. Novitsky and Babkina, p. 42.
87. S. Smirnov, 'The Employment of Old-Age Pensioners in the USSR', *International Labour Review*, vol. 116, no. 1 (July–August, 1977) p. 89.
88. Novitsky and Babkina, pp. 42–3.
89. Lantsev, p. 140.
90. Lantsev, p. 134.
91. *Izvestia*, 26 July 1977, p. 2.
92. *Izvestia*, 18 April 1973, p. 3, trans. in *CD*, vol. xxv, no. 16, pp. 22–3.
93. Ibid.
94. *Izvestia*, 14 June 1977, p. 5, trans. in *CD*, vol. xxix, no. 37, p. 4; Novitsky and Babkina, pp. 47–8.
95. *Izvestia*, 18 April 1973, p. 3.
96. Kogan, p. 85.
97. *Literaturnaia Gazeta*, 13 September 1972, p. 12, trans. in *CD*, vol. xxv, no. 1, p. 15.
98. Smirnov, p. 89.
99. *Izvestia*, 26 July 1977, p. 2.
100. Novitsky and Babkina, p. 47.
101. *Izvestia*, 26 July 1977, p. 2.
102. Lantsev, p. 134.
103. Kogan, p. 89.
104. Ibid., p. 88.
105. *Izvestia*, 5 April 1964, p. 5, trans. in *CD*, vol. xvi, no. 14, pp. 29–30.
106. *Nedelia*, no. 15, 9–15 April 1979.
107. Smirnov, p. 90.
108. The discussion of the 1964 law is drawn from *Pravda*, 16 July 1964, pp. 1–2, and *Izvestia*, 16 July 1964, p. 2, trans. in *CD*, vol. xvi, no. 29, pp. 23–5.
109. A. A. Kartskhiia, *Pensionnoe Obespechenie po Starosti* (Moscow, 1978) p. 13.
110. Women collective farmers who have given birth to 5 or more children and reared each to 8 years of age can retire at age 55 if they have worked a minimum of 15 years.
111. Kartskhiia, p. 35.
112. Ibid., pp. 66–121.
113. Ibid., p. 105.
114. Ibid., p. 95.
115. *Izvestia*, 31 May 1977, p. 2, trans. in *CD*, vol. xxix, no. 22, p. 26; *Izvestia*, 3

August 1977, trans. in *CD*, vol. xxix, no. 31, p. 21.
116. *Literaturnaia Gazeta*, 7 August 1968, p. 12.
117. *Literaturnaia Gazeta*, 19 November 1969, p. 10.
118. Ibid.
119. *Izvestia*, 14 June 1977, p. 5.
120. *Izvestia*, 18 April 1973, p. 3.
121. *Izvestia*, 31 October 1973, p. 5, trans. in *CD*, vol. xxv, no. 44, p. 19.
122. A. Ia Semenchenko *et al.*, *Tretii Semestr* (Moscow, 1975) pp. 172–3.
123. *Izvestia*, 31 October 1973, p. 5; Semechenko, p. 9.
124. Semenchenko, p. 27.
125. L. Sbytova, 'Sources of Labour Power Under Current Conditions' *Voprosy Ekonomiki*, 1978, no. 6, pp. 33–43, trans. in *Problems of Economics* (May 1979) vol. xxii, no. 1, p. 33.
126. *Izvestia*, 31 October 1973, p. 5.
127. Ibid.
128. Sbytova, p. 33.
129. *Trud*, 24 June 1972, p. 1.
130. Semenchenko *et al.*, p. 8.
131. Ibid., pp. 61 and 119.
132. Ibid., p. 121.
133. *Literaturnaia Gazeta*, 30 June 1966, p. 2.
134. *Pravda*, 16 October 1979, p. 3, trans. in *CD*, vol. xxxi, no. 42, p. 17.
135. *Narodnoe Khoziaistvo SSSR v 1980g*, p. 462.
136. *Literaturnaia Gazeta*, 30 August 1978, p. 12.
137. *Literaturnaia Gazeta*, 12 June 1968, p. 13.
138. Novitsky and Babkina, pp. 45–6.
139. *Literaturnaia Gazeta*, 12 June 1968, p. 13 and 24 October 1973, p. 12.
140. *Literaturnaia Gazeta*, 12 June 1968, p. 13.
141. *Izvestia*, 25 December 1971, p. 2, trans. in *CD*, vol. xxiii, no. 52, p. 21.
142. Semenchenko *et al.*, p. 140; *Trud*, 17 July 1974, p. 4.
143. *Trud*, 30 June 1972, p. 4.
144. Semenchenko *et al.*, p. 140.
145. *Trud*, 17 July 1974, p. 4.
146. Semenchenko *et al.*, pp. 96–7, 110 and 169.
147. Ibid., p. 170.
148. *Pravda*, 10 May 1970, p. 3.
149. *Narodnoe Khoziaistvo SSSR v 1970g*, p. 620.
150. Semenchenko *et al.*, p. 19.
151. *Izvestia*, 31 October 1973, p. 5.
152. Semenchenko *et al.*, p. 145.
153. *Pravda*, 14 April 1969, p. 1.
154. G. A. Severukhina, 'Sravnitel'nyi Analiz Biudzhetov Vremeni Rabochei i Studencheskoi Molodezhi', *Tezisy Dokladov* (Sverdlovsk, 1973) p. 308.

3 SEASONAL AND TEMPORARY WORK

1. A. L. Epshtein, *Sezonnye i Vremennye Rabotniki* (Moscow, 1975) p. 50.
2. S. D. Tseitlin, *Vremennye i Sezonnye Rabotniki* (Moscow, 1963) p. 27.

3. *Pravda*, 20 November 1966, pp. 2–3, trans. in *CD*, vol. xviii, no. 47, pp. 20–1; *Literaturnaia Gazeta*, 14 June 1978, p. 11.
4. Tseitlin, p. 25.
5. Ibid., pp. 5–6.
6. Ibid., p. 7; Epshtein, p. 8.
7. Epshtein, p. 9.
8. E. Manevich, 'Ratsional'noe Ispol'zovanie Rabochei Sily', *Voprosy Ekonomiki*, no. 9 (September 1981) p. 60.
9. A. Glukhov, 'Ispol'zovanie Trudovykh Resursov v Sel'skom Khoziaistve', *Ekonomicheskie Nauki*, no. 2 (1964) p. 24.
10. *Literaturnaia Gazeta*, 13 October 1971, p. 11.
11. Based on total state farm labour force data found in *Narodnoe Khoziaistvo SSSR v 1969g*, p. 530.
12. V. Litvinova, 'Ob Uluchshenii Ispol'zovaniia Rabochei Sily v Sovkhozakh', *Ekonomicheskie Nauki*, no. 2 (1964) p. 35.
13. *Kopanka 25 let Spustia* (Moscow, 1965) p. 111.
14. *Literaturnaia Gazeta*, 19 March 1975, p. 10, trans. in *CD*, vol. xxvii, no. 41, p. 32.
15. Epshtein, p. 17.
16. Ibid., p. 19.
17. Ibid.
18. Tseitlin, p. 8.
19. *Literaturnaia Gazeta*, 19 March 1975, p. 10; trans. in *CD*, vol. xxvii, no. 41, p. 21; *Literaturnaia Gazeta*, 13 October 1971.
20. *Literaturnaia Gazeta*, 15 March 1978, p. 11.
21. *Literaturnaia Gazeta*, 13 September 1978, p. 11.
22. *Literaturnaia Gazeta*, 14 June 1978, p. 11.
23. *Kommunist*, 7 April 1976, p. 2, trans. in *CD*, vol. xxviii, no. 26, p. 22.
24. *Kommunist*, 8 April 1976, p. 2, trans. in *CD*, vol. xxviii, no. 26, p. 26.
25. *Literaturnaia Gazeta*, 14 June 1978, p. 11, trans. in *CD*, vol. xxx, no. 31, p. 12.
26. *Literaturnaia Gazeta*, 13 October 1971.
27. 'Tem, Kto Pomogaet Selu', *Trud*, 6 April 1973, p. 4.
28. *Literaturnaia Gazeta*, 17 January 1968, p. 10, trans. in *CD*, vol. xx, no. 5, p. 6.
29. *Literaturnaia Gazeta*, 14 June 1978, p. 11.
30. On this subject see, for example, James R. Millar, 'The Prospects for Soviet Agriculture', *Problems of Communism* (May–June 1977) pp. 11–12.
31. *Literaturnaia Gazeta*, 13 October 1971; *Pravda*, 20 November 1966.
32. *Trud*, 7 April 1976, p. 2.
33. *Kommunist*, 7 April 1976, trans. in *CD*, vol. xxviii, no. 26, p. 26; *Literaturnaia Gazeta*, 14 June 1978; *Pravda*, 8 September 1976, p. 2, trans. in *CD*, vol. xxviii, no. 36, p. 21.
34. *Pravda*, 20 November 1966.
35. *Literaturnaia Gazeta*, 13 October 1971.
36. *Pravda*, 20 November 1966. Collective farms do not actually pay the workers. They are paid by construction organisations through a local branch of *Gosbank*.
37. Epshtein, p. 20.

38. *Izvestia*, 28 May 1967, p. 2, trans. in *CD*, vol. XIX, no. 14, p. 37.
39. Epshtein, p. 22.
40. Ibid., p. 24.
41. *Trud*, 20 October 1976, p. 2.
42. *Izvestia*, 28 May 1967. Bagasse is crushed, juiceless sugar cane which is used for fuel.
43. Tseitlin, p. 39; *Izvestia*, 28 May 1967.
44. Epshtein, p. 51.
45. Ibid., p. 40.
46. Tseitlin, pp. 43–4.
47. Epshtein, pp. 40–1.
48. Tseitlin, p. 38.
49. Epshtein, pp. 41–2.
50. Tseitlin, p. 20.
51. Epshtein, p. 26.
52. *Trud*, 13 December 1974, p. 4.
53. Epshtein, pp. 16–17.
54. For example, see *Literaturnaia Gazeta*, 26 July 1978, p. 11; *Literaturnaia Gazeta*, 15 March 1978, p. 11.
55. Manevich, p. 60.
56. *Literaturnaia Gazeta*, 15 March 1978 and 26 July 1978.
57. *Literaturnaia Gazeta*, 17 January 1968.
58. *Trud*, 16 September 1978, p. 2.
59. *Literaturnaia Gazeta*, 10 October 1973, p. 13, trans. in *CD*, vol. XXV, no. 49, p. 16.
60. *Pravda*, 20 November 1966.
61. *Zarya Vostoka*, 28 December 1979, p. 2, trans. in *CD*, vol. XXXII, no. 5, p. 17.
62. Litvinova, p. 35.
63. *Literaturnaia Gazeta*, 19 March 1975 and 14 June 1978.
64. *Literaturnaia Gazeta*, 13 October 1971.
65. *Literaturnaia Gazeta*, 19 March 1975.
66. *Kommunist*, 7 April 1976.
67. *Literaturnaia Gazeta*, 14 June 1978.

4 OVERTIME WORK

1. *Trud*, 2 March 1973, p. 4.
2. For example, see *Trud v SSSR*, 1968, pp. 239–40.
3. The Soviets use the terms 'iskliuchitel'nost' i chrezvychainost''. See L. A. Muksinova, *Problemy Regulirovaniia Rabochego Vremenii v SSSR* (Moscow, 1969) p. 198.
4. *Trud*, 13 January 1971, p. 4.
5. A. A. Kliuev and A. V. Iarkho, *Profaktivu o Kontrole za Rabochim Vremenem i Vremenem Otdykha* (Moscow, 1975) p. 37.
6. P. D. Vladimirovich, *Sverkhurochnye Raboty. Rabota v Vykhodnye i Prazdnichnye Dni. Dezhurstva* (Moscow, 1961) p. 5.
7. Kliuev and Iarkho, p. 32; Vladimirovich, p. 6.

8. Kliuev and Iarkho, pp. 37–8.
9. Ibid., p. 35.
10. 'Ogranichenie etc.,' p. 4. Formerly it was after the fourth month that women were excused from overtime work; now anytime a doctor certifies they are pregnant.
11. The discussion of the role of trade unions is drawn from *Pravda*, 14 August 1960, p. 3, trans. in *CD*, vol. xii, no. 33, pp. 21–2; *Trud*, 13 January 1971; *Trud*, 23 September 1975, p. 2; Kliuev and Iarkho, pp. 34–5.
12. Ibid., p. 40; Vladimirovich, p. 9.
13. This discussion is drawn from Kliuev and Iarkho, pp. 38–40 and *Trud*, 13 January 1971.
14. Vladimirovich, p. 13.
15. *Izvestia*, 13 April 1972, p. 5, trans. in *CD*, vol. xxiv, no. 15, p. 20.
16. *Trud*, 11 October 1972, p. 4. The Russians use the term *otgul* to refer to the day off during the week in lieu of having had to work on a Saturday or Sunday.
17. Interview with Soviet emigrés, Springfield, Illinois, USA, 1981.
18. *Pravda*, 12 March 1968, p. 1, trans. in *CD*, vol. xx, no. 11, 1 April 1968, p. 26; *Pravda*, 25 April 1968, p. 3, trans. in *CD*, vol. xx, no. 17, pp. 20–1.
19. The holidays are 1 January, 8 March (International Women's Day), 1 and 2 May, 9 May (Victory Day), 7 and 8 November (Celebrating the Bolshevik Revolution) and 7 October (Constitution Day, formerly 5 December). The discussion on holiday employment is from *Trud*, 14 January 1972, p. 4 and Vladimirovich, pp. 18–19.
20. Vladimirovich, pp. 14–15.
21. *Trud*, 6 October 1972, p. 4.
22. The discussion on state agriculture is drawn from A. V. Iarkho, *Sverkhurochnye Raboty. Rabota v Vykhodnye i Prazdnichnye Dni* (Moscow, 1965) pp. 24–5 and Kliuev and Iarkho, pp. 104–5. The treatment of public catering and the fishing industry is from Iarkho, pp. 26–7 and 31.
23. G. A. Prudenskii, *Problemy Rabochego i Vnerabochego Vremeni* (Moscow, 1972) p. 304.
24. Ibid.
25. *Komsomolskaia Pravda*, 4 March 1969, p. 2, trans. in *CD*, vol. xxi, no. 18, p. 30.
26. *Nash Sovremennik*, no. 6 (June 1975) pp. 118–131, trans. in *CD*, vol. xxvii, no. 32, p. 5.
27. The discussion of PGS is taken from L. Ia. Gintsburg, *Regulirovanie Rabochego Vremeni v SSSR* (Moscow, 1966) pp. 285–9.
28. Muksinova, p. 197.
29. Kliuev and Iarkho, p. 41; Alec Nove, *An Economic History of the USSR*. (Penguin, 1969) p. 81.
30. Alec Nove, *An Economic History of the USSR* (Penguin, 1969) p. 81.
31. For example, see *Izvestia*, 31 October 1975, p. 5, trans. in *CD*, vol. xxv, no. 44, p. 25; Muksinova, p. 212; *Pravda*, 14 August 1960.
32. *Izvestia*, 31 October 1975.
33. Ibid., and Vladimirovich, p. 38.
34. *Izvestia*, 31 October 1975.
35. Muksinova, pp. 212–13.

36. A. V. Netsenko, *Sotsial'no-Ekonomicheskie Problemy Svobodnogo Vremeni Pri Sotsializme* (Leningrad, 1975) p. 75.
37. Kliuev and Iarkho, p. 33.
38. *Izvestia*, 31 October 1975.
39. *Trud*, 14 October 1955, p. 2, trans. in *CD*, vol. VII, no. 39, p. 9; *Komsomolskaia Pravda*, 4 March 1969.
40. *Pravda*, 25 August 1974, p. 2; trans. in *CD*, vol. XXVI, no. 34, p. 5.
41. *Trud*, 14 October 1955, p. 2; trans. in *CD*, vol. VII, no. 39, p. 9.
42. Some of the best literature on the subject includes: Gregory Grossman, 'The "Second Economy" of the USSR', *Problems of Communism*, (September–October, 1977) pp. 25–40; Grossman, 'Notes on the Illegal Private Economy and Corruption', *Soviet Economy in a Time of Change*, 10 October 1979 (Joint Economic Committee, Washington, D.C.) pp. 834–55; A. Katsenelinboigen, 'Coloured Markets in the Soviet Union', *Soviet Studies*, vol. XXIX, no. 1 (January, 1977) pp. 62–85.
43. *Literaturnaia Gazeta*, 28 June 1978, p. 13.
44. *Literaturnaia Gazeta*, 7 March 1973, p. 12, trans. in *CD*, vol. XXV, no. 38, pp. 5–6.
45. Conversations with Soviet emigrés, Springfield, Illinois, USA, 1981; *Literaturnaia Gazeta*, 8 August 1973, p. 11, trans. in *CD*, vol. XXV, no. 38, p. 7.
46. *Literaturnaia Gazeta*, 8 August 1973, p. 11, trans. in *CD*, vol. XXV, no. 30, p. 6.
47. For example, see Alec Nove, *The Soviet Economy* (Praeger, 1961) p. 160.

5 LEISURE

1. B. Grushin, *Svobodnoe Vremia: Aktual'nye Problemy* (Moscow, 1967) pp. 76–7.
2. G. M. Podorov, *Rabochee i Svobodnee Vremia* (Moscow, 1975) pp. 136–9.
3. V. A. Artemov *et al.*, *Statistika Biudzhetov Vremeni Trudiashchikhsia* (Moscow, 1967) p. 119.
4. G. T. Zhuravlev, 'Svodobnoe Vremia i Kul'turnaia Zhizn' Rabotnikov Promyshlennogo Predpriiatiia', G. V. Osipov and Ia. Shchepan'skii (eds), *Sotsial'nye Problemy Truda i Proizvodstva* (Moscow, 1969) pp. 373–4.
5. *Literaturnaia Gazeta*, 9 April 1975, p. 13; L. A. Gordon, E. V. Klopov, and L. A. Onikov, *Cherty Sotsialisticheskogo Obraza Zhizni: Byt Gorodskikh Rabochikh Vchera, Segodnia, Zavtra* (Moscow, 1977) p. 95.
6. B. T. Kolpakova and V. D. Patrusheva (eds), *Biudzhet Vremeni Gorodskogo Naseleniia* (Moscow, 1971) p. 179.
7. G. E. Zborovskii and G. P. Orlov, *Dosugi: Deistvitel'nost i Illuzii* (Sverdlovsk, 1970) p. 21.
8. Gordon *et al.*, p. 16.
9. M. A. Gurevich, 'Voprosy Organizatsii Svobodnogo Vremeni v Plane Sotsial'nogo Razvitiia Kollektiva', *Tezisy Dokladov Nauchno-Prakticheskoi Konferentsii "Vnerabochee Vremia i Sotsial'noe Planirovanie"* (Sverdlovsk, 1975) p. 109.
10. I. E. Ermolaev, 'Ob Izmerenii Potrebnostei Realizuemykh v Sfere

Svobodnogo Vremini', *Tezisy Dokladov*, pp. 121 and 124.
11. A. G. Davydov, 'Vnerabochee i Svobodnoe Vremia Uchenogo', *Tezisy Dokladov*, p. 152.
12. Ibid., pp. 153–4.
13. M. T. Iovchuk and L. N. Kogan (eds), *Dukhovnyi Mir Sovetskogo Rabochego* (Moscow, 1972) p. 334; V. N. Pimenova, *Svobodnoe Vremia v Sotsialisticheskom Obshchestvæ* (Moscow, 1974) p. 257; F. S. Faizullin, 'Rol' Planirovaniia Sotsial'nogo Razvitiia Gorodov v Upravlenii Svobodnym Vremenem', *Tezisy Dokladov:*, pp. 88–9.
14. *Literaturnaia Gazeta*, 12 March 1969, p. 12.
15. *Literaturnaia Gazeta*, 15 February 1967, p. 11.
16. *Literaturnaia Gazeta*, 12 March 1969, p. 12.
17. G. P. Orlov, *Svobodnoe Vremia Kak Sotsiologicheskaia Kategoriia* (Sverdlovsk, 1973) p. 125.
18. Pimenova, p. 257.
19. For example, see *Ekonomicheskaia Gazeta*, no. 17 (1967) trans. in *CD*, vol. xix, no. 20, p. 12; *Literaturnaia Gazeta*, 21 June 1972, p. 12; A. I. Ivan'kov, 'Biudzhet Vremeni Trudiashchikhsia i Plan Sotsial'nogo Razvitiia Predpriiatiia', *Sotsial'nye Problemy Novykh Gorodov Vostochnoi Sibiri*, vol. 2 (Irkutsk, 1974) p. 87.
20. Iovchuk and Kogan, p. 392.
21. *Izvestia*, 26 May 1973, p. 5, trans. in *CD*, vol. xxv, no. 21, p. 23.
22. *Literaturnaia Gazeta*, 18 July 1973, p. 12, trans. in *CD*, vol. xxv, no. 30, pp. 16 and 29.
23. Iu. V. Arutiunian, *Sotsial'aia Struktura Sel'skogo Naseleniia SSSR* (Moscow, 1971) p. 63.
24. M. T. Iovchuk and A. S. Kulagin, 'Nekotorye Aktual'nye Problemy Razvitiia Sotsialisticheskoi Kultury na Sele', *Sotsiologicheskie Issledovaniia*, no. 4 (1975) p. 37.
25. Arutiunian, p. 63.
26. *Statistical Abstract of the United States* (1981) pp. 245 and 342.
27. *Izvestia*, 3 December 1967, p. 1, trans. in *CD*, vol. xix, no. 48, p. 13.
28. N. M. Blinov, 'Sotsiologicheskie Issledovaniia Truda i Vospitaniia Sovetskoi Molodezhi 20-Kh Godov', *Sotsiologicheskie Issledovaniia*, no. 1, 1975, p. 149.
29. Gordon *et al.*, p. 156.
30. *Pravda*, 21 February 1978, p. 3, trans. in *CD*, vol. xxx, no. 8, p. 13.
31. *Statistical Abstract of the United States*, 1978, p. 595.
32. A. G. Kharchev and S. I. Golod, *Professional'naia Rabota Zhenshchin i Sem'ia*, Leningrad, 1971, p. 108.
33. B. M. Firsov and K. Muzdybaev, 'K Postroeniiu Systemy Pokazatelei Ispol'zovaniia Sredstv Massovoi Kommunikatsii', *Sotsiologicheskie Issledovaniia*, no. 1, 1975, p. 115.
34. Gordon *et al.*, p. 60.
35. Iovchuk and Kogan, p. 365.
36. *Statistical Abstract of the United States*, 1981, p. 559.
37. Zhuravlev, p. 384.
38. Gordon, Klopov and Onikov, p. 61.
39. Ibid, p. 76.

40. V. G. Baikova, A. S. Duchal and A. A. Zemtsov, *Svobodnoe Vremia i Vsestoronnee Razvitie Lichnosti* (Moscow 1965), pp. 88 and 90.
41. I. P. Trufanov, *Problemy Byta Gorodskogo Naseleniia SSSR* (Leningrad, 1973) p. 100.
42. Gordon, Klopov and Onikov, p. 150.
43. Ibid, p. 151.
44. Trufanov, p. 77.
45. Kolpakova and Patrusheva, p. 140.
46. *Trud*, 25 August 1978, p. 2, trans. in *CD*, vol. xxx, no. 34, 30 September 1978, pp. 13–14.
47. Trufanov, pp. 63–4.
48. A. G. Levitskaia, 'Sotsial'nye Sfery Novogo Goroda', *Sotsial'nye Problemy Novykh Gorodov Vostochnoi Sibiri*, vol. 2 (Irkutsk, 1974) p. 17.
49. *Sotsial'noe i Natsional'noe* (Moscow, 1973) p. 173.
50. *Trud*, 25 August 1978, p. 2.
51. *Literaturnaia Gazeta*, 10 November 1976, p. 11, trans. in *CD*, vol. xxviii, no. 47, p. 18.
52. *Literaturnaia Gazeta*, 10 November 1976, p. 11.
53. Kolpakova and Patrusheva, p. 140.
54. *Literaturnaia Gazeta*, 10 November 1976, p. 11.
55. *Trud*, 25 August 1978, p. 2.
56. Keith Bush, 'Books in the Second Economy' (Papers from the Conference on the Second Economy of the USSR, Kennan Institute for Advanced Russian Studies, January 1980).
57. L. I. Petrovicheva, *Sovetskii Rabochii-Chitatel'* (Minsk, 1978) p. 81.
58. E. K. Vasil'eva, *Sotsial'no-Professional'nyi Uroven' Gorodskoi Molodezhi* (Leningrad, 1973) p. 23.
59. *Kniga i Chtenie v Zhizni Nebol'shikh Gorodov* (Moscow, 1973) p. 281.
60. Ibid.
61. I. I. Tsofnas and N. F. Korneinko, 'Struktura i Osobennosti Ispol'zovaniia Svobodnogo Vremeni Stroitelei', *Tezisy Dokladov*, p. 147.
62. Ibid.
63. *Kniga i Chtenie etc*, p. 282.
64. G. I. Mel'nikov, V. N. Sudakov, 'Nekotorye Voprosy Adaptatsii Molodykh Rabochikh', *Sotsial'nye Problemy Novykh Gorodov Vostochnoi Sibiri* (Irkutsk, 1971) p. 63.
65. Gurevich, p. 111.
66. *Pravda*, 1 September 1974, trans. in *CD*, vol. xxxvi, no. 35, p. 26.
67. *Izvestia*, 26 December 1974, trans. in *CD*, vol. xxvi, no. 52, pp. 22–3.
68. *Literaturnaia Gazeta*, 11 July 1973, p. 12, trans. in *CD*, vol. xxv, no. 40, p. 14.
69. Iovchuk and Kogan, p. 402.
70. *Literaturnaia Gazeta*, 9 April 1975, p. 13.
71. V. N. Kudriavtsev, *Prichiny Pravonarushenii* (Moscow, 1976) p. 170.
72. *Zhurnalist* (January, 1977) pp. 54–6, trans. in *CD*, vol. xxix, no. 8, p. 14.
73. G. P. Orlov, *Svobodnoe Vremia Kak Sotsiologicheskaia Kategoriia* (Sverdlovsk, 1973) pp. 125 and 127.
74. *Literaturnaia Gazeta*, 4 January 1967, p. 7.
75. Gurevich, p. 111.

76. G. E. Zborovskii and G. P. Orlov, *Dosugi: Deisvitel'nost' i Illuzii* (Sverdlovsk, 1970) p. 233.
77. Gordon, *et al.*, p. 151.

6 HOLIDAYS

1. Archibald A. Evans, *Flexibility in Working Life* (Organisation for Economic Co-operation and Development: Paris, 1973) pp. 67–8.
2. *Narkhoz SSSR v 1980 g*, p. 367. There are two other forms of paid leave (*otpuska*) which Soviet citizens can receive: sick leave and paid leave for school work, e.g. to study and take exams. Neither of these receives further consideration in this study.
3. M. Iu. Gol'dshtein and V. S. Korotkov, *Rabochee Vremia i Vremia Otdykha Rabochikh i Sluzhashchikh v SSSR* (Moscow, 1959) p. 65.
4. V. I. Azar, *Otdykh Trudiashchikhsia SSSR* (Moscow, 1972) p. 7.
5. The discussion on the historical background of holiday policy, unless otherwise stated is from L. Ia. Gintsburg, *Otpuska Rabochikh i Sluzhashchikh* (Moscow, 1961) pp. 17ff.
6. This discussion is drawn from Gintsburg, pp. 29ff., and Gol'dshtein and Korotkov, pp. 47ff.
7. Gol'dshtein and Korotkov, p. 58.
8. Ibid.
9. *Literaturnaia Gazeta*, 3 December 1969, p. 11.
10. Azar, p. 48.
11. *Literaturnaia Gazeta*, 3 December 1969, p. 11.
12. V. P. Stauskas, 'Otdykhaiushchii i Kurorty', *Tezisy Dokladov Naucho Prakticheskoi Konferentsii "Vnerabochee Vremia i Sotsial'noe Planirovanie"* (Sverdlovsk, 1973) p. 191.
13. *Literaturnaia Gazeta*, 24 June 1970, p. 12.
14. *Literaturnaia Gazeta*, 26 March 1969, p. 12.
15. *Literaturnaia Gazeta*, 25 October 1972, p. 13.
16. *Literaturnaia Gazeta*, 10 October 1979, p. 13.
17. *Literaturnaia Gazeta*, 20 July 1977, p. 12, trans. in *CD*, vol. xxix, no. 29, pp. 5–6.
18. *Literaturnaia Gazeta*, 2 July 1975, p. 13.
19. Azar, p. 18.
20. *Literaturnaia Gazeta*, 20 July 1977, p. 12.
21. *Literaturnaia Gazeta*, 30 August 1978, p. 12, trans. in *CD*, vol. xxx, no. 36, p. 5.
22. *Literaturnaia Gazeta*, 20 September 1967, p. 13.
23. Azar, p. 15.
24. *Literaturnaia Gazeta*, 20 July 1977, p. 12.
25. Ibid.
26. *Literaturnaia Gazeta*, 3 December 1969, p. 11.
27. *Literaturnaia Gazeta*, 28 June 1972, p. 12.
28. *Literaturnaia Gazeta*, 3 December 1969, p. 11.
29. *Literaturnaia Gazeta*, 28 May 1966, p. 1.
30. *Literaturnaia Gazeta*, 2 July 1975, p. 13.

31. Azar, p. 47.
32. *Sovetskaia Rossia*, 24 November 1979, p. 4, trans. in *CD*, vol. xxx, no. 51, p. 17.
33. Azar, p. 41.
34. *New York Times*, 27 March 1983, p. 1.
35. *Doma Otdykha: Sbornik Statei i Materialov (1920–1923)* (Moscow and Petrograd, 1923).
36. I am indebted to Mark Field for providing a precise definition of the two institutions.
37. *Literaturnaia Gazeta*, 30 August 1978, p. 4, trans. in *CD*, vol. xxx, no. 36, p. 5.
38. Azar, pp. 33–4.
39. *Literaturnaia Gazeta*, 21 August 1968, p. 13.
40. Ibid.
41. *Pravda*, 2 November 1972, p. 3.
42. Azar, p. 42.
43. *Komsomolskaia Pravda*, 18 September 1960, pp. 2–3, trans. in *CD*, vol. xii, no. 44, p. 14.
44. *Komsomolskaia Pravda*, 5 February 1961, p. 2, trans. in *CD*, vol. xiii, no. 9, pp. 29–30.
45. Azar, p. 11.
46. Ibid., p. 10.
47. *Pravda*, 26 July 1973, p. 6, trans. in *CD*, vol. xxv, no. 30, p. 16.
48. *Izvestia*, 26 July 1973, p. 5, trans. in *CD*, vol. xxv, no. 30, p. 15.
49. Ibid.
50. *Literaturnaia Gazeta*, 18 July 1973, p. 12.
51. *Literaturnaia Gazeta*, 18 July 1973, p. 12.
52. *Literaturnaia Gazeta*, 20 July 1977, p. 12, trans. in *CD*, vol. xxix, no. 29, p. 5.
53. *Pravda*, 15 July 1972, p. 6.
54. *Izvestia*, 28 August 1976, p. 5, trans. in *CD*, vol. xxviii, no. 35, pp. 22–3.
55. I. F. Dement'eva, 'Obshchestvennaia Znachimost' Turizma v Usloviiakh Nauchno-Tekhnicheskogo Progressa', *Tezisy Dokladov Nauchno Prakticheskoi Konferentsii 'Vnerabochee Vremia i Sotsial'noe Planirovanie'* (Sverdlovsk, 1975) pp. 182–3.
56. I. Velichene, 'Trud i Zdrov'e Zhenshchiny-Rabotnitsy', *Problemy Byta, Braka i Sem'i* (Vilnius, 1970) p. 97.
57. Azar, p. 46.
58. L. G. Dzis'ko, E. A. Znamenskaia and N. A. Shkliaev, *Kurortnoe Stroitel'stvo v SSSR* (Moscow, 1975) p. 85.
59. *Sotsial'noe i Natsional'noe* (Moscow, 1973) p. 174.
60. Azar, p. 85.
61. Ibid., p. 15.
62. *Izvestia*, 23 April 1971, p. 4, trans. in *CD*, vol. xxiii, no. 16, p. 46.
63. *Literaturnaia Gazeta*, 18 June 1966, p. 2.
64. *Literaturnaia Gazeta*, 20 September 1967, p. 13.
65. *Izvestia*, 23 April 1971.
66. *Literaturnaia Gazeta*, 18 June 1966, p. 2.
67. *Literaturnaia Gazeta*, 28 April 1966, p. 2.

68. *Literaturnaia Gazeta*, 20 July 1977, p. 12, trans. in *CD*, vol. xxix, no. 29, pp. 5–6.
69. *Literaturnaia Gazeta*, 26 March 1969, p. 12.
70. *Pravda*, 5 September 1969, p. 3, trans. in *CD*, vol. xxi, no. 36, p. 25.
71. *Literaturnaia Gazeta*, 26 March 1969, p. 12.
72. Ibid.
73. *Pravda*, 5 September 1969, p. 3.
74. *Pravda*, 26 July 1973, p. 6.
75. *Pravda*, 17 January 1971, p. 3, trans. in *CD*, vol. xxiii, no. 4, p. 29.
76. *Sovetskaia Kultura*, 30 March 1973, p. 6, trans. in *CD*, vol. xxv, no. 19, p. 18.
77. *Pravda*, 11 October 1971, p. 2, trans. in *CD*, vol. xxiii, no. 41, p. 34.
78. Azar, p. 19.
79. *Sovetskaia Kultura*, 30 March 1973, p. 6; *Literaturnaia Gazeta*, 30 August 1978, p. 12.
80. Azar, p. 19.
81. *Literaturnaia Gazeta*, 28 April 1966, p. 2.
82. *Pravda*, 19 October 1972, p. 3, trans. in *CD*, vol. xxiv, no. 42, p. 19.
83. *Pravda*, 3 August 1963, p. 3, trans. in *CD*, vol. xv, no. 31, p. 24.
84. *Literaturnaia Gazeta*, 15 September 1971, p. 12.
85. *Pravda*, 6 April 1958, p. 3, trans. in *CD*, vol. x, p. 14; *Literaturnaia Gazeta*, 15 September 1971, p. 12.
86. *Literaturnaia Gazeta*, 1 July 1966, p. 2.
87. *Literaturnaia Gazeta*, 15 September 1971, p. 12.
88. Azar, p. 52.
89. *Literaturnaia Gazeta*, 30 April 1969, p. 12; *Literaturnaia Gazeta*, 15 October 1969, p. 12.
90. *Pravda*, 17 January 1971, p. 3.
91. *Literaturnaia Gazeta*, 15 October 1969, p. 12.
92. *Literaturnaia Gazeta*, 10 November 1976, p. 13.
93. *Literaturnaia Gazeta*, 20 July 1977, p. 12.
94. *Literaturnaia Gazeta*, 23 August 1972, p. 10.
95. *Literaturnaia Gazeta*, 30 April 1969, p. 12; *Izvestia* 26 July 1973, p. 5, trans. in *CD*, vol. xxv, no. 30, pp. 15–16.
96. *Pravda*, 11 October 1971, p. 2, trans. in *CD*, vol. xxiii, no. 41, p. 34.
97. *Literaturnaia Gazeta*, 20 July 1977, p. 12. I have not seen any cost data which supports the argument that the average size of facilities are not cost effective.
98. *Literaturnaia Gazeta*, 10 September 1966, p. 1.
99. *Pravda*, 1 July 1974, p. 3, trans. in *CD*, vol. xxvi, no. 22, pp. 14–15 and *Pravda*, 13 September 1974, trans. in *CD*, vol. xxvi, no. 37, p. 23.

7 WOMEN AND THE SERVICE SECTOR

1. See also Z. Iankova, 'O Bytovykh Roliakh Rabotaiushchei Zhenshchiny', *Problemy Byta, Braka i Sem'i* (Vilnius, 1970) p. 43.
2. G. A. Slesarev and Z. A. Iankova, 'Zhenshchina na Promyshlennom Predpriiatii i v Sem'e', in G. V. Osipov and Ia. Shchepanskii (eds), *Sotsial'nye Problemy Truda i Proizvodstva* (Moscow, 1969) p. 432.

3. Z. A. Iankova, 'Razvitie Lichnosti Zhenshchiny v Sovetskom Obshchestve', *Sotsiologicheskie Issledovaniia*, no. 4, 1975, p. 48.
4. Slesarev and Iankova, p. 437.
5. A. E. Kotliar and S. Ia. Turchaninova, *Zaniatost' Zhenshchin v Proizvodstve*, pp. 93, 124 and 129.
6. *Ekonomika i Organizatsiia Promyshlennogo Proizvodstva*, no. 3 (1978) pp. 19–29, trans. in *CD*, vol. xxx, no. 30, p. 4.
7. Kotliar and Turchaninova, p. 90.
8. See A. V. Netsenko, *Sotsial'no-Ekonomicheskie Problemy Svobodnogo Vremeni Pri Sotsializme* (Leningrad, 1975) p. 75 and L. S. Kolobov, 'Rezhimy Truda i Otdykha i Vnerabochee Vremia Trudiashchiknsia', in V. S. Patrushev (ed), *Opyt Ekonomiko-Sotsiologicheskikh Issledovanii v Sibiri*, p. 92.
9. I. Velichene, 'Trud i Zdrov'e Zhenshchiny-Rabotnitsy', *Problemy Byta, Braka i Sem'i*, p. 97.
10. *Ekonomika i Organizatsiia Promyshlennogo Proizvodstva*, no. 3 (1978) pp. 57–64, trans. in *CD*, vol. xxx, no. 31, p. 9.
11. E. Z. Danilova, *Sotsial'nye Problemy Truda Zhenshchiny-Rabotnitsy* (Moscow, 1968) p. 50.
12. Slesarev and Iankova, p. 431.
13. A. G. Kharchev and S. I. Golod, 'Proizvodstvennaia Rabota Zhenshchin i Sem'ia', in G. V. Osipov and Ia. Shchepanskii (eds), *Sotsial'nye Problemy Truda i Proizvodstva*, p. 446.
14. A. Pimenova, 'Uslugi v Sem'e', *Problemy Byta, Braka, i Sem'i*, p. 151.
15. Slesarev and Iankova, p. 432.
16. A. Kharchev, 'Byt i Sem'ia Kak Kategorii Istoricheskogo Materializma', *Problemy, Byta, Braka i Sem'i*, p. 19.
17. For a more complete treatment of the subject see William Moskoff, 'Divorce in the USSR', *Journal of Marriage and the Family* (May 1983) pp. 414–25.
18. Danilova, p. 49.
19. *Literaturnaia Gazeta*, 15 March 1978, p. 13.
20. V. G. Baikova, A. S. Duchal and A. A. Zemtsov, *Svobodnoe Vremia i Vsestoronnee Razvitie Lichnosti* (Moscow, 1965) p. 65.
21. N. V. Panova, 'Voprosy Truda i Byta Zhenshchin', *Problemy Byta, Braka i Sem'i*, p. 89.
22. *Literaturnaia Gazeta*, 15 March 1978, p. 13.
23. Velichene, pp. 96 and 98.
24. Slesarev and Iankova, p. 423.
25. A. G. Kharchev and S. I. Golod, *Professional'naia Rabota Zhenshchin i Sem'ia* (Leningrad, 1971) p. 45.
26. Netsenko, p. 66.
27. Ibid., p. 67.
28. Kharchev and Golod, *Professional'naia Rabota etc*, p. 94.
29. A. G. Kharchev and S. I. Golod, 'Proizvodstvennaia Rabota Zhenshchin i Sem'ia', in Osipov and Shchepanskii, *Sotsial'nye Problemy Trudy i Proizvodstva*, p. 450.
30. N. Volga, 'Issledovanie Dinamiki Razvitiia Semei Dlia Sovershenstvovaniia Tipov Zhilishcha', *Problemy Byta, Braka i Sem'i*, p. 57.

31. For example, see *Izvestia*, 17 April 1976, p. 2, trans. in *CD*, vol. XXVIII, no. 15, pp. 7–8.
32. E. Z. Danilova, p. 46; L. A. Gordon, E. V. Klopov and L. A. Onikov, *Cherty Sotsialisticheskogo Obraza Zhizni: Byt Gorodskikh Rabochikh Vchera, Segodnia, Zavtra* (Moscow, 1977) p. 37.
33. A. G. Levitskaia, 'Sotsial'nye Sfery Novogo Goroda', *Sotsial'nye Problemy Novykh Gorodov Vostochnoi Sibiri*, vol. 2 (Irkutsk, 1974) pp. 17–18.
34. *Izvestia*, 27 November 1976, p. 4, trans. in *CD*, vol. XXVIII, no. 48, pp. 21–2.
35. *Pravda*, 17 July 1971, p. 3, trans. in *CD*, vol. XXIII, no. 29, p. 9.
36. Ibid., pp. 8–9.
37. *Literaturnaia Gazeta*, 24 June 1970, p. 11.
38. *Literaturnaia Gazeta*, 4 June 1969, p. 12.
39. Ibid.
40. Ibid. and Danilova, p. 46.
41. *Literaturnaia Gazeta*, 24 June 1970, p. 11.
42. Danilova, p. 47.
43. *Literaturnaia Gazeta*, 24 June 1970, p. 11.
44. Ia. Andriushkiavichene, 'Zhenskii Trud i Problema Svobodnogo Vremeni', *Problemy Byta, Braka i Sem'i*, p. 80.
45. *Literaturnaia Gazeta*, 24 June 1970, p. 11.
46. Danilova, p. 47.
47. Kharchev and Golod, *Professional'naia Rabota*, p. 44.
48. *Komsomolskaia Pravda*, 28 March 1974, p. 2, trans. in *CD*, vol. XXVI, no. 45, p. 18.
49. Ibid.
50. Danilova, p. 53.
51. *Literaturnaia Gazeta*, 29 March 1967, p. 12, trans. in *CD*, vol. XIX, no. 15, p. 15. An equally strong denunciation can be found in *Literaturnaia Gazeta*, 22 February 1967, p. 12.
52. Kharchev and Golod, *Professional'naia Rabota*, p. 83.
53. Slesarev and Iankova, p. 428.
54. Levitskaia, p. 17.
55. Kharchev and Golod, *Professional'naia Rabota*, p. 83.
56. G. S. Petrosian, 'Vnerabochee Vremia Trudiashchikhsia v Period Razvernutogo Stroitel'stva Kommunizma', *Voprosy Filosofii*, no. 2 (1965) p. 42.
57. *Literaturnaia Gazeta*, 12 May 1971, p. 11 and a conversation with a Soviet emigré.
58. G. S. Petrosian, *Vnerabochee Vremia Trudiashchikhsia v SSSR* (Moscow, 1965) p. 154.
59. *Literaturnaia Gazeta*, 14 May 1969, p. 12, trans. in *CD*, vol. XXI, no. 20, p. 21; *Pravda*, 22 May 1970, p. 1, trans. in *CD*, vol. XXII, no. 21, p. 22.
60. *Pravda*, 28 December 1982, p. 3, trans. in *CD*, vol. XXXIV, no. 52, p. 6.
61. *Pravda*, 11 January 1983, p. 1, trans. in *CD*, vol. XXXV, pp. 10–11.
62. S. G. Kosiachenko, *Sebestoimost', Tarify i Rentabel'nost' Bytovykh Uslug* (Moscow, 1971) pp. 11 and 13.
63. Pimenova, p. 144.

64. N. Tatarinova, *Stroitel'stvo Kommunizma i Trud Zhenshchin* (Moscow, 1964) p. 85.
65. Ibid.
66. Slesarev and Iankova, p. 431.
67. *Pravda*, 7 August 1977, p. 3, trans. in *CD*, vol. xxix, no. 32, p. 68.
68. Gordon *et al.*, p. 37.
69. *Pravda*, 22 May 1970, p. 1, trans. in *CD*, vol. xxii, no. 21, p. 22.
70. Andriushkiavichene, p. 81.
71. S. Vainshtein and Iu. Evreinov, 'Puti Razvitiia Tipovykh Zhilykh i Obshchestvennykh Zdanii', *Problemy Byta, Braka i Sem'i*, p. 68; Kharchev and Golod, *Professional'naia Rabota*, p. 81.
72. *Pravda*, 22 May 1970, p. 1, trans. in *CD*, vol. xxii, no. 21, p. 22.
73. *Pravda*, 16 June 1978, p. 3, trans. in *CD*, vol. xxx, no. 24, p. 21.
74. B. G. Kriazhev, *Vnerabochee Vremia i Sfera Obsluzhivaniia* (Moscow, 1966) p. 124.
75. Gordon, Klopov and Onikov, p. 36.
76. Baikova *et al.*, p. 62.
77. Pimenova, p. 142.
78. Vainshtein and Evreinov, p. 68.
79. *Pravda*, 29 July 1971, p. 3.
80. Gordon, Klopov and Onikov, p. 35.
81. Kriazhev, p. 118.
82. Discussion with Veronica Shapovalov, July 1981.
83. Tatarinova, p. 84.
84. Danilova, p. 53.
85. Petrosian, p. 153.
86. Kriazhev, p. 118.
87. *Pravda*, 4 August 1970, p. 1, trans. in *CD*, vol. xxii, no. 31, p. 14.
88. *Pravda*, 20 January 1958, trans. in *CD*, vol. x, no. 3, pp. 30–1.
89. Petrosian, p. 155.
90. Gordon, Klopov and Onikov, p. 35.
91. *Izvestia*, 28 August 1976, p. 5, trans. in *CD*, vol. xxviii, no. 35, pp. 22–3.
92. Kosiachenko, p. 70.
93. *Literaturnaia Gazeta*, 28 June 1978, p. 13.
94. V. I. Dmitriev, 'Vyezdnaia Forma Obsluzhivaniia Naseleniia', *Sotsiologicheskie Issledovaniia*, no. 1 (1975) p. 106.
95. Ibid., p. 107.
96. Andriushkiavichene, p. 81.
97. Tatarinova, p. 86.
98. Gordon, Klopov and Onikov, pp. 34–5.
99. *Izvestia*, 17 July 1971, p. 2, trans. in *CD*, vol. xxiii, no. 29, pp. 9–10.
100. Ibid.
101. *Literaturnaia Gazeta*, 29 March 1967, p. 12, trans. in *CD*, vol. xix, no. 15, p. 14.
102. Trufanov, p. 131.
103. A. M. Geliuta and V. I. Staroverov, *Sotsialnyi Oblik Rabochego-Intelligenta* (Moscow, 1977) p. 179.
104. Andriushkiavichene, p. 81.

105. For example, see William Moskoff, 'The Male-Female Income Gap in the Soviet Union', *The ACES Bulletin* (Spring 1979) pp. 21–31.
106. Pimenova, p. 146.
107. V. A. Artemov *et al.*, *Statistika Biudzhetov Vremeni Trudiashchikhsia*, p. 120. Unfortunately, the appliances involved are not mentioned.
108. *Pravda*, 7 August 1977, p. 3, trans. in *CD*, vol. xxix, no. 32, p. 17.

8 THE RURAL SECTOR

1. *Narkhoz v 1980 g*, pp. 7, 254 and 363.
2. *Literaturnaia Gazeta*, 11 June 1966, p. 2.
3. 365 days less 102 Saturdays and Sundays less 8 paid holidays less 22 paid leave days plus one *subbotnik* (unpaid work day) equals 234.
4. *Literaturnaia Gazeta*, 17 December 1969, p. 10.
5. *Kopanka 25 let Spustia* (Moscow, 1965) p. 64.
6. Kh. B. Zharekeshev, 'Izmenenie Struktury Svobodnogo Vremeni i Problemy ego Ispol'zovaniia v Formirovanii Lichnosti Sovremennogo Sel'skogo Truzhenika', *Kommunisticheskoe Vospitanie Truzhenikov Sela i Voprosy Povysheniia Kul'tury Sel'skogo Byta* (Moscow, 1975) p. 211.
7. *Pravda*, 4 February 1980, p. 7, trans. in *CD*, vol. xxxii, no. 5, p. 8.
8. V. G. Baikova *et al.*, *Svobodnoe Vremia i Vsestoronnee Razvitie Lichnosti* (Moscow, 1965) p. 223.
9. Ibid., pp. 223–4.
10. Iu. V. Arutiunian, *Sotsial'naia Struktura Sel'skogo Naseleniia SSSR* (Moscow, 1971) p. 133.
11. Ibid., p. 135.
12. Ibid., p. 136.
13. I. M. Slepenkov and B. V. Kniazev, *Molodezh' Sela Segodnia* (Moscow, 1972) p. 143.
14. Baikova *et al.*, p. 249.
15. Karl-Eugen Wadekin, *The Private Sector in Soviet Agriculture* (University of California: Berkeley, 1973) p. 297.
16. N. A. Aitov, 'Izmeneniia Sotsial'noi Prirody i Klassovykh Osobennostei Krest'ianstva', *Sotsiologiia v SSSR* vol. 1 (Moscow, 1965) p. 367; V. A. Artemov *et al.*, *Statistika Biudzhetov Vremeni Trudiashchikhsia* (Moscow, 1967) p..66.
17. Artemov *et al.*, p. 87.
18. I. Levikin, *Nekotorye Metodologicheskie Problemy Izucheniia Psikhologii Krest'ianstva* (Orel, 1970) p. 55.
19. Arutiunian, pp. 186–7 and 214.
20. S. G. Kosiachenko, *Sebestoimost', Tarify i Rentabel'nost' Bytovykh Uslug* (Moscow, 1971) pp. 11, 15 and 16.
21. Arutiunian, p. 166.
22. 'Kakie Izmeneniia Proiskhodiat v Strukture Svobodnogo Vremeni', *Politicheskoe Samoobrazovanie*, no. 7 (July 1962) p. 71.
23. Baikova *et al.*, p. 242.
24. *Pravda*, 16 January 1967, p. 2, trans. in *CD*, vol. xix, no. 3, p. 26.
25. *Sotsial'noe i Natsional'noe* (Moscow, 1973) p. 217.

26. For example, see *Pravda*, 14 June 1972, p. 3.
27. G. Sarkisian, 'Sblizhenie Urovnei Zhizni Gorodskogo i Sel'skogo Naseleniia', *Politicheskoe Samoobrazovanie*, no. 6, 1968, p. 124.
28. *Izvestia*, 25 February 1975, p. 5, trans. in *CD*, vol. xxvii, no. 8, p. 27.
29. Ibid.
30. N. A. Builo, *Novyi Byt Kolkhoznoi Derevni* (Minsk, 1976) p. 93.
31. V. Sinitsyn, 'Pereustroistvo Byta Derevni', *Kommunist*, no. 3, (February 1965) p. 81.
32. Builo, p. 42.
33. *Selo, Plan, Chelovek*, p. 146.
34. Slepenkov and Kniazev, p. 83; M. T. Iovchuk and A. S. Kulagin, 'Nekotorye Aktual'nye Problemy Razvitiia Sotsialisticheskoi Kul'tury na Sele', *Sotsiologicheskie Issledovaniia*, 4 November 1975, p. 36.
35. *Pravda*, 2 January 1967, p. 2, trans. in *CD*, vol. xix, no. 1, pp. 18–20.
36. Builo, pp. 41–2.
37. P. I. Simush, *Sotsial'nyi Portret Sovetskogo Krest'ianstva* (Moscow, 1976) p. 59.
38. Arutiunian, p. 153.
39. Ibid., p. 151.
40. *Sotsial'noe i Natsional'noe*, p. 111.
41. Sinitsyn, pp. 83–4; Shkurko, p. 164.
42. Sinitsyn, p. 84.
43. V. N. Shkurko, *Problemy Formirovaniia Vsestoronne Razvitoi Lichnosti, Kolkhoznika* (Minsk, 1971) p. 164.
44. T. Kudrina, 'Nekotorye Sotsial'nye Problemy Kul'tury Sovremennogo Sela', *Sotsial'nye Problemy Kul'tury Sovremennogo Sela*, issue 1 (Moscow, 1974) p. 12.
45. Slepenkov and Kniazev, p. 168.
46. Arutiunian, p. 146.
47. *Izvestia*, 4 April 1974, p. 5, trans. in *CD*, vol. xxvi, no. 14, p. 19.
48. Ibid., p. 140.
49. Arutiunian, p. 146.
50. Shkurko, p. 240.
51. Arutiunian, p. 63.
52. I. V. Zhuravleva and L. S. Shilova, 'Sredstva Massovoi Informatsii na Sele', *Tezisy Dokladov Nauchno-Prakticheskoi Konferentsii "Vnerabochee Vremia i Sotsial'noe Planirovanie"* (Sverdlovsk, 1975) p. 143.
53. Sinitsyn, p. 83.
54. Simush, p. 125.
55. Ibid., p. 124.
56. Slepenkov and Kniazev, p. 171.
57. *Selo, Plan, Chelovek*, p. 146.
58. Zhuravleva and Shilova, p. 145.
59. I. Bodol, *Preodolenie Sushchvestvennykh Razlichii Mezhdu Gorodom i Derevnei v Usloviiakh Moldavskoi SSR* (Kishinev, 1967) p. 80.
60. Arutiunian, p. 159.
61. Slepenkov and Kniazev, p. 171.
62. Simush, p. 124.
63. Arutiunian, p. 156.

64. Shkurko, p. 163.
65. Arutiunian, p. 178.
66. G. S. Entelis, *Preobrazhenie Sotsial'no-Klassovoi Struktury Sel'skogo Naseleniia* (Kishinev, 1974) p. 182.
67. Simush, p. 124.
68. *Sotsial'nyi Oblik Kolkhoznoi Molodezhi. Po Materialam Sotsiolicheskikh Obsledovanii 1939 i 1969* (Moscow, 1976) pp. 223 and 276.
69. Sinitsyn, p. 83.
70. *Selo, Plan, Chelovek*, p. 147.
71. Slepenkov and Kniazev, p. 168.
72. Shliapentokh and Maslova, p. 60.
73. *Sel'skaia Zhizn'*, 29 May 1975, p. 3.
74. Arutiunian, p. 158.
75. Ibid., p. 178.
76. Slepenkov and Kniazev, pp. 169–70.
77. Aitov, p. 367.
78. Arutiunian, pp. 151–2.
79. K. N. Kulmatov, 'Bor'ba za Sotsialisticheskuiu Kul'turu Byta Sel'skuiu Naseleniia-Vazhnyi Uchastok Ideologicheskoi Raboty', *Kommunisticheskoe Vospitanie Truzhenikov Sela i Voprosy Povysheniia Kul'tury Sel'skogo Byta* (Moscow, 1975) p. 197.
80. *Selo, Plan, Chelovek*, p. 147.
81. Simush, p. 134.
82. Ibid., p. 90.
83. *Sel'skaia Zhizn*, 17 July 1973, p. 5.
84. Kudrina, p. 12.
85. Slepenkov and Kniazev, p. 158.
86. Simush, p. 126.
87. *Sotsial'noe i Natsional'noe*, pp. 112–13.
88. Arutiunian, pp. 183–5.
89. Builo, p. 60.
90. Entelis, p. 185.
91. Simush, p. 113.

Index

absenteeism, x
agriculture
  definition of the good life, 193-4
  eligibility for pensions, 42
  housework, 173-7
  leisure activities, 183-95
  length of work day, 158-61
  old-age pensioners, 36, 41-4
  overtime work, 71-2
  satisfaction with leisure activities, 193
  seasonal work, 52
  student employment, 47
  time budgets, 166-77
  use of urbanites, 55, 56
  work-leisure trade-off, 176-7
alcohol, 98
amateur activities, 83

blue-collar workers
  desired leisure activities, 110-11
  influence of television on leisure, 100
  leisure, 86, 92-3, 94
  length of work week, 19-20
  weekly work load, 19-20
books
  in second economy, 105
  number published, 105
Brezhnev, Leonid, xv

central planning, as cure for holiday deficiencies, 132-3
child care, 138-41, 13
children, 83, 85, 93
  barrier to attending school, 102
  effect on housework, 15-16
  effect on leisure time, 90-1

city size
  commuting time, 23
  housework, 18
  effect on leisure activities, 86, 95-7
  owning gardens, 103-4
  working pensioners, 37
collective farms
  eligibility for pension, 42-3
  hours of work, 159-61
  housework, 173-7
  leisure activities, 183-95
  ownership of television sets, 186-8
  public services and private appliances, 177-83
  right to do seasonal work, 55
collective gardens, 5, 102-4
  criticisms, 104
  official recognition, 104
collective nature of leisure, xv
commuting, 22-3
consumption, per capita, xi

dachas, 103, 120, 126
dissatisfaction with leisure activities, 107-9
double burden, 136-41

education
  as determinant of desire for leisure, 111
  effect on housework, 17
  effect on leisure activities, 91-2
  relation to time budgets, 12
electrical appliances, 150-5
  among Tatar families, 153, 155
  in rural areas, 180-3
  ownership by income level, 155

electrical appliances – *continued*
  ownership by sex and level of income, 154
engineering-technical workers
  desired leisure activities, 110
  leisure, 93–4

five-day work week
  differential impact on men and women, 20–1
  effect on leisure, 97–8
  effect on time budgets, 19–22
free time, *see* leisure

hobbies, 85, 86, 93
holidays
  at the Black Sea, 120
  by time of year, 118–19
  determinants of activities, 127–8
  differential holiday entitlement by occupation, 117–18
  foreign travel, 122
  holiday passes, 123
  houses of rest, 123, 124–5
  length in Soviet Union, 114–15
  length in USA and Western Europe, 113–14
  organised and unorganised, 118–22
  policy from 1917 to Second World War, 115–16
  preferences of holiday-makers, 128
  quality of facilities, 130–2
  rural areas, 192–3
  sanatoriums, 123, 124–5
  shortage of facilities, 129–30
  tourism, 125–6
home workers
  legislation, 32
  number working, 33
  pensioners working, 41
  productivity, 33
  remuneration, 33
hotels, shortages, 129–30
hours of work, 5, 19
  agriculture, 158–61
  by sex, 5, 7
  five-day work week, 19–22
  overtime employment, 73
  part-time workers, 26–7

houses of rest, 123, 124–5
housework, 12–18
  city size, 18
  effect of five-day work week, 19–22
  effect of income, 16–17
  effect of number and age of children, 15–16
  effect of sex and education, 17–18
  effect of type of living space, 18
  electrical appliances, 150–5
  male–female differences, 6–7, 8
  public services, 141–50

income
  effect on desire for part-time work, 32
  effect on housework, 16–17
  effect on time budgets, 12
intelligentsia, leisure activities, 94

Kazan
  holidays, 127
  leisure, 90
kolkhozy, *see* collective farms

labour force
  absenteeism, x
  inefficient use of, ix–xi
  number of working pensioners, 34
  redundancy, x
  pensioners as percentage of, 35
  potential impact of part-time work, 28
  shortage, ix–x
  turnover, ix
labour turnover, ix
large cities
  leisure, 83, 95
  percentage owning gardens, 103
labour productivity
  old-age pensioners, 41
  part-time workers, 28
laundries and dry cleaners, 144
leisure, 81–112
  collective gardens, 102–4
  collective nature of, xv
  desired activities, 110–11
  determinants, 87–97: city size, 95–7; education, 91–2; income,

89–90; male–female differences, 87–8; marital status and children, 90–1; occupation, 92–4
dissatisfaction with, 107–9
effect of five-day week, 97–8
going to school after work, 100–2
historical trends, 83–4, 88
holidays in rural areas, 192–3
household expenditures, 98
philosophical perspective, xiv, xv
reading, 104–5
rural areas, 183–95
television, 98–100
Leningrad
  going to school after work, 102
  time budgets, 19
  use of public services, 141, 143
libraries
  holdings, 105
  in homes, 106
  rural areas, 190–1

marital status
  and time budgets, 9
  as determinant of holiday activity, 127
  effect on leisure, 90
Marx, Karl, xiii–xiv, 33
meeting with friends, 83, 85, 93
men and women, differences in vacation activity, 127–8
moonlighting
  and overtime work, 77–8
  costs to state, 62–3
  earnings, 57–8
  official attitudes towards, 63
Moscow
  leisure activities, 86
  old-age pensioner employment by sex and age, 36
movies, theatres and concerts, 83, 85, 88, 93
multiple job holders, 106–7

occupation
  and time budgets, 9–11
  effect on leisure, 92–4
old-age pensioners
  age of retirement, 34

as percentage of total labour force, 35
effects of legislative changes, 37–8
length of work life after retirement, 40
motives for working, by sex, 39, 40, 41
number working, 34
participation by sector of the economy, 35
participation by sex, 36–7
percentage continuing to work after retirement, 40
pension laws, 37–8
percentage of retirement age, 34
productivity, 41
proposals for increasing pensioner participation in labour force, 43–4
wages, 37–8
white-collar workers, 44
working as home workers, 41
working in agriculture, 41–4
overtime work
  as trade-off with leisure, 66
  benefits to state, 79
  compensation, 69–72
  hours worked, 73
  illegal uses of, 76–7
  in public catering enterprises, 72
  legal basis for, 67–8
  motivation to work overtime, 69
  on state farms, 72
  part-time workers, 26
  planned overtime, 73–4
  role of trade unions, 68
  second economy, 77–8
  subbotnik, 74–6

part-time work
  defined, 26
  effect of income, 32
  Estonian experience, 29, 30
  household reluctance, 29
  labour productivity, 28
  length of work week, 26–7
  percentage employed, 27
  potential impact on labour force, 28
  reasons against, 28–9

part-time work – *continued*
  Russian Republic, 27
  similarities to West European flexitime, 29
  students, 48
  USA and East Germany, 27
  women's motives, 29–30
pension rights
  collective farmers, 42: compared with state sector, 42–3
  part-time workers, 26
  seasonal workers, 59–60
physical activities, 83, 85, 88
Pravda, 105
prepared foods, 147–8
private plot, 102, 161–6
  and urban workers, 5, 102–4
  income derived from, 162
  time spent on, 163–5
public catering
  overtime employment, 72
  shortages on holiday, 131
  utilisation by households, 145–7
public services, 138–50
  in rural areas, 177–81
  utilisation of services, 143

radio, 83, 85, 88
  in rural areas, 186–8
reading, 83, 88, 93, 104–6
  in rural areas, 186–91
reduced work day, 26
redundant labour force, x
repair services, 149–50
retirement
  motives for, 39, 40
  see also old-age pensioners
Russian Republic
  homework, 33
  part-time work, 27

sanatoriums, 123, 124–5
seasonal work
  composition of work-force, 55
  costs and benefits to state and individual, 61–3
  definition, 52
  fringe benefits, 59–60
  in agriculture, 53

income, 56–8
informal recruitment, 56
non-agricultural labour force, 53, 55
number employed, 53, 54
organised recruitment procedures, 55
rights of collective farmers, 55
role in economic planning, 51
urbanite participation, 55, 56
violations of the law, 53
see also moonlighting
second economy
  connection with overtime work, 77–8
  connection with seasonal work, 64
sexual inequality, *see* hours of work; housework
shift work, 135–6
shopping, 13, 148–9
sovkhozy see state farms
state farms
  holidays, 192–3
  overtime work, 71–2
  time budgets, 171–3
storming, x
Strumilin, S., 2–3
student construction detachments, 44–7
student workers, 44–50
  agricultural employment, 47
  areas of employment, 46
  contracts between educational institution and an enterprise, 47
  costs and benefits to state, 49
  during school year, 47–8
  higher education students working, 45, 46
  part-time work, 27, 48
  pay, 48–9
  problems, 49–50
  student construction detachments, 44–7
studying, 83, 85, 88, 93
  children as barrier, 102
  determinants, 101
  enrolments, 101
  going to school after work, 100–2
subbotnik, 74–6

television, 83, 85, 88, 93, 98–100
  effect on other cultural activities, 100
  rural areas, 186–8
temporary work
  definition, 52
  fringe benefits, 60
  number employed, 53, 54
  role of, 51
  types of work, 52
time budgets, 2
  and education, 11–12
  and income, 11–12
  and marital status, 9
  and occupation, 9–11
  early methodology, 2–3
  five-day work week
  sex differences, 6–7, 10, 20–1
  urbanites, 4–9
tourism, 125–6

urbanites, time budgets, 2–9

vacations, *see* holidays

waiting in queue, 22
white-collar workers
  leisure activities, 94
  pensioners, 44
women
  complaints about job, 135
  discontinuities in labour-force participation, 31
  length of time out of labour force
  motives for part-time work, 29–30, 39
  numbers wanting part-time work, 30–1
  part-time work, 27–8, 29–33
  work plans, 31
  working pensioners, 36–7